Beezy Marsh is an international number one bestselling author who puts family and relationships at the heart of her writing. She writes fiction as well as memoir and biography and still finds time to blog about her life in Oxfordshire, as an imperfect mum to two boys. She's also an award-winning investigative journalist, who spent more than twenty years making the headlines in newspapers including the *Daily Mail* and the *Sunday Times*. Beezy is a firm believer that sisters, mothers and wives are the glue that binds everything together and ordinary lives are often the most extraordinary.

Also by Beezy Marsh

All My Mother's Secrets
Keeping My Sisters' Secrets
Mad Frank and Sons
Mr Make Believe

Her
Father's
Daughter

BEEZY MARSH

PAN BOOKS

First published 2019 by Pan Books
an imprint of Pan Macmillan
20 New Wharf Road, London N1 9RR
Associated companies throughout the world
www.panmacmillan.com

ISBN 978-1-5098-9268-6 (UK)
ISBN 978-1-5290-3061-7 (Canadian edition)

1 3 5 7 9 8 6 4 2

A CIP catalogue record for this book is available from the British Library.

Typeset by Palimpsest Book Production Ltd, Falkirk, Stirlingshire
Printed and bound by CPI Group (UK) Ltd, Croydon, CR0 4YY

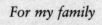

For my family

'There is no gate, no lock, no bolt that you can set upon the freedom of my mind'

– Virginia Woolf, *A Room of One's Own*, 1929

Introduction

As the storm clouds of war gathered over Britain in the late 1930s, working-class families braced themselves to make more sacrifices.

Brothers, husbands and fathers had been lost on the fields of France and Flanders in 'the war to end all wars' of 1914–18, but now another generation readied itself to take up arms to defend the nation.

Those lucky enough to survive the First World War had returned to battles on the home front: the daily struggle to make ends meet, the fight against deadly diseases with no money to pay for medical care, and the reality of life on the dole or on the breadline throughout the hungry years of the 1920s and 1930s.

Yet through it all, against the odds, families survived.

Children thrived, women coped, and people made the best of it. The turbulent years between the wars saw huge social changes and upheaval, with mass unemployment, marches and strikes as unions fought for better pay and conditions. Working-class men and women gained the vote for the first time. It was inconceivable to many ordinary folk that they now had their say at the ballot box but there was no turning back. However, many would grumble that the vote didn't put bread on the table or mend the holes in their kids' shoes.

For most women, day-to-day life went on much as it had done for their mothers and grandmothers. Keeping the family clothed, clean, fed and healthy was a full-time and gruelling job. It was a thankless task, but it was done with love and the support of an extended network of aunts, cousins, grannies and neighbours, who were there to provide a listening ear, words of comfort or just a nice cup of tea when the going got rough. Hopes were brewed, poured and sipped at in Britain's sculleries, as they had been for generations.

The old adage that kindness cost nothing was woven into the very fabric of the clothes that were knitted and sewn and mended by the hearth, in the failing light of gas lamps. All life's troubles were scrubbed away at the washboard and run through the mangle in the back yard before being hung out to dry in the alley in the cold light of day, because all the neighbours knew your business anyway.

In the cramped rows of two-up, two-downs, the spirit of community was forged in the pit of poverty and despair.

This is the true story of a family who lived through these trying times and their journey through the first half of the twentieth century, which tested the mettle of the entire nation.

Annie, calm, kind, accepting of her lot, was like so many other working-class women, mothers and wives. She was raised in Soapsud Island, the close-knit community of

London's laundries, and her expectations extended little beyond the washtubs where she worked from the tender age of twelve to earn her keep.

Her mother, Emma, a respected and highly skilled silk ironer, kept a secret from Annie to spare her the shame of a choice she'd made in the grief of widowhood when Annie was just a baby. Annie and her brother George grew up believing their father had died a hero in the First World War. But after Annie discovered the truth about George's parentage, which is revealed in the prequel to this book, *All My Mother's Secrets*, she began to understand why her mother had lived a lie. The bonds between them were strengthened by the half-truths told in order to survive in a world which judged women harshly. Annie vowed to keep the shocking truth from her brother George, just as her mother had done.

She accepted, as so many did, that some secrets are kept for a reason; some secrets must never be told.

Her mother Emma got married for a second time, to laundry hand Bill, and they had two daughters, who Annie helped raise from the age of fifteen, as well as working all the hours she could. She was selfless and single until her mid-thirties, when she fell in love with their lodger, Harry. On the eve of the Second World War, Annie married Harry, a dependable union representative from the local factory, and all her dreams of starting a family of her own began to come true.

She was in awe of Harry, who was eight years her senior, taciturn, political, well read but strangely reluctant to talk about his upbringing in the Northern powerhouse of Newcastle, where coal and shipbuilding were king. Harry received letters from his sister, Kitty, a mysterious and forthright woman who worked as a journalist at a time when women simply did not do such things, but Harry never invited her to stay.

When war came to their doorstep with the harsh reality of the Blitz, the world as they knew it was turned upside down and the past came back to haunt Harry and threaten Annie's happiness.

This is their true story, of loss and hope, of enduring love and the unshakeable bonds that bind generations through all life's hurts. It is one of secrets and lies and the will to survive.

It is the true story of a family facing extraordinary choices to keep living ordinary lives in a world where nothing would ever be the same again.

Prologue

Kitty

Newcastle upon Tyne,
August 1911

Kitty had got used to the sound of crying in the house since her father had gone.

Mum made no attempt to hide her sobbing and most evenings, as she sat in her armchair in the parlour, she'd put down her sewing and let grief wash over her.

Kitty would go to her then, knowing that words were useless because nothing could bring him back. The clock on the mantelpiece would strike nine and then ten but their loss had no respect for seconds or minutes or hours. They were caught by it, suspended like flies in amber.

The cries coming from upstairs grew louder, but it was too early for Mum to be back from work.

Kitty hesitated for a split second on the stairs, catching sight of her reflection in the hallway mirror. She'd glanced at herself hundreds of times going up and down those stairs in all the years they'd lived in Lily Avenue. It had been her little secret before she went to school, checking if her collar was straight and her unruly auburn hair tied neatly with a velvet ribbon, just the way the teacher liked it.

So much had changed in the past year. She didn't care one jot what she looked like these days. People stared at her and so she'd got used to staring back at them, almost daring them to mention her father's name.

She'd reached the top of the stairs now. The sobbing was coming from her little brother Harry's room. Kitty pushed open the bedroom door and Harry looked up at her, grey eyes filled with shame and anger, his lip cut and bleeding and a livid purple bruise darkening on his cheek. 'I don't want you to see me like this, Kit,' he howled, hurling himself face down on the bed. 'Just leave me alone, will you?'

She ran to him and kneeled at his side, watching his shoulders heave with each sob. The back of his shirt was streaked with dirt where he'd been knocked to the ground.

'I promised Dad before he went: I won't leave you ever, so don't be a soft lad and keep asking me to go,' she said, fighting back tears of her own. 'Who did this to you? Was it the Jesmond Dene gang again, that bunch of layabouts?'

He turned his face to the wall and her hand found his. He didn't speak but he clasped her fingers tightly, just as he had the first time she'd held him, when he was just a baby.

'It's you and me, Harry, against all of them,' she whispered. 'We're family, don't ever forget that.'

1

Annie

Acton, May 1940

Night, when it fell in London, was as dark as it had been in the years Annie spent as a child at her aunt's farm in Suffolk, with only the stars and the moon to guide her home from the fields.

But there was no thrill in looking up at the twinkling blanket overhead these days, just the fear of what might be coming their way from Germany. Even the sound of footsteps approaching in the gloom of the terraced streets that she knew so well made her nervous. Then there were the lamp posts to contend with. Her stepdad, Bill, had got himself a proper shiner when he'd walked slap bang into one the other night on the way home from the pub.

He'd blamed Hitler, of course, but most folks managed to spot the white stripes that the Air Raid Precautions' wardens had carefully painted on the posts at waist height to help guide people home in the blackout. You couldn't blame him for having a drink or three; poor Bill, he was too old to fight, and he was scared out of his wits by the fear of invasion.

Mum joked that he'd wage a war of words fierce enough to defeat Jerry and he was keeping an old shillelagh under the bed 'just in case'. They never spoke about the real reason he'd hit the bottle – he was worried sick about the strain of the war on Mum's heart. She'd given them all a few scares and the doctors had warned her not to overdo it, but Mum soldiered on regardless.

Annie pulled the sides of her coat together against the chill of the night air. She couldn't fasten it any more. She was seven months gone now and with every passing day she felt more like one of the floppy, grey barrage balloons bobbing about on wires above the depot at Acton station. The baby kicked, and she patted her belly and whispered, 'We'll be home soon, don't you worry.'

She'd only popped out to take Mum some tea, but they'd spent ages in the scullery, nattering over a cuppa that was as weak as dishwater but warming nonetheless, so you couldn't grumble, really. She didn't like leaving Mum on her own too much while Bill was out down the boozer, and with her old man Harry out at the Air Raid Precautions' station with all the other wardens, she was glad of the company, even if it meant a short walk home alone in the dark.

Besides, her youngest half-sister Elsie had clocked off at the cardboard-box factory and gone off dancing up in the West End again, which was giving Mum more grey hairs.

'I don't know what's got into her lately,' Mum had confided, as she fried a solitary egg on the range. 'All she talks about is the dances these days. She used to be such a sensible girl. It's like the world's turned upside down with this fighting. At least Ivy's already turned in. I don't have to worry about her.'

Ivy was Elsie's older sister and she was keen on her beauty sleep these days, having just accepted a proposal of engagement from Charlie, a local painter and decorator. Ivy was always more sensible than Elsie, planning carefully for the future, but when the pair of them got together they were still as thick as thieves and neither was averse to making a bit of mischief at Annie's expense, just as they had done when she was helping to raise them. Annie was fifteen when Ivy was born, because Mum had remarried during the First World War, so both the girls treated Annie as more of a mother than a sister. Annie's dad had died long before then, when she was just a baby, and it was no secret that she and Bill had never quite seen eye to eye. Bill doted on his daughters and it was as plain as the nose on his face that Annie was second best in his eyes, but he'd mellowed with age and Annie, well, she was kind and forgiving to a fault. She knew Bill worshipped the ground that Mum walked on and that was enough for her, even if he did like to pinch all the best bits of bacon for himself. Mum slid the egg onto one of her best blue and white china plates with great care, offering it to her daughter.

Annie looked up at her mother's careworn face. 'Bill will want this for his breakfast, won't he?'

Eggs had been scarce since food rationing had started a few months ago but Mum always seemed to find some little extra morsel to feed her.

'Well, what he don't know about can't hurt him,' she said, tapping the side of her nose conspiratorially. 'I hid it behind the cod liver oil in the larder because he can't abide the stuff, so I knew it would be safe there. And anyway, you're carrying my grandchild. Your need is greater than his.'

He'd been grumbling about anything and everything since war broke out and Annie got the impression he was getting on Mum's nerves a lot. The house was a smart three-bedroomed terrace in Grove Road, just off Acton High Street, and the yard out the back had a strip of garden wide enough for Bill to dig down and install an Anderson shelter. Of course, he moaned he'd put his back out doing it.

Annie balanced the plate on her knees as Mum offered her a crust of bread to dip in the runny yolk, which was the best bit. She was constantly hungry with this baby growing inside her. She'd spent the first four months barely able to keep anything down but since the morning sickness had stopped, she'd been ravenous. She tried her best not to think about it when she went to bed hungry, because it seemed a bit unpatriotic to complain when there was a war on.

It wasn't a case of starving on rations – she went along with her coupons to the butcher's and the grocer's like everyone else and she was allowed to go to the front of the queue because she was in the family way. Harry always made sure she had the biggest cuts of meat and the most potatoes, because he could get extra to eat down at the ARP centre on the night-shift.

Anyway, it seemed to make Mum feel better to feed her up a bit.

It was so cosy in the scullery at her mum's with the wireless tuned in to the BBC, which was playing cheery songs from the varieties up North tonight. The front room had a couple of nice armchairs in it but they were covered with sheets unless they had company – and by that Mum meant the vicar – so that room was kept for best. Mum always had one ear out for any broadcasts about the forces and when the news was on, the world stood still and you could hear a pin drop.

Finishing up the last of her egg, Annie spotted Mum holding a letter between trembling fingers. 'Is it another one from George?'

Mum nodded solemnly. Annie's younger brother George had been among the first to volunteer for active service when war had been declared and was over in France, with the British Expeditionary Force. He was a despatch rider for Lord Gort, the head of the whole army.

George wrote home regular as clockwork, but of course he couldn't say too much, other than that the French food wasn't a patch on his mum's cooking and so on. Mum had got quite a collection of letters together and they took pride of place on the mantelpiece over the range in the scullery during the day, next to a picture of him in his uniform, and then they were carried up to bed, with a candle, to be pored over once more before she went to sleep at night.

'Well,' said Annie brightly, 'what's the latest? I bet he's having the time of his life with all the French girls! Ooh la la!'

It was a running joke between her and Mum that George would come swanning in one day in his khakis with a raven-haired mademoiselle on his arm and walk her up the aisle in Acton, which would really set tongues wagging. But Mum didn't laugh at the joke like she normally did.

'He says they're on the move again but there's something up,' she said, her eyes flickering across the page. 'I can feel it in my water. It's as if he's saying goodbye.'

Annie stood up, heaving herself out of the chair, and went to her mother's side. 'What do you mean?'

'It's right here, plain as the nose on your face,' said Mum. 'He's signed off differently, look.'

Annie read her brother's words: *Take care, kiss Annie for me, and the baby when it comes. I will always be your George. I hope I can make you proud . . .*

Annie reached over and untied the bundle of letters on the mantelpiece. 'But he always says "take care" and mentions the baby!' she said. 'Don't upset yourself over nothing.'

'I just know he's in danger,' said Mum, clutching at her chest for an instant as the colour drained from her face. 'You'll understand when you've had the baby. It's a mother's instinct.'

'But, Mum,' said Annie, 'all the newspapers have been full of stories about our boys going off to Belgium and being welcomed like heroes! People have been chucking flowers at them. We've got the Germans on the run.'

Mum just shook her head. It had taken another cup of tea and a slug of brandy from the cupboard under the stairs to calm her down after that and Annie couldn't help noticing the tears in her mum's eyes when she left.

Annie hurried on past the shops of Churchfield Road, their blinds drawn, sandbags piled high under the windowsills. It took a while for her eyes to get used to the dark, but the moon was out tonight and that helped light the way. Her younger half-sister Elsie had been hankering after a set of buttons for her coat which would glow in the dark and all the newspapers were telling people to wear white to make it easier to be spotted. That was all very well, but white clothes got dirty so quickly and what with cleaning and shopping and all the rest of it, that just wasn't practical. And in any case, who had the money to buy a new white dress or a skirt? Only the posh folk, that was for sure.

It was just a brisk ten-minute walk to their flat on Allison Road but with every passing week, Annie couldn't help noticing how out of breath she was by the time she got there. She'd married Harry just before the war broke out, but she still got butterflies every time she put the key in the lock and pushed open the front door; this was their home, a place to call their own. They had the two down-stairs rooms in an Edwardian terraced house, a kitchen and a bedroom. They didn't have to share it with anyone else in their family, which round these parts was quite something. An elderly couple had the flat upstairs and they shared the outside lavvy with them, and the copper on washdays, but Annie didn't mind that. In fact, she'd help them out by running their sheets through the mangle in the back yard when she could because old Mrs Hill's legs gave her trouble getting up and down the rickety back stairs which led from the upstairs flat directly into the yard. It was the same with shopping: Annie would take Mrs Hill's coupons down to the butcher's and the grocer's for her, as she was headed there anyway.

Harry had a good job, as an engineer calibrating and testing the pumps for diesel engines down at Charles Anthony Vandervell and Co, which was known locally as C.A.V., one of the big factories about half a mile away, down Acton Vale. That's how they'd met, when she was working there as a machine hand four years ago. Annie hadn't taken to him at first, because he was a union rep, a serious, quiet, political sort and a good eight years older than her, not to mention the fact that she was a Londoner and he was from Newcastle upon Tyne.

But beneath his gritty exterior lay a man whose twinkling grey eyes made her heart flip and whose sense of humour was enough to give them both a fit of the giggles over the silliest of things. He'd won her heart when he'd come to lodge with them for a time at Mum and Bill's in Grove Road and the next thing she knew, she was walking up the aisle, sewing curtains and expecting the patter of tiny feet.

All the factories in Acton were given over to the war effort now, and C.A.V. was no exception. Harry worked his shifts there but fitted in his ARP volunteering around them too.

A lot of folk moaned about the blackout and the precautions and got a bit shirty with the wardens hammering on their front doors with orders to 'put that light out!' Some called it a 'Phoney War' because there was no sign of Herr Hitler trying to set foot in the country and they were getting sick and tired of lugging gas masks everywhere, bumbling around in the pitch black, going without and queuing for one of the grocer's carefully measured twists of sugar in a little paper bag, a pat of butter or a sliver of meat from the butcher.

But Harry insisted it wasn't a waste of time. 'The Nazis won't rest until we're all speaking German, you mark my words,' he'd bark at people who failed to observe the blackout. 'Don't make it easy for them by lighting the way to your home so they can drop bombs on it, you blethering idiots.'

Once she was inside the front door, Annie fumbled in the dark for the candle and the box of matches she left on the table in the hallway and lit it. It threw shadows up the stairwell, which was dingy at the best of times, painted a grim shade of mustard brown. She wandered down the passageway into the scullery at the back, checking the blackout curtain was still pinned firmly in place before lighting the gas lamp on the wall. There was enough milk for her to have some Ovaltine, which was a bit of a treat before bed. Easing off her shoes – which were pinching something terrible these days, with her feet swelling so much – she sat down at the table and rubbed some life back into her toes.

The wireless sat on a cabinet next to the stove. George had made the cabinet for her and Harry, as a wedding gift, before the nightmare had started, when people still hoped against hope that another generation of young men wouldn't have to take up arms, as their fathers had done before them, in the Great War. The wireless had been his parting gift to her, his green eyes alive with the excitement of going off to serve his country, like so many other eager recruits around town.

He'd shown her how to work the radio, tinkering about with the dial as Harry sat in his favourite armchair rolling a smoke and smiling at them both.

'You'll be able to hear everything I get up to on this, Annie,' he said, as she saw him, for the first time, not as her little brother, but a grown man; how very handsome he looked, with his new short back and sides, his uniform pressed to perfection by Mum and his shoes polished so you could almost see your face in them. Annie was proud but nervous too, because George had been so sick with TB when he was little, it had given them all a fright. She'd always be his big sister, she couldn't help feeling that way, but she tried to push her protective instincts to one side now.

'Well, you'd better behave yourself over in France, then, or the BBC will be putting out a special announcement and we will hear it all, right here in Acton!' said Annie, poking him in the ribs.

It all seemed such a long time ago, but he'd only been gone a few months.

She heard a voice saying, 'Oh, George . . .' and then realized it was her own. She'd promised herself she wouldn't cry. Not tonight. It wasn't good for the baby, all this sadness, was it?

Annie stood up and put her hands on the small of her back, which had started to ache again. She'd made another promise, to Harry, that she wouldn't listen to the news broadcast before bed, but as her fingers flicked the switch and she twisted the dial, hearing the familiar crackle of the airwaves, she knew she was powerless to resist.

There was something comforting about it, even though Harry said it was probably the worry keeping her awake at night rather than the baby, who had the sharpest elbows and a kick so strong, it was surely going to be a boy, and a footballer at that.

The announcer's voice enveloped her with a kind of warmth as she shuffled over to the stove and lit the gas ring to heat the milk in the pan. She dried her eyes.

'This is the BBC Home Service. Here is the midnight news and this is Alvar Lidell reading it . . .'

Harry was a lump in the bed beside her, snoring softly as dawn broke.

Annie felt the chill of the lino under her feet as she padded across the bedroom and down the hallway to the scullery to make herself a cuppa. She switched on the wireless again, just to pass the time until she could pop out to the shops and get something for Harry to eat. He was on a late shift at the factory today.

The kettle was just coming to the boil, the steam working itself up into a high-pitched whistle, when the pips went to mark the top of the hour. Annie stopped in her tracks.

'Good morning, this is the BBC Home Service. German forces have invaded Holland, Belgium and Luxembourg

by air and land. The invasion began at dawn with large
numbers of aeroplanes attacking the main aerodromes
and landing troops,' the presenter announced. '*British and*
French troops have moved across the Belgian frontier in
response to appeals for reinforcements.

'*In London, it has been announced that Winston*
Churchill will lead a coalition government after Prime
Minister Neville Chamberlain said he was stepping
aside . . .'

Annie opened her mouth to scream but no sound came
out. She clutched her stomach and sat down, the screech
of the kettle filling the kitchen. Harry blundered in, half
asleep, grumbling, 'You could wake the dead with that
racket, our Annie. I was trying to get some kip.'

She didn't budge.

In an instant, he read the fear in her eyes and sat down
beside her, putting his arm protectively around her shoulders. 'What's wrong, pet?'

'The news,' she said. 'The Germans have invaded Belgium
and Holland.' She burst into tears. 'What if we're next?'

'Well,' said Harry, giving her a little squeeze, his brow
furrowing as he spoke. 'You know, it happened before in
the last war, when the Hun broke through our lines in one
area, but we beat them back in the end. They will never
win.'

They sat in silence for a moment.

Annie nodded as if she was calmed by his answer, but
a niggling doubt was gnawing away at her. She didn't
want to say it out loud, but what if Mum had been right
last night? What about her brother, George?

2

Annie

Acton, May 1940

All the housewives seemed to take out their frustrations about being at war with a renewed fervour for cleaning, and Bessie was no exception.

She stood, feet firmly planted, beating the living daylights out of a rag rug on the line she'd strung up across the patch of earth she called a back garden.

'Oh, I'd like to give that Mr Hitler what for, I would,' she said, whacking it with fresh vigour, sending dust and dirt flying all over the place.

Annie nodded in agreement. Bessie had forearms like two giant hams from all the years she'd spent scrubbing at the washtubs in the laundries. There were so many laundries crammed into the little terraced streets of South Acton it had the nickname Soapsud Island and the area had been the lifeblood of Annie's family for as long as she could remember. She had worked there as a laundry maid when she was young; her stepdad, Bill, had spent long years as a dollyman, heaving wet blankets out of the tubs; and her mum still took in ironing for the laundry bosses as a favour now and again, because she was such a skilled silk presser. The family had toiled long and hard at one of the small hand laundries, Hope Cottage, before it closed and then Mum went on to one of the new power laundries with all the steam irons and presses, which she still grumbled about for being 'newfangled'. Her methods had been tried and tested for generations. She still preferred to use the heavy 'sad' irons which she warmed on the range before working them with almost lightning speed across crumpled garments and turning out clothes which would be fit to hang in a shop window.

Some of the Soapsud Island washerwomen were as tough as old boots and Bill said only last night that Churchill should have thought of sending an army of them over to bash the Germans. 'They wouldn't stand a chance against the likes of Bessie! They'd be better at fighting than the bloody Belgians.' The mere thought of Bessie knocking Hitler and his cronies for six was enough to raise a smile, even if they were all still worried sick about what was happening to George.

All the talk was of how the Belgian army had surrendered and the whole town was picking over every little bit of news they could get about what was happening to our boys at the front. Everyone had a brother, husband or uncle fighting over there.

'Now,' said Bessie, 'Let me get you that shawl I've been knitting for the baby. Not long to go now, Annie. You sure you ain't carrying twins?'

Annie looked down at the bump in front of her. She hadn't seen her toes since Easter and her belly was straining against the thin cotton of the maternity smock she'd made for herself.

'Doctor says it's just one, but I've got to go up to the hospital in Willesden Lane when the time comes to have it,' said Annie.

'What for?' said Bessie. 'You're fit as a fiddle! I thought you'd be having it round your mum's in Grove Road.'

It was a bit embarrassing really, but all Annie's medical forms had the words 'elderly mother' written over them in red ink. She didn't feel old, at thirty-five, but compared to the rest of the mums going for their check-ups at the mother and baby clinic in Gunnersbury Lane, she was positively ancient. She'd worked all the hours God sent in the laundry from the age of twelve and then she'd helped her mum raise her half-sisters, Elsie and Ivy, so there hadn't been much time for romance until Harry walked into her life, when she – and everybody else – thought she'd been left on the shelf.

Annie felt herself colouring up.

'Sorry, love,' said Bessie, realizing she'd hit a raw nerve. 'It's none of my business. It's just if you were my daughter, I'd want to be there with you, at home, where I could be with you all the way through, that's all.' She patted Annie on the shoulders. 'Doctor knows best, though.'

Bessie had known her since she was a girl and was a bit like a second mum to her, so she hadn't meant to upset her at all. She was always fussing around people she cared about because she'd lost her only son in the Great War.

'Will it hurt when the baby comes, do you think?' said Annie, almost in a whisper.

No one really talked about it, giving birth. People exchanged glances and gossiped in hushed tones about 'women's troubles' after they'd had a baby, but no one really explained it, not even her friend Esther, who had three of her own.

'It's best not to focus on the pain of it,' Bessie said. 'It goes very quickly and then you forget it because you have a beautiful baby in your arms. Just ask your mum.'

Annie didn't want to bother her mum with her fears about giving birth, not now, not when everyone was so worried about the threat of invasion that the whole country had been told to go to church at the weekend to pray for the troops abroad.

Bessie bustled Annie inside to her upstairs flat. She had a couple of rooms in one of the run-down terraces in Stirling Road. 'You look like you could use a brew. It's not good for a woman to be standing up too long in your condition.' Annie knew that protesting was useless. Bessie in full flow was more forceful than one of Hitler's tanks, which meant she probably had some titbit of gossip to share.

Soapsud Island was still home to Annie in a lot of ways. Her family had moved across the High Street, yes, but she'd never escape the feeling that this was where she really belonged, in the grimy streets where kids made their own fun with a tin can, or a plank and some old pram wheels, and everyone knew everybody else's business. Grove Road was a bit posher and people were friendly but they were in and out of each other's houses a lot less than people from Soapsud Island.

Some might think the way of life in Soapsud Island was nosy, but there were plenty of old folk left without family to care for them because their relatives had gone away to fight. South Acton looked after its own. Neighbours would cook up a pie or plate up a meal for each other, help with the cleaning or just pop in to pass the time of day.

Bessie poured them both some tea out of her enormous brown pot, covered with a cosy she'd knitted specially, in a Union Jack flag design. 'Now,' she said, settling down on a rickety wooden chair, her haunches spilling over the sides, 'have you heard from Vera lately?'

Annie shook her head. Vera was one of her oldest pals from her days as a laundry maid, her best-looking and most fun friend, but their paths seemed to have taken them in different directions since Annie got married just before the war broke out. Mum didn't shed too many tears about that because she thought Vera was trouble with a capital T. Annie didn't see it that way; Vera was more spirited and stubborn than most and she had got herself into some scrapes but it wasn't her fault that life had been so tough. Her dad came back from the First World War a broken man and hit the bottle almost as hard as he belted Vera's mum. Vera had learned, early on, she would have to stand up for herself if she was going to make it in this world. Bessie had a big heart and she'd always done her best to take Vera under her wing and keep her on the straight and narrow but something about her tone of voice made Annie wonder whether things had changed.

'I saw her up the wet fish shop on Acton Lane the other day,' said Bessie. 'It ain't my place to say but I thought she looked a bleeding mess. Hair like a haystack, thin as a stick and bruises all up her arms and legs where she'd been falling down drunk coming out of the pub, if you please! She'd been entertaining some handsome young chaps in uniform it seems and was one over the eight.

'Mrs Parker said she'd practically picked her out of the gutter. It ain't right, Annie, not for a lovely girl like that. People will talk.'

'People *are* talking,' said Annie, raising an eyebrow. It was lost on Bessie, who ploughed on: 'I'm not one to gossip, as you know, but there's a war on and girls like her, well, they can get themselves a bad reputation for' – Bessie lowered her voice to a stage whisper – 'spreading diseases.'

It took a few days for Annie to pluck up the courage to go around to Vera's house in Stirling Road, which was just a few doors down from Bessie's. It wasn't that she didn't like her friend any more, she just didn't know quite how to tell her what people were saying behind her back.

Vera's mum, Old Mrs O'Reilly, had given birth to more kids than Annie had eaten hot dinners and since her husband upped and died, Vera had moved back in to help with the rent and raising her nieces and nephews. Her other siblings had their hands full making ends meet and there were a few who were on their own because their other halves were at Her Majesty's Pleasure in the Scrubs, but no one liked to mention that. There were always hordes of little O'Reillys stampeding in and out of that house in Stirling Road, being chased out of shops, across the railway tracks or climbing into people's garden sheds. You couldn't stray far through South Acton without bumping into one, their startling blue eyes and nit-ridden mop of blond hair a dead giveaway for the local bobby, who'd grab them by the scruff of their neck and march them home.

Annie knocked on the door and Mrs O'Reilly answered, her hair done up in rollers and covered with a hairnet, a snotty-nosed toddler on her hip and another clinging forlornly to her legs. 'Oh, hello love,' she said, eyeing Annie up and down. 'When's it due, then?'

'Couple of months,' said Annie.

'I didn't even know you was in the family way!' she said, her eyes narrowing a little. 'Haven't seen much of you lately, have we? Where've you been hiding?'

Annie shuffled about a bit, wondering how to explain her absence. She needn't have bothered because Mrs O'Reilly wasn't one to bear grudges. 'Oh, it don't matter now! Vera'll be so pleased you've called around. I know how it can be when you're setting up home. Bet your mum's happy to be having a little grandkid on the way, ain't she? Mind you, I can always loan her one of mine if she fancies . . .'

Right on cue, a couple of little O'Reillys came tumbling head first down the stairs and landed with a bump, by Mrs O'Reilly's worn slippers. 'Get out of it!' she chided. 'Go on and play in the street.'

'Is Vera in?' said Annie, peering into the darkest recesses of the hallway, which was even grimier than she remembered.

'No, love,' said Mrs O'Reilly. 'I just sent her up to the shops with me ration book. Why don't you take a walk up there and see if you can find her? She's been gone ages.'

Annie lumbered her way up Acton Lane towards the grocer's shop. Things were much quieter these days, with a shortage of petrol meaning fewer cars on the road. The delivery motorbikes, which her brother George used to love zooming around on, had all but disappeared. People still used buses and the trams if they were going further afield, of course, but most folk were just on Shanks's pony – their own two legs. Hers were killing her from the effort of heaving the baby bump around in front of her like some great zeppelin.

Women stood nattering to their neighbours on their front steps, just as they always had done, but their windows were now criss-crossed with tape to stop the glass shattering if a bomb dropped. That now seemed even more of a possibility than ever before. The notion of there being a Phoney War had ebbed away with the situation in Belgium and Holland, and the atmosphere around town was tense.

She reached the grocer's, which had some new posters up in the window, warning people not to be 'squander-bugs' when they went to the shops. A cartoon figure of an insect called the squanderbug had a little moustache on it, like Hitler's, and was covered in Swastikas, the sight of which made Annie feel queasy. 'Beat the squanderbug, keep your war savings!' warned another poster. Well, Annie and her family didn't really have much in the way of savings anyway, like most folk around these parts. They barely had two brass farthings to rub together by the end of the week, but she supposed the government knew what it was doing telling people to be careful what they spent their money on.

There was a long queue of customers waiting to be served, with their cardboard boxes on string slung over their shoulders. Annie had nearly gone out without her gas mask the other day and was only reminded by a notice chalked on the pavement to go back and get it. All the women were chatting but Annie quickly spotted one among them who was being studiously ignored by the rest. Her hair was pinned up at the sides and pulled into a fashionable roll at the front. She had too much red lipstick on, her skirt was tight and her blouse had a few too many buttons undone. On her feet she wore the most ridiculously high-heeled peep-toe shoes. It was Vera.

'Annie!' she cried, loud enough to wake the dead, as she caught sight of her friend. 'As I live and breathe! How are you, girl?'

A couple of women in the queue exchanged glances and tutted.

Annie made her way over to Vera's side and they hugged. 'Oh my Gawd! You look like the back end of a bus!' said Vera, giggling. 'When's it due?'

'I've still got a couple of months to go,' said Annie, as the rest of the queue looked on reprovingly.

Just then, a paperboy came running past, waving a newspaper in the air. 'Read all about it! The miracle of Dunkirk! Our boys rescued from the jaws of defeat by the navy and our little ships!'

There was a stampede out of the shop as mothers, sisters and wives fought to get the latest news on what had happened in France; even the grocer stopped serving and went out the back to switch on the wireless. The colour drained from Annie's face and she felt the room starting to spin.

'Steady on, girl,' said Vera, grasping Annie by the arm. 'I think we need to find you somewhere to sit down.'

'It's George,' said Annie, her voice little more than a croak. 'He's over there . . . what if he's . . .'

'Now, now, don't you be talking nonsense,' said Vera, marching her friend out of the shop. 'It sounds like it's good news, not bad, so keep your pecker up!'

Annie allowed herself to be walked, gently, arm in arm with her friend, up Acton Lane and onto the High Street. Even with the war on, it was still as busy as ever. People always had a reason to go up to the shops, even if it was merely to get a bit of gossip. Just being in the fresh air had stopped Annie feeling dizzy. Vera had to pause every few yards to adjust the strap on the back of her shoes which kept slipping off, because they were a size too big.

'I know they don't fit me right, but I just loved them so much, I had to have 'em!' she said. 'Make me feel like a film star. In fact, I've got an idea. How do you fancy coming to the pictures with me?' she said, turning to Annie.

Vera was pretty, her blonde pin curls framing a doll's

face, with an upturned nose and a rosebud mouth, but when she spoke, Annie couldn't help noticing some of her friend's teeth were black and there was a whiff of booze on her breath.

Annie didn't want to offend her, but she really wasn't in the mood to sit through a film. 'I think I'd rather get home,' she said, smiling apologetically.

Vera looked crestfallen. 'I'm not talking about just having a good time to take your mind off it all,' she said. 'It's the newsreel they have on first, before the film. We might get to see if George is on one of them boats. Just think how happy that would make you, and your mum – she must be worried sick. Be good to check, won't it?' She puffed her chest out with pride at her great idea.

'I'm not sure,' said Annie. 'Perhaps we could make it another day?'

But Vera would not be dissuaded. 'Oh, come on!' she chided. 'You know we always have fun when we're together. You need something to get you out of the doldrums and this is just the ticket.'

A couple of soldiers, who barely looked old enough to lather up shaving soap, were hanging around outside the Crown Cinema. Annie pulled some coins out of her purse to pay for herself and Vera. It was only a shilling each but Vera had a ten-bob note and she didn't want to break into that so Annie stumped up for both of them. As Vera and Annie made their way in, with Vera wiggling in her too-tight skirt, one of the soldiers let out a low wolf whistle. She turned and flashed them a broad grin while Annie turned scarlet with embarrassment.

There was a Laurence Olivier and Vivien Leigh film showing and, on any other occasion, Annie would have been delighted to sit through it, but right now, it felt like the weight of the world was pressing down on her shoulders with the worry of what was happening over in France.

The cinema lights had already been dimmed and they shuffled their way along the back row, where there were double seats, because Vera had decided there would be more room for Annie to sit comfortably. There were a few old blokes dotted about, whiling away the hours until they could get another pint, some youngsters who were skiving off school and a few smoochy couples who planned to make good use of the darkness to get up to no good. God only knows what Harry would make of her going to such a notorious fleapit, and that was before she got onto the fact that she was there with Vera. Annie couldn't quite get the way those women in the grocer's were so openly snubbing her friend out of her mind.

She didn't have time to dwell on it because the Pathé newsreel started up and the voice of the news announcer filled the cinema. '*Our man has risked his life to bring you these images of the beaches of Dunkirk under enemy fire, our own guns replying.*'

Annie's mouth fell open as she watched the scenes on the big screen before her, the sky filled with the thickest pall of black smoke she had ever seen. This was war, real war, and it was horrific. The noise of gunfire was deafening as the announcer continued: '*And here, on their way home, home from the hell that is Dunkirk, our brave boys*

from the army are rescued by the navy. Alongside them,
the little ships that turned a military disaster into a miracle
of deliverance.'

Hundreds and hundreds of soldiers were crammed onto
the decks of boats of all shapes and sizes. It was a wonder
they could stay afloat. 'See how many of them are getting
out?' said Vera. 'There's blooming loads of them. Look!
That boat is stuffed to the gunnels. Oh, I think I just saw
George!'

'Shhhh!' said a man in the row in front. 'I'm trying to
watch the news!'

'So are we!' said Vera, angrily tapping him on the
shoulder. 'And what's more, she's in the family way and
her brother is over there fighting rather than sitting on his
bum in this cinema. So, we can talk if we like.'

The man tutted his disapproval and the usherette
appeared, shining her torch right into Annie's face, making
her squint. 'Sorry,' Annie mouthed.

The usherette shone the torch over them both, caught
sight of Annie's pregnant bump, rolled her eyes and
walked away.

'You could get away with murder with that baby inside
you, Annie,' said Vera. 'People treat you with respect.' She
clasped her hands in front of her for a moment. 'Not like
me . . .'

It was a relief when the news came to an end and the
film started up. Annie allowed herself to be transported
into another world, in *21 Days Together*, where
Laurence Olivier and Vivien Leigh had but twenty-one
days to spend together, before he would be hanged for

a murder he'd committed as a crime of passion. As the credits rolled and they strolled out into the foyer, Annie turned to Vera and said, 'Thanks for making me come along.'

Vera had been right: watching the film had made her feel a bit better. Of course, she hadn't seen George on the grainy black and white newsreel; there were so many soldiers crammed into those ships, all looking exhausted and filthy, more like a rag-tag bunch of tramps than an army. It would be a wonder if their own mothers could recognize them. But at least she had some hope now.

Pressing her hands together to give herself the strength to broach the subject, Annie turned once more to her friend as they left the cinema. 'Vera,' said Annie, struggling to find the right words, 'there's something I wanted to ask you. Bessie told me about the other night—'

But a tall chap, handsome and in uniform, with slicked-back hair, and a toothy grin, cut in. 'Afternoon, ladies. I was wondering if you might be free later to come to a dance up in Shepherd's Bush?'

He caught sight of Annie's bump and took a step back. 'Oh, pardon me, I didn't mean to intrude.'

'No, don't go,' said Vera, eagerly reaching out to him. 'She's my pregnant sister. I was just taking her out because our brother's away in Dunkirk and we wanted to try to spot him. She's got to go home now, haven't you, Annie?'

Annie nodded, watching Vera depart on her new shoes that were slightly too big, walking with a wobble, leaning on the soldier.

Just before they rounded the corner, Vera looked back

over her shoulder and gave Annie a knowing wink. As she did so, Annie felt her heart sink, right into her poor swollen feet. She walked home alone.

3

Annie

Acton, June 1940

'And what time of day do you call this, young lady?'

Bill stood in the hallway at Grove Road, his shaving mug in his hand and his braces dangling over his trousers, as he caught his youngest daughter Elsie trying to creep in through the front door.

He raised his hand to slap her, his salt and pepper hair flopping forward over his face, which was puce with anger. 'I've a good mind to knock you into the middle of next week. You can't be stopping out all night like some common . . .'

Annie came out of the kitchen, where she'd been sitting up with Mum half the night, and moved towards him, to stop him doing something he'd regret.

Bill halted in front of Elsie, at the foot of the stairs, with the words he wanted to say lodged in his throat. He couldn't bring himself to do it, not to his favourite. All the years he'd raised her, taught her manners, set her on the right path. And then the war had come along and filled her head with silly ideas and she wasn't his sweet-natured good girl any more. She was going off with the other factory workers, the brazen lot, putting on rouge and powder, curling her hair in rollers and dancing till dawn with God knows who. Well, he was going to put a stop to it.

'You can't treat us like this, me and your mother . . .'

Elsie reached out to him. 'I'm sorry, Dad. I just got carried away and I missed the last bus back, so I stayed around at Joan's place in Notting Hill. I didn't mean to worry you and I promise I wasn't doing anything to make you ashamed of me.'

He recoiled from her touch, turning away to shuffle back off down the hallway as Elsie stood there, shame-faced.

Annie went to her side. 'What on earth were you thinking? You should have come home. Mum has been scared sick about you and so have I, on top of all the worry about George. You could have been lying dead in the gutter, knocked down by a car in the blackout . . . Anything could have happened to you.'

Elsie rolled her eyes and started to climb the stairs. 'I don't know what's wrong with everybody. I'm fine, aren't I? I wasn't in any kind of danger, I just stayed out overnight. Lots of the factory girls do it. I'm nearly twenty-one! I'm not a child.'

Annie followed her, slowly, because she was finding stairs so difficult now, and went into Elsie's room. Elsie started unbuttoning her blouse, revealing her curvaceous shape. She was a much bigger build than either Annie or her mum, just the sort of fresh-faced, rounded girl that soldiers liked to press against as they did a foxtrot around the dance floor, that was for sure.

As she was standing there in her brassiere and skirt, Annie spotted a red mark just above her sister's collarbone.

'Oh Lord,' said Annie, peering at her. 'Is that a love bite?'

Elsie's hand flew up to cover her chest and then she sat down on the bed, all the wind knocked out of her sails.

'You'd better find a way of covering that up or your dad will go crackers,' said Annie, making her way over to the chest of drawers where Elsie kept her make-up. She pulled out some powder and handed it to her. Elsie dabbed a bit on and then looked up at Annie. 'It's useless! You can still see it, can't you? Oh God, what was I thinking?'

'I don't know,' said Annie, sitting down next to her sister. 'Who is he, then? I hope he is worth all the trouble he's causing.'

Elsie bit her lip and looked at the floor. 'Just a fella I've seen at the dances a few times.'

Annie's face darkened. 'Tell me you didn't . . .'

'No!' cried Elsie. 'What do you take me for? I just had a bit of a cuddle in the back alley behind the Shepherd's Bush Empire, that's all, and I think I let him go a bit further than I wanted because he's just joined the navy.'

'He's going away to sea, so you let him take a bite out of you?' said Annie, nudging her sister in the ribs to make her laugh.

Elsie shook her head. 'Oh, Annie. I know I shouldn't have let him, but it felt, well, it felt nice. And all the blokes seem to want to do more with us girls now, because they're going away to the war and they don't know if they are ever coming back. It doesn't seem fair to say no to them.'

Annie looked into her sister's eyes. She'd held her as a baby and helped raise her, so in some ways they were more like mother and daughter than sisters. 'I understand. You want to have some fun, but you need to be careful about letting them go too far. You don't want to get yourself into trouble or you'll find yourself with a bad reputation.' In her mind's eye, Annie saw Vera tottering off out of the cinema with a soldier on her arm. 'Did you really stay at Joan's place?'

'Yes, I did,' said Elsie. 'Cross my heart, I did.'

'Look, Elsie, you are a grown woman, but you are living at home still, so you've got to think about Mum and Bill and their feelings and their rules because you are under their roof. You can't stay out like that. I had to come down here because Mum was up all night worrying about George and she had a bit of a funny turn when you didn't come home. We've hardly had any sleep.'

Annie rubbed her eyes. She was dog-tired but with the baby kicking her half the night, she could barely get any kip at the moment, no matter what Elsie had been up to. But she wasn't going to let on about that.

'I'm sorry,' said Elsie, staring at the floor.

Annie stood up and pulled open a drawer, rummaging about for another blouse for her sister. She picked the one with the highest neck she could find and told her to put it on.

Right on cue, Elsie's older sister Ivy appeared in the doorway.

She wagged her finger. 'Who's been a dirty stop-out then? Come on, tell me, who is he?'

Elsie quickly buttoned her blouse up before Ivy could spot the love bite.

'Do you think he's going to put a ring on your finger?' said Ivy, brandishing the sapphire engagement ring that Charlie had bought her. She was proud of being a fiancée and you couldn't blame her, but Annie wished she'd picked another moment to flaunt it. The last thing the family needed was for Elsie to start charging up the aisle with some bloke she'd snogged around the back of the Shepherd's Bush Empire.

The scullery was more like a funeral parlour than the cheery, bustling heart of their Grove Road home for the rest of the morning. Mum managed to say two words to Elsie by lunchtime, but only after she'd promised never to stay out like that again. Mum's face was grey with worry and she'd barely eaten, not even after Bill made her favourite bread and dripping to try to tempt her.

It had only been a few days since the first reports about Dunkirk in the papers and Mum sat there in her rocking chair, poring over every last detail in the *Evening News* and the *Daily Mirror*, while keeping her ears pricked for further updates from the BBC Home Service.

Bill did his best to cheer everyone up, practically standing to attention every time the announcer mentioned Lord Gort, the head of the British Expeditionary Force, who George reported to directly. 'Impressive man, very impressive. He stands over six feet tall, you know? Man's a bleeding giant. He'll squash that Hitler like a little cockroach.'

Elsie rolled her eyes and said, 'Yes, Dad, we know. You've only told us about fifty times already!'

But Annie indulged him. 'Don't be like that, Elsie. Lord Gort is such a great leader and to think George reports directly to him! It's something we should all be very proud of.'

A few neighbours had popped around to see how they were getting on, knowing that George was involved in all the drama in France. No one could make it better, of course, but just knowing that people cared was enough to lift Mum's spirits a bit.

Around tea time, there was another knock at the door and Elsie said, 'Don't worry, Mum, I'll get it.'

The shriek she let out brought the whole family running, even Annie, who almost got wedged sideways in the door as both she and Bill tried to squish through it at the same time.

There, dishevelled, filthy, thin as a rake, wearing ragged trousers and a woollen jumper three sizes too big with a maple leaf on the front of it, with a gaggle of schoolkids cheering in his wake, was George.

'Hello, Mum,' he said.

'My boy!'

Mum was like a woman possessed, grabbing hold of George, kissing his face, hugging him, laughing and crying all at the same time, as half the street gathered outside the front door, celebrating his safe return from the beaches of France.

'But how did you get here? Won't you be in trouble with Lord Gort?' said Bill, shifting anxiously from foot to foot. 'You're supposed to be with him, aren't you?'

George shrugged his shoulders. 'I jumped off the train at Acton station 'cos I knew you'd want to know I was safe. The rest of my regiment – what's left of it – are on the way back to barracks. Expect I'll get a couple of days in chokey for it but after what I've been through, that's nothing. I'll take the punishment. I just wanted to see you all.'

He leaned down and kissed Mum on the cheek. 'I missed your cooking, just like I said.'

Her eyes filled with tears as they hugged for what seemed like an eternity.

Eventually, she stepped back and had a good look at him. 'Oh, good Lord, what on earth have you been doing?' cried Mum, as George started to scratch at his head and his armpits. To her, he was just a grubby little schoolboy again, rather than a soldier who had fought his way through enemy lines to get back to Blighty. 'You're crawling with lice. We'd better get you cleaned up. Elsie! Ivy! Get the copper filled up. Go on out the back, George, and get those filthy clothes off.'

He was manhandled down the hallway by all three of his sisters. As he squeezed past Annie, he quipped, 'You look like you've got a whole loaf in the oven there, my girl, never mind a bun,' which made everyone collapse in gales of laughter.

'Feels like it too,' said Annie, giving him a big hug and wiping her eyes. 'It's a proper little wriggler this baby, I expect it will be trouble. Just like you. Now, I'd better get some fresh things for you to put on.'

'I expect the sergeant major will have me peeling spuds for a month but it's worth it just to see you all,' said George.

By the time the water had heated for George to have a bath in the tin tub and he had scrubbed himself clean, Mum had used up the entire week's ration of bacon in a fry-up; even Bill couldn't begrudge him that.

George wolfed it down, followed by two strong cups of tea, and then began to tell them of his miraculous escape from the hell that was Dunkirk.

'It had all started so well. We had such a success of it in Belgium, with people welcoming us like heroes. We couldn't believe it when Jerry broke through with tanks and the Belgian army just bloody well rolled over and surrendered, the useless sods,' said George, catching his mother's eye. 'Pardon my French, Mum.

'Everyone was ordered to retreat to the coast. Our boys were hiding in ditches and barns, taking out the enemy where they could, but, oh my God, the poor Belgian people . . .' He put his head in his hands. 'They were blown to bits on the road, the German swines showed no mercy. They were just trying to get away from the fighting.'

A shiver ran down Annie's spine at the horror of it all.

'But what about Lord Gort?' said Bill, who was on the edge of his seat, absorbing every word of the despatches from the frontline so that it could all be repeated, at length, to his mates down the boozer later on. 'Surely he had a plan?'

'Yes,' said George, 'he did, but there was so much

confusion with everything that was going on with the French generals and the Belgians and the higher-ups over here. Boulogne and Calais had fallen and the German Panzer tanks were smashing their way across the countryside from the north so we were caught in a pincer movement and the game was up. It's all very well for people in London to make plans but when you are caught up in it, it's chaos. We had no way out but those beaches in the end.

'I got separated from my regiment but I had orders to burn my motorbike and despatch bag in case any of the papers fell into enemy hands if I was captured, so I did, and then I had to get to Dunkirk. I had to hide out in a pigsty for a day and there was a boy there, can't have been more than twelve years old. I did the only thing I could think of and I gave him my army greatcoat and some rations. In the next village, I borrowed a bicycle from a Frenchman. I don't think he minded, he couldn't stand the smell of me.'

Bill gave a hollow laugh as he caught George giving him a little wink.

'But when I got there, Dunkirk was on fire and there were thousands and thousands of men just hiding in the dunes or waiting on the beaches. I didn't know it then, but we'd be there for days. We had no water, we were so thirsty, we were looking at the sea with nothing to drink, and then the bombing started.' George's hands started to shake.

'Don't upset yourself, George,' said Mum, putting her arms around him. 'It's over now.'

'Oh God, Mum, the cheers when there was a dogfight overhead and our boys took down the Krauts. I think you could have heard it in Dover,' he laughed, pouring himself yet another cup of tea.

Then his voice fell to a whisper. 'I saw men go mad. Fellas just stripped off and walked into the sea and swam out and they were like little blobs on the horizon and then I lost sight of them and I didn't think about them any more. I just thought about getting home to you, so I knew I wasn't going to go doolally.'

Elsie and Ivy were listening, open-mouthed.

'So,' said Bill, shifting in his chair. 'How did you get back? Was it on one of those big navy ships? Annie said she saw some on the newsreel at the cinema the other day and they were jam-packed.'

'I saw so many of them on fire,' he said. 'It wasn't always a good thing to be on one of the big ships . . .'

'But you made it out all right,' said Bill, patting him on the knee, waiting for him to continue.

'Yes,' said George. 'We boarded a boat off a jetty that some of the lads had built on top of burned-out trucks. They put these duckboards over the top of them so that when the tide came in, we could clamber out along them.

'The first boat wasn't very big, and it was so crowded it was a wonder we were even floating. It didn't matter because we'd only been on it about half an hour when we got fired on by a Stuka and half of us ended up overboard. I suppose we were the lucky ones because some of the lads didn't even make it over the side.'

His eyes filled with tears. 'I spent hours in the Channel, just trying to keep my head above the water. I lost track of the time. It was getting dark then, which was a mercy because at least the Germans couldn't see to strafe us with their machine guns. We were shouting to each other, to keep our spirits up, but some of the voices went quiet as the night went on; there were boys from all over the place, a few of us from London, and we tried to talk about where we grew up, people we knew, anything really, just to stay awake.

'I kicked off my boots and just sort of floated for some of it. There was no point struggling and the sea was calm as a millpond. The next thing I knew, dawn was breaking and I saw the most beautiful sight. It was the *Maid of Orleans*, a blooming great steamship. We waved and shouted and she came alongside us and the squaddies lowered lifeboats over the side and we clambered in. As I climbed aboard the boat, I heard a voice saying, "All right, son, we've got you." This big Canadian geezer, he must have been six foot four, whipped off his sweater and gave it to me.

'He didn't even hesitate, Mum. He took it off his own back and handed me a good shot of whisky too, the finest thing I ever tasted.'

The room was eerily silent as he finished his story.

George had survived but Annie had a feeling that for the rest of them, the war was just beginning.

4

Annie

Acton, June 1940

'It's so good to know he's home safe, I knew he'd make it, but he probably didn't tell you the worst of it, and just as well,' said Harry, hugging Annie tightly as they lay in bed together back at the flat.

'Men see things in war that they can't forget and don't want to talk about.' He rolled over to face the wall, just as he always did when he was going to go to sleep.

Annie lay there in a dark, wondering for a moment about what Harry meant, before turning to him.

'Is that why you won't talk about your scar?' she whispered.

It was about the size of a florin; a raised, red reminder of the Great War, on his right side, and it had shocked her the first time they had got into bed together on their wedding night. He had a much bigger scar on his back, about the size of a fist, where the bullet had passed clean through him, narrowly missing his vital organs. He'd confessed that much, but he never wanted to talk about how he got it, only once telling her, 'I'm lucky to be alive and that's enough for me, Annie.'

Annie had never forced the issue; her Uncle Arthur had fought in the trenches and returned a changed man, like many around Acton. He bore no scars from fighting but the war had left its mark on him in other ways, with his incessant rubbing of his hands and his need to be alone most of the time. He used to scare the living daylights out of Annie when she was a girl because of his strange habits and silent ways but the family looked after him. He lived with one of her aunts for a long time and she took care of him. Then, shortly before the war, he married a widow from the laundries who was as quiet as a mouse, so Mum said they were both right for each other.

But Harry was different. He was the lifeblood of the union at work, always ready to offer sensible advice to anyone with a problem. He was so looking forward to the baby coming and fussed over Annie almost as much as Mum did. But he can't have been much more than a boy when he went away to fight, Annie had worked that much out. She took a deep breath and falteringly began, 'Do you want to talk about it, Harry? About what happened to you in the war?'

She always felt she was prying when she tried to talk to Harry about his feelings. It wasn't like her side of the family, with Elsie and Ivy bickering, Bill grumbling and Mum making everyone cups of tea in the cramped scullery at Grove Road. He fitted in there but when anyone asked how his folks back in Newcastle were getting on, he'd fall silent.

He was such a private person, really, and he never spoke

much about his mum because it upset him to talk about her; she wasn't in the best of health and his sister, Kitty, looked after her, he'd said that much. Kitty had the poshest job Annie had ever heard of for a woman – she worked for a shipping journal in Newcastle, tapping away at a typewriter and checking all the facts and figures, helping to edit it. Harry always talked about Kitty with such pride and Annie longed to meet her, but it seemed such a long way away, Newcastle upon Tyne.

Annie had even asked him if they could go and visit, but he'd just flicked open his evening newspaper and said, 'Oh, Annie, pet, it's too far to go, especially now there's a war on.' He wrote letters, lots of them, and he got letters back too. Annie supposed they must be from Kitty and his mother, but she'd never read them. He'd read her bits of news about what was happening at the shipyards but she didn't like to ask too much more because, well, he seemed to like a bit of privacy. He kept the letters locked away in an old tea chest and he carried the key around in his jacket pocket.

Annie reached out and stroked his back, feeling the softness of his flannel pyjamas at her fingertips, silently thanking God that his life hadn't been claimed by a German bullet in the trenches of the First World War.

Her question hung in the air. Harry lay motionless and Annie supposed, from the sound of his deep breathing, that he was already asleep.

The next morning, Annie was on her way down to her mum's when she caught sight of Vera walking along wearing an ARP tin hat at a jaunty angle and whistling

'Knees Up Mother Brown', relishing every moment of the attention she was getting from people queuing with their coupons along Churchfield Road for the butcher's and the grocer's.

'Hello, hello,' said Vera, sidling up to her friend with a wicked grin on her face. 'Put that light out, then!'

'Vera!' said Annie, pointing to the hat. 'You'll get into trouble wearing that, it's for official use only, you know.'

'I am official,' she chimed, puffing her chest out. 'I've only gone and joined the air-raid wardens, haven't I!'

Annie tried to ignore the filthy looks and tutting noises of the two old ladies outside the butcher's as Vera said, 'They were only too pleased to have me, an' all. They need all the help they can get, with things being the way they are after Dunkirk. I felt it was me patriotic duty to volunteer.'

'That's . . . lovely,' said Annie, struggling to imagine Vera reporting for night duty at the air-raid wardens' HQ without taking a detour to the pub first. 'I wanted to tell you our big news. George got home safely from Dunkirk. I need to get down to Mum's to see him again before he goes back to barracks.'

'Oh, Annie,' said Vera, flinging her arms around her friend. 'I just knew it was going to be all right, didn't I? Your mum must be over the moon about it. Send him my best, won't ya? I should be getting on, I've got important air-raid warden business to attend to.'

Annie smiled to herself as she watched Vera strutting off down the road in her heels but just as Vera was passing a pile of sandbags by the old cemetery, Annie spotted someone else falling into step with her friend. It was

Herbie, the local second-hand car dealer, who'd been keeping himself very busy of late, if rumours were to be believed.

Things had always had a strange habit of dropping off the back of lorries and into Herbie's hands but since the war had broken out there had been a constant stream of goods going into and out of his yard down in South Acton – at least, that's what Bessie had told her.

And the moment Hitler invaded Poland, he'd raised the wall of his front garden by a couple of feet; folks said he'd put a big metal tank in there, behind the hedge, and filled it with petrol. Anyone who needed extra coupons seemed to be able to find them thanks to Herbie and cigarettes were always in plentiful supply when he popped into the pub.

There was something greasy-looking about him, despite his neatly tailored pinstriped suit; the turn-ups on his trousers were just a bit too wide and his shoes so highly polished that they almost gleamed. Herbie wore his black hair slicked back and he had a thin, pencil moustache which twitched whenever he spoke. He carried a little notebook in his breast pocket and he was forever taking it out and noting down what people owed him. He had a silly saying he'd trot out whenever he did that: 'It's all a game, business, ain't it? And it's my game.'

'He's a parky little so-and-so, that Herbie,' Bill would grumble to anyone who'd listen, after he'd put yet another packet of fags on tick. 'Sell his own grandmother if he thought he could get a bob for her.'

Thankfully Herbie hadn't spotted Annie because she didn't want to be seen talking to the likes of him. But he had seen Vera all right and he popped his arm around her in the chummiest manner as they rounded the corner.

Elsie was on her hands and knees in front of the scullery cupboard, yanking pots and pans onto the red-tiled floor, making the most dreadful din.

'For Gawd's sake!' cried Mum, covering her ears as she ushered Annie in to sit down and take the weight off her feet. 'George is trying to sleep upstairs! He'll think the Germans have landed. What on earth are you doing, girl?'

Elsie turned around, sweeping a lock of her chestnut hair from her face, which was red with exertion from pulling out every kitchen pot they owned, it seemed. 'War effort!' she panted. 'It's a scrap metal drive. They want every home to donate some saucepans so that they can melt them down and make aeroplanes. I think it's a brilliant idea! Joan's going to get her mum to put loads of their things in.'

'Oh, is she now?' Mum retorted, grabbing her favourite cast-iron stockpot before Elsie could get her hands on it. She cradled it in her arms. 'Well, no one is touching my pans without my say-so, war or no war!'

'Oh, Mum,' cried Elsie, putting a few aluminium sauce-pans in a little heap, 'we've got to give something. I just saw Esther with the Women's Voluntary Service down on the High Street and they've got a lorry-load going off to that Beaverbrook fella, the Minister for Aeroplanes. I promised her we'd donate.'

Annie smiled to herself. She was desperate to see her friend Esther but they hadn't spoken since last week; Esther had been so busy organizing the Women's Voluntary Service war efforts there just hadn't been time for much else. She had turned into a whirling dervish since her three kids had been evacuated to Wales and her husband, Paul, had joined the RAF. 'It's like being in an empty nest, Annie,' she had told her friend the last time they'd bumped into each other at the shops. 'I've got to keep myself busy, so I'm taking in a couple of Belgian refugees as well as volunteering. The poor souls have nowhere else to go.'

Esther's eyes shone with tears as she spoke. Her family had fled persecution in Belarus before the Great War, saving money from their shoemaking business and fleeing to a new life in England, so she felt more keenly than most how terrible it must be to have to start again from scratch in a foreign land. Annie had always been struck by how kind Esther's family were; they'd helped her out when she'd rowed with Bill and had nowhere else to turn. There would always be food on the table and a warm welcome for her.

Annie couldn't imagine cramming refugees into her flat or her mum's house, but Esther lived in a house on the smarter side of Acton, off Twyford Avenue, because her husband had found a job as a bank clerk and they'd gone up in the world. She never put on airs and graces like some people, though. She was still the same Esther who had washed shirts with Annie back in the laundry when they were little more than girls. She'd even promised to give Annie some of her kids' old baby clothes, which would really help Annie out.

There was a footfall on the stairs and George ambled in, rubbing sleep out of his eyes with his hair all over the place.

Mum practically clucked like a mother hen as she handed him some toast, spread thickly with butter, and started to pour him a cup of tea. She handed him his army uniform trousers, which had been patched and pressed to perfection overnight, as if by a miracle.

'Thanks, Mum,' he said. He kissed Annie on the cheek and sat down at the table. 'I'd better be off sharpish after this. I'll be for the high jump if I stay much longer.'

'Harry's planning to pop in on his tea break, can't you just wait a little longer?' said Annie, reaching out to hold his hand. 'He'll be so disappointed if he misses you.'

George glanced at his sister, smiled and nodded in agreement.

Annie watched him as he ate his breakfast, trying to freeze time. She'd always looked out for him when they were growing up together but the battles that were to come in this war were his to fight. 'You will come back to us safely, won't you?' she said.

He held her hands in his. 'Of course I will,' he replied gently. 'You know, Annie, you mustn't worry about me. You've got to think about the baby now. In fact, I'm going to write to the little one, from wherever I end up. I'll send postcards to you, I promise. And when this war is over, we can all look through them together. How about that?'

Annie found herself fighting back tears. 'That's so kind, George.'

While they were chatting, Elsie was edging her way towards the door with her scrap metal contribution, but she was cut off at the pass by Mum, who made a last-ditch effort to snatch one pan back. The pair of them were still tussling when Harry appeared in the hallway and Mum relented and went back to the washing-up.

He joined them at the table but Annie watched with a growing sense of unease as Harry listened to George tell him more about his miraculous escape from Dunkirk. His jaw was rigid, and his eyes started to dart about the room. In the end, he got up and came back with a bottle of sherry from the larder and poured himself a glass.

He liked a pint did Harry, but sherry was for Christmas and celebrations, so it was strange to see him choosing a drink like that and at this time of day. Mum raised an eyebrow as he knocked it back and, glancing at the clock on the mantelpiece, said, 'Well, it's almost time for the news.'

They switched on the wireless to listen to the BBC Home Service and the room fell silent. The announcer spoke solemnly about an important speech Prime Minister Winston Churchill had made to parliament, in the face of the German invasion of France and the fall of the Low Countries.

Churchill's words carried across the airwaves into their little terraced home. They were all relying on him now, more than ever, to guide them through this war. '*We shall go on to the end. We shall fight in France, we shall fight on the seas and oceans, we shall fight with growing confidence and growing strength in the air, we shall defend our island, whatever the cost will be.*'

There was flicker of terror on Harry's face, before he put his head in his hands for a moment. George stood up; it was time for him to go.

'*We shall fight on the beaches, we shall fight on the landing grounds, we shall fight in the fields and in the streets, we shall fight in the hills. We shall never surrender.*'

The neighbours turned out to wave George off and Harry strolled along with him, to get back to work at the factory. Annie and her mum watched from the doorstep as the two men made their way down towards Acton High Street. George would need to catch the tram up to town and return to his regiment, which was stationed up North, near Leeds, where he'd be expected to explain his absence to his superiors.

Annie felt so exhausted and queasy from the emotion of saying goodbye, she went upstairs for a lie-down and the next thing she knew, it was tea time and Mum was at her side, gently shaking her awake.

She tried to sit up but had the most sudden and shocking pain, letting out a yelp. 'Ooh,' she said, as she curled into a ball and her stomach went rigid. 'I think I might be better standing.'

As she swung her legs over the side of the bed, there was a sudden gush of liquid all over the bed and the floor.

'Oh my God,' cried Annie. 'I didn't mean to do that, I've ruined the bedspread. I'm sorry.'

'Stop fussing,' said Mum, rolling up her sleeves. 'It's just your waters breaking. I'll get some towels. Now, just relax.'

'But I'm supposed to go to the hospital!' cried Annie, panic etched on her face. 'I'm too old to have it at home. The doctor said so!'

'Stuff and nonsense,' said Mum. 'You're as fit as a fiddle.'

Annie eased herself out of her underwear and lay on her back as the contractions started to get closer together, gasping, 'I need to get up to the hospital!'

'No time for that,' said Mum matter-of-factly. 'This baby's got other ideas . . .'

She was such a perfect, wriggling lump of humanity, with a pink, screwed-up face, and hair as black as coal.

She'd only taken a few hours to arrive and Annie knew, as she looked down at the baby in her arms, that their world would never be the same now that she was here.

'What shall we call her?' said Annie, gazing up at Harry, who looked fit to burst with pride. Bill had been despatched to get him from the factory, with the news that the baby was on the way.

Harry thought for a moment and then said, 'How about Anita? It means little Annie, and she does look just like you . . .'

As Annie lay back, exhausted, the baby wriggled again in her arms and started to cry. Annie stroked the baby's face for a moment and felt a deep pull of love inside her, when tiny fingers clasped hers.

Harry came to Annie's side and picked up the baby, soothing her. 'There, there, little Annie. Everything's going to be all right.'

She stopped crying and looked right at him.

'My daughter, my little girl, Daddy's here,' he said.

5

Annie

Acton, September 1940

'They were more like a bunch of street urchins than my own children,' said Esther, as she helped Annie push the baby around Springfield Gardens one beautiful, sunny afternoon. 'As soon as I laid eyes on them, I knew I had to bring them home.'

Esther's three kids were playing chase, whooping with delight, their gas masks in cardboard boxes strung across their bodies. Leonard, her eldest, still didn't have a picking of fat on him and his younger sisters Florrie and Clemmie had a terrible, exhausted look about them, with dark circles under their eyes.

'I wish I'd had Bessie with me when I went to get them back and found out what had been going on,' said Esther. 'She would have given that beastly farmer's wife what for. I should never have let them be evacuated in the first place.'

'Don't torment yourself,' said Annie. 'Everyone thought that sending them out of London was the right thing to do.'

Poor Esther. She'd trusted that the farm in North Wales where the children had been evacuated would be a kind place, where they could run about in the fresh air and enjoy the country life. Instead they were used as cheap labour, forced to milk the cows and feed the pigs and muck out the stables before breakfast, and after school they had more chores before the farmer's wife would even think about feeding them. Clemmie, the youngest, found it the hardest because she got terribly homesick and when she lost her coat, she was left without one all winter and got sick with the flu.

It was only when Leonard managed to smuggle a letter to the parish priest to send to his mum that Esther realized something was wrong. They'd been struggling as evacuees for more than nine months by the time she brought them home to London. Now they were back where they belonged and Esther had a full house, what with the kids and the Belgian refugees she'd taken in, but everyone seemed to get along just fine.

'I don't think I will ever forgive myself,' Esther said, as Clemmie ran to her for a hug. 'Just don't you let little Anita get sent away, will you?'

'Of course not,' said Annie. 'She's staying right here with me, where she's safe.'

They wandered past rows and rows of vegetables which had been planted thanks to the Dig for Victory campaign. The lawns at Springfield Gardens had always been so well tended, but now they'd been turned over into mounds of earth and they looked like a market garden, with Acton's Gardening Society volunteers hard at it, tending their crops. The veg was sold 'off the rations' in the market place just off the High Street. The fact that you weren't limited by coupons meant there was always something to chuck in the pot to make a stew go that bit further.

People had been pulling together since Dunkirk, preparing for the worst. There were pillboxes popping up all over the place around Acton, disguised as police telephone kiosks and even an ice cream stall. Kids played around them, but Annie knew that if it came to it and Germany invaded, they'd be used as vantage points for the Home Guard to fire weapons at the enemy. Every street had volunteer firewatchers and there were signs painted in white in front of the houses: 'P' meant there was a stirrup pump kept there and 'L' meant ladder. Kids liked to join in too, so they'd chalk 'B' for 'bucket' on the pavement outside their front doors.

Things at Grove Road were quite cheerful because Ivy and Charlie were tying the knot soon and there was all the excitement that that brought with it. Annie was helping Ivy to make her dress, because she was a dab hand with a needle and thread, but her sister had lost so much weight recently, Annie was sure she'd have to take it in again. Ivy had always been slimmer than Elsie, with a heart-shaped face, but now she had a gaunt look and her clothes had started to hang off her. Of course, all brides lost a bit of weight before their big day, with the nerves of it all, but Annie couldn't help worrying about her. In her heart of hearts, she feared something was wrong but Ivy just brushed her concerns to one side whenever Annie tried to ask her if she needed to talk.

'Is Elsie going to be a bridesmaid?' asked Esther. 'I expect she'll be wanting to walk up the aisle next, won't she?'

But Annie's reply was drowned out by the deafening wail of the air-raid siren. Esther and Annie looked at each other in horror. Time stood still. They heard the drone of aircraft approaching from above and then the boom of the anti-aircraft guns less than a mile away at Gunnersbury Park. Then there was another sound, more terrifying: the sickening thud of bombs exploding.

There was little time to think. Esther's children ran, screaming, towards them, in a welter of flailing arms and legs. Annie grabbed Anita from the pram, tucking her under one arm. She seized Clemmie's hand and started to run towards the public air-raid shelter at the far end of the park. It was buried deep underground and had grass over the top, so that all you could see were a couple of little periscopes sticking out, to give people inside fresh air.

She'd had a quick look around one morning while she was out with the baby, just out of curiosity, really, pushing open the metal door, peering inside and wrinkling her nose at the dank smell. But now, this grim underground concrete bunker was their best hope of survival and she'd never been more grateful for it.

Esther was hot on her heels, with Leonard and Florrie at her side. Gardeners chucked their spades to the ground and threw off their gumboots to sprint across the park to safety, as the sky above filled with enemy planes, sounding, for all the world, like a horrid black cloud of droning insects.

Annie's heart was pounding as she hurried Clemmie down the narrow concrete steps which led into the shelter in front of them. The metal door was propped open and half a dozen people were already sitting in there, blanching with fear under the electric lights. There were slatted wooden benches at either side of the shelter and some metal bunk beds at the far end. Once the last of the gardeners had made it to safety, the door clanged shut and the fetid atmosphere closed in on them.

'Do you think there will be anything left of Acton when we get out of here?' said Esther, her eyes widening as the thudding of bombs grew nearer.

'Of course there will,' came a man's voice from the bench opposite. 'And if there ain't, we'll rebuild it.'

Annie could only hope that her family had got to safety in the Anderson shelter in the back garden. And, please God, let Harry have made it into the factory shelter down at C.A.V. She clasped her hands together around the baby, willing them all, through divine intervention, to get through this and trying to ignore a dark swell of terror inside her about what may become of them if they took a direct hit.

The baby started to grizzle. She was hungry.

Annie knew she was going to have to feed her but the whole idea of doing it in front of strangers seemed to have robbed her of the use of her fingers. Esther leaned across and whispered, 'It's all right, Annie, no one will care. Just get on with it. Here, let me help while you get yourself sorted. I'll hold her for you for a minute.'

Annie turned scarlet with humiliation and fumbled to undo the buttons on the front of her blouse. It was such a private thing, a precious moment between her and her child, and now she was having to do it in front of people she'd never met before. A woman at the other end of the shelter untied her headscarf and brought it to Annie, gently laying it over her shoulder to protect her modesty. She was about the same age as her own mother. 'There you go, love, you carry on, it's only natural,' she said, giving Annie's arm a little squeeze.

Men looked at the floor or started twiddling their thumbs. One lit up a smoke, his match flaring.

The reality of being in the middle of an air raid seemed to sink in after a while, and Clemmie began to sob quietly, until an old woman started humming 'We'll Meet Again'. Before long, all three of Esther's children were singing along. One of the gardeners produced a hunk of bread from his jacket pocket and shared it with them. Annie gazed down at Anita, who was now sleeping soundly through the most horrifying racket outside: the booming of the ack-ack guns punctuated by the thudding of a stick of bombs raining down from the sky.

More than an hour went by before the all-clear sounded, and when they emerged, blinking, into the remains of the day, there was an eerie quietness and the acrid smell of burning filled the air. Birds were still twittering in the trees, but the park was strewn with abandoned wellies, gardening equipment and Annie's overturned pram, as if a whirlwind had whipped through their world and then, just as suddenly, departed.

'Well,' said one gardener, shrugging his shoulders, 'it don't look that bad! I'd better get back to me spuds.'

They all took great lungfuls of air, shook hands with each other and said their goodbyes, as they were now certainly more than just strangers. They had survived this together.

The horizon seemed to be on fire, glowing red, with palls of black smoke rising in the distance. Annie and Esther hugged each other tightly. Who would have thought that the war would come to London?

With Anita still fast asleep, Annie hurried with her pram to her mum's house in Grove Road, her heart thumping ten to the dozen. Churchfield Road hadn't been hit but some shopkeepers were dragging more sandbags up in front of their windows, in case of any further attacks.

People were standing on their doorsteps talking animatedly and children started coming out of the houses in dribs and drabs, to play in the streets, just as they always did on fine evenings. One little boy kicked over a dustbin which clattered as Annie went past, almost making her jump out of her skin.

Mum was standing on the front step looking out for her as she came rushing down the road with the pram, at full pelt. They almost collided with each other and then Mum threw herself into Annie's arms, hugging and kissing her.

'Oh, thank the good Lord above, you're safe!' cried Mum. 'Come inside, love, I'll put the kettle on.'

Just then, Elsie came lumbering down the stairs with a huge bundle of bedding, which she dropped as soon as she laid eyes on Annie and the baby. 'Oh, Annie,' she cried, rushing down the last few steps and ignoring Mum's tutting at the mess she'd just made. 'I thought we were all goners! Where were you?'

'I was caught in the park with Esther,' said Annie, lifting the baby out of the pram. 'We made it into the underground shelter. It wasn't that bad. Folks were quite nice, actually.' The last thing she wanted was to have to spend every air raid in there with Anita, but she was determined to put a brave face on it.

'Love,' said Mum, brushing some hair back from Annie's forehead, 'why don't you and little Annie come and stay down here in the evenings? It would be much better. We can all be together in the Anderson.'

Bill's head appeared around the scullery door. 'But there's barely enough room in there as it is! We'll be squished like sardines!'

He caught the look in Mum's eye and thought better of continuing, muttering, 'All right, all right, it'll be fine. We'll make room.' He grabbed his coat and made for the front door before Mum could flick a tea towel in his general direction. 'I s'pose I'd better go and see if I can find another chair or two down at the totter's in South Acton.'

'Well,' said Elsie, giving the baby a quick hug as Bill set off, 'when the siren went, I grabbed my lippie and my best blouse, and three guesses what Ivy ran back into the house for?'

'I'm up here!' came a voice from the landing. 'I can hear you, Elsie, you cheeky minx.'

'Yes,' said Elsie, waving her arms melodramatically. 'The dress!'

Annie called up to her sister: 'Do you need it pinning again?'

'The waist's gone all baggy,' Ivy wailed. 'Oh Gawd, Annie, I look a sight. No man's going to want to marry me looking like this.'

Mum and Annie exchanged glances before Annie said, 'I'll be up in a minute, then, just let me sort the baby out.'

She was climbing the stairs to help her sister with her wedding dress when Harry burst through the front door, still wearing his black tin hat with ARP on it. He pulled her into an embrace. 'Oh, Annie! All I could think about was you and the baby staying safe. I couldn't bear to lose you.'

'We're fine,' said Annie, gazing into his grey eyes, which melted her heart. 'We'll get used to this. We can't let them beat us.'

Annie knew then, beyond any doubt, that the battle for Britain's future, for all their lives, would be waged on their doorsteps.

6

Annie

Acton, October 1940

The bombing went on, night after night.

The incessant wail of the air-raid siren in the early hours of the morning became as much a part of everyone's daily routine as the pips marking the top of the hour on the BBC Home Service.

Daylight raids were rare because of the ack-acks and spitfires but the bombers flew in under the cloak of darkness with alarming regularity, leaving a trail of destruction in their wake.

The East End had been flattened in the first attacks, with huge damage to the docks and factories on both sides of the Thames. Annie got used to seeing small gaggles of survivors, with all their worldly goods in bundles, at bus and tram stops in the town as they headed further west, to get out of London, to the safety of the countryside. Others queued patiently outside the town hall, waiting to hear if they could be rehoused.

But German bombers were having a field day in Acton

too. Horn Lane, which lay less than half a mile away, had been hit three times in as many weeks and the last bomb demolished an entire house, leaving a hole the size of a trolley bus on the corner of Acacia Road.

Annie couldn't imagine ever getting used to what was happening to the area she loved so much.

She'd be wheeling her pram through streets she'd known for years, only to round a corner and find a bombed-out home standing there, like a doll's house with the front blown off and all the furniture smashed to smithereens. Clothes, photographs, children's toys – all the little treasures that people liked to keep, to make their mark in this life – were strewn in every direction. People helped, of course, to go through the wreckage, to salvage any belongings from the Blitz, offering comfort to those who were lucky enough to have survived.

After one nightly raid, when Annie was on her way down to Soapsud Island to see Bessie, she passed a bomb site and spotted a photographer from the local paper taking a picture. The fella who'd lived there was kneeling down beside some things he'd pulled from the wreckage: an old suitcase, a table and – miraculously – some china. His house lay in ruins behind him. 'That's right,' said the photographer, 'let's show old Hitler we're not beaten yet.' The man smiled for the camera, giving a cheesy grin, as his life lay in tatters and the flashbulb went off.

The hostilities with Germany seemed to have led to an uneasy truce between Bessie and the lady downstairs over who had the rights to the copper in the scullery on washday, although there was always the possibility of a skirmish on the stairs.

Annie parked the pram outside and left the baby there to sleep, while a couple of girls in tatty pinafores played hopscotch nearby. Bessie's front door was open, so she walked in, just as she always did, making her way up the creaky staircase. She rapped lightly on the door to Bessie's kitchen and pushed it open. It was spotlessly clean, as ever, and smelled faintly of carbolic soap.

Bessie was sitting on her favourite chair at the kitchen table, her grey hair pulled up into a bun, with a heap of rags at her feet. Her eyes lit up when she saw Annie, but her fingers kept working, prodding strips of material through an old jute potato sack with a wooden clothes peg. 'Oh, Annie, love! Nice to see you. How've you and the baby been keeping?'

'We're fine,' said Annie, pulling up the only other chair in the room to sit beside Bessie. 'I can't say I'm getting much sleep but then, I suppose nobody is these days.'

'Changes your life for the better, having a little one, though, don't it?' Bessie said, beaming at Annie. 'Here, hand me another pile of those rags, will you? My lumbago is killing me from the washboards yesterday.' Bessie was around the same age as Mum, but she still worked shifts at one of the local laundries down Bollo Lane. It was back-breaking work, for just a few pounds a week, but it was all she had ever known.

Annie handed her the strips of material and then stood up to pop the kettle on the stove in the corner. There was a scratching sound at the back door, which led, via a rickety wooden staircase, to the yard below. She opened it and a fat, ginger tomcat strutted in. He wandered over to a china saucer of milk by the fireplace and began to lap at it; he was all the family Bessie had, so even on rations, he wasn't going to go hungry.

'They say it's going to be a bomber's moon tonight,' said Bessie, her brows knitting in concentration as she held up her rag rug to check it for evenness. 'Seen much of Vera lately?'

'No,' said Annie. 'She popped round to see the baby a few weeks ago but I haven't seen hide nor hair of her since, because she's joined the ARP, you know? Harry sees her from time to time. Says she's actually quite a good worker.'

'Mmm,' said Bessie, fixing Annie with a gimlet eye. 'I've heard she's making the most of being an air-raid warden.'

'What do you mean?' said Annie, trying to ignore the sinking feeling in her stomach.

'Well, she's been seen hanging around with that Herbie a lot lately and you know he's a right little so-and-so.'

'But Bessie,' said Annie, stiffening, 'at least she's got a job and she's doing something for the war effort. More than me, in fact. And she's known Herbie since school, their families are friends from way back.'

'Hasn't stopped her taking liberties on account of her position, though, has it? And that's before we get onto her flashing her knickers at anything and everything in uniform,' said Bessie, putting down her rug, smoothing her pinny and walking to the stove, where the kettle had sprung to life and was whistling its head off.

'I don't know anything about that, so I wouldn't want to gossip . . .' said Annie.

'Well, neither would I!' said Bessie huffily. 'But I know she's been seen handing packets of tea to that Herbie and the other day, someone swore blind they saw her pulling some rashers of bacon out of her drawers, like some kind of bleeding hoister!'

'But—' Annie began.

'Everyone knows the ARP are getting extra rations down at their headquarters! Everything from milk and butter to tea and bacon and eggs, if you please! Everyone knows it, while the rest of us are scraping by on what we can get on the coupons. It don't seem fair, Annie, because it ain't, and Vera's making money out of it. I'm not saying she ain't doing her bit, with all the other ARP girls, but why should she be getting extra helpings?' Bessie folded her arms across her ample bosom and glared at Annie.

'I don't think it's fair to have a go at Vera about the extra rations at the ARP,' Annie murmured. 'I mean, Harry is getting extra too, you know, for working the nightshifts.'

Bessie coloured up. 'Oh, I'm not having a go at Harry, goodness me, no! I couldn't begrudge a working man like him, doing shifts at the factory and then volunteering on top of it all. He's entitled to it. It's just Vera being on the take that rankles. Besides, she's getting a bit podgy around the middle, if you ask me.'

Annie looked at her friend, who was almost shaking with anger as she spoke. She had no answers to give her. The silence was punctuated by the crying of Anita, who had woken in her pram outside and was exercising her lungs as best she could.

'I'd better go,' said Annie with a sigh, 'or the woman downstairs'll complain about the racket.' She was secretly quite relieved to be going. 'I'll try to talk to Vera about it the next time I see her.' Although God only knows how she was going to manage to broach this lot with her friend.

Annie paused for a moment, walking over to Bessie and giving her shoulder a gentle squeeze. 'Perhaps you shouldn't dwell on what is going on with Vera. I know you wouldn't spread gossip about her, but I just think the less said, the better.'

Bessie tutted at her, shook her head and went back to her rag rug.

'Suit yourself, Annie,' she muttered under her breath. 'But it ain't gossip, because it's all true.'

As night fell, Annie was only too happy to be down at Grove Road with her mum, sisters and Bill, huddled in the Anderson shelter in the back garden. It was not much more than six feet long and about four feet across, so everyone had to sit cheek by jowl in there. Mum had tried her best to make it comfortable, with an old camp bed covered with blankets and a couple of chairs with cushions on. But because it was made of corrugated iron, it was blooming chilly inside, even with earth piled on top of it, which is what the government had told everyone to do for extra protection.

Bill had hung a picture of the King on the wall, for patriotic reasons, and Mum had all their important papers

– health insurance policies, birth certificates, the rent and the tallyman's books – safely tucked inside, in an old tin box, in case the house took a direct hit. When the air-raid siren went, everyone would tip themselves out of bed, chuck on a dressing gown or jumpers and a coat, and shoes, and rush downstairs. Bill kept a paraffin lamp and matches by the back door and it was only a few steps to the bottom of the garden in any case, so it didn't take long to get inside.

The baby was everyone's priority. Mum had made her a little cot in the shelter, out of an old drawer, and the bedding was changed nightly to stop it getting damp. Inside the house, she slept with Annie, in Elsie's bed, while Elsie and Ivy bunked up together, top to tail – which was the source of a lot of rows, but everyone tried to make the best of it.

In the dim glow of the paraffin lamp, with Anita wrapped snugly as the ground shook, it seemed to Annie that their whole world was shrinking. Jerry liked to drop a stick of bombs, in fours or sixes, so the explosions went off one after the other. They'd close their eyes and hold hands, praying, *Dear God, please let it pass us by*, as they waited for the all-clear to sound, but always with a horrible guilt that the bombs had landed on some other poor souls in Acton. Then, they'd push open the shelter door, shout hello to the neighbours over the garden fence, who were bumbling their way back into their own home – 'That was a close one!' – and go back to bed, to try to snatch some sleep until the siren went again.

When dawn broke and Annie opened the curtains, it was always with a sense of trepidation, to see what was left standing in the neighbourhood. Harry would usually bring news of what had happened, popping in for a quick kiss and a cuppa before heading back to their flat for a few hours' kip before his factory shift. But as the days of bombings turned into weeks, he said less and less about what he'd seen during his nights on the air-raid wardens' watch.

The worst thing was, one night, there was a direct hit in Soapsud Island, on Church Path, which flattened half the street. Everyone felt it happen; the foundations in Grove Road – less than half a mile away – shook with the impact. Eight houses went down, along with the corner shop. It was a dreadful blow to the community – unspeakable. Half a dozen lost their lives, including people her mum and Bessie had worked with in the laundries for years.

Harry barely said a word when he came around, ashen-faced, the next morning after his ARP shift, to check on her and the baby. She didn't push him. It just felt wrong. Someone had to remove the dead bodies and search for the living, calling out, 'Is anybody there?' into the rubble, as volunteers frantically lifted bits of masonry aside. All too often, they were searching in vain or there was little they could do to save people, due to the force of the blast.

Even then, in its darkest hour, Soapsud Island showed it wasn't beaten. When the funeral services were over, mourners went back to Church Path and draped Union Jacks over the ruins.

They stood together, arm in arm, heads bowed, and vowed never to give in to Nazi Germany.

*

'Ivy, you are going to look pretty as a picture!' said Mum, as Ivy teetered in her high heels and wedding dress on a chair in the bedroom, while Annie pinned the hem to get it just right.

'Do you really think so?' said Ivy. 'I hope Charlie likes it.'

Annie gazed up at her younger sister for a moment. She was as pale as a ghost, with a cloud of dark hair framing her face, which used to be like Mum's, but now seemed to have developed high cheekbones. Her dress was of cream satin and fell from her nipped-in waist, making it look impossibly tiny. Annie had worked hard to create the puffed sleeves and sweetheart neckline that Ivy wanted but if she lost any more weight, the bust would need taking in too.

Elsie was busy practising a few dance steps across the wooden floorboards in her knee-length dress, which had the same puff sleeves as her sister, but was in peach artificial silk. Annie had picked a couple of dress lengths of material up at Derry and Tom's in Kensington High Street for next to nothing back in the summer when they'd had a sale on and there was just enough of the peach material left over for her to make herself a blouse. She was planning to wear it on the big day, along with her best woollen skirt and shoes, as matron of honour.

Charlie had volunteered and was away square-bashing in Kent with the army, so Ivy hadn't seen him for a couple of weeks, but she tended to pop down to his mum's in Soapsud Island, because she wanted to get along with her mother-in-law and Charlie liked her being around there. They were planning to rent an upstairs flat nearby, in Steele Road. 'It's next door to the stone-mason's yard,' Mum had confided in Annie, 'which means the first thing Ivy'll see every morning when she draws back the curtains is a bunch of headstones. That's not very cheerful, is it?'

Elsie sashayed back and forth across the floorboards, swishing her dress about as she went. 'Do you think you could make me a siren suit for the shelter, Annie, if you have time? We could use one of our old blankets and fashion it with arms and legs.' She picked up a blanket from the foot of her bed. 'The suits are quite stylish. Joan's got one.'

'Oh, I bet she has,' said Mum, handing Annie some extra pins. She had little time for Elsie's friend; for a start, she blamed her for luring her daughter out gallivanting all over the place with men in uniform.

'I'll see what I can do,' said Annie. 'Perhaps I will get some time next week.'

In truth, she was barely sleeping and the last thing she felt like doing was taking on another sewing project, but at least if Elsie had a siren suit, she'd be more likely to be in the air-raid shelter at Grove Road, rather than going out dancing at all hours of the night.

The wedding was quite a small family affair on a brisk and sunny Saturday morning but the whole neighbour-hood wanted to share in the excitement of it.

Mum had used up all the dried fruit she'd been hoarding for Christmas to make a fruit cake, and Bessie chipped in with a bag of currants and some spare sugar.

There was no question of icing it, so Mum did what most people had to do nowadays and created a cake-shaped cover in white cardboard to look like icing, with some flowers on the top.

Bill had borrowed one of the laundry delivery vans to take Ivy down to All Saints Church on Acton Green. While Ivy was getting dressed, Annie and Elsie spent ages fixing a length of white ribbon to the bonnet to make it pretty. The big surprise was that George had been allowed some home leave for the wedding, and as Ivy came out of the house and realized it was her big brother sitting there at the wheel of the van, grinning from ear to ear, she almost burst into tears.

'Now, now,' said Mum, dabbing at her daughter's face with a hankie, 'no tears yet or you'll ruin your face for Charlie!'

'Come on, Ivy,' said George, 'you don't want to keep him waiting too long. Hop in!' A crowd of kids had already gathered to peer at the blushing bride and housewives waved and shouted their good wishes to her as the van made its way down Grove Road. George planned to drive her up and down the High Street a few times to give the rest of the wedding party a chance to get to the church first.

Harry slipped his hand into Annie's as they walked down Acton Lane in all their finery. He'd put on his best suit, of dark navy wool, and last night he'd spent ages polishing his shoes. Annie leaned into him as they fell into step together, pushing the baby in the pram as they went. It reminded her of her wedding day, just before the war broke out, when things were the way they'd always been and bombs didn't rain down from the sky every night.

Mum's sister, Aunt Clara, was waiting in the church with her friend Dora, who'd lived with her for as long as anyone could remember. They'd organized some of the washerwomen to help decorate the church and they'd done a beautiful job with the flowers which were tied to the end of each pew. Bessie was bustling about checking that everything was just as it should be, and she sat, with some ceremony, with Mum and the rest of the family, as a mark of her status in the proceedings.

Charlie was there early, waiting at the altar, as thin as a reed in his khaki uniform. Above his high forehead, he had a shock of black hair, which stuck up on end no matter how hard he tried to comb it down. He smiled as Ivy entered the church, and his blue eyes sparkled but Annie couldn't help thinking there was something flinty about his gaze.

Ivy's bouquet of pink carnations was shaking in her hands as she made her way up the aisle on Bill's arm, with Annie and Elsie following close behind. Everybody wanted it to be such a great occasion, a little sparkle of happiness in the midst of so much death and destruction, and Ivy looked like the expectation of it was weighing on her every step.

But as she reached Charlie, she smiled and it was like the sun coming out. All the nervousness disappeared. She gazed up at Charlie adoringly as the vicar began: 'Dearly beloved, we are gathered here today in the presence of Christ . . .'

*

Everyone came back to Grove Road for a reception of sherry, cake and sandwiches with the happy couple before heading off down the pub for a bit of a knees-up.

Mum was just slicing the fruit cake into thin pieces so that there would be enough to go around when Charlie came over to Annie and embraced her.

'Congratulations, Charlie,' she said. 'You must be over the moon.'

'Yes,' he said, running his hands through his hair, which, close up, reminded Annie of a lavatory brush. 'Ivy's a lovely girl. But Harry's a lucky man, isn't he? I mean, you got your figure back quickly, didn't you?' He put his hands in his pockets as he appraised her form in her blouse and tight-fitting skirt. 'Let's hope it runs in the family.'

Ivy came to his side with two pieces of cake on a plate; he took one and bit into it, chewing thoughtfully. 'Very nice.'

Ivy made to pick up the other slice but in a split second, his hand covered hers. Annie watched as Ivy returned the cake to its resting place on the plate in front of her.

She tilted her chin towards him, her lips slightly parted. Then she kissed him.

7

Annie

Acton, November 1940

Annie and Harry passed like ships in the night.

He still found time to dandle the baby on his knee but what with the factory and his duties with the ARP, they were barely spending any time together as a family.

Anita was nearly five months old now, able to hold her head up well and stare at people with such a direct gaze, she seemed to look right into their souls. Harry doted on her; he still insisted on Annie and the baby sleeping down at Grove Road as much as possible because of the bombing.

Bill had spent ages out in the back garden making the Anderson shelter cosier for the winter. He'd made bunk beds, using wire and some planks of wood from one of the timber yards down in South Acton. The whole project seemed to have involved a lot of splinters and a fair amount of swearing.

Annie had sewn the siren suit for Elsie out of an old blanket, just as she'd promised, and Elsie had taken to sleeping in it most nights; what's more, with no Ivy kicking her in the shins, she could make the most of having a bed to herself again.

When Harry had rest days from his ARP work, they'd stay up at their flat on Allison Road, even though it meant a sprint over the road to the public air-raid shelter in Springfield Gardens when the siren went. It was either that or hiding out under the kitchen table and praying to God that they wouldn't take a direct hit. She'd started calling that dreaded siren the 'Moaning Minnie' and the shelter was 'the bunker'. She hated that place – it was dank and sometimes the people in there got a bit rowdy, especially if they'd been down the pub first. No one wanted to have to bring their baby into that kind of atmosphere, but it really was a matter of life and death and it wasn't as bad as some of the other shelters, which were so waterlogged you needed your wellies or you'd be up to your ankles in it.

She was hoping that tonight would be different, and the bombers wouldn't come over, so they'd get a quiet night in together. She'd made a little stew, carefully dicing the veg and seasoning it just as he liked it. But Harry didn't come home for his tea after work as they had planned. The hours ticked by and she busied herself, ironing the baby's clothes, cleaning the kitchen floor, and doing some knitting for winter. By eleven o'clock, she'd sorted through all her clothes drawers and hung all Harry's work shirts, nice and tidily, back in the wardrobe, trying to ignore a knot of worry that was building in her stomach.

She heard the front door open and bang shut, his footfall down the hallway, and then the scullery door swung open and Harry appeared. His tie and collar were undone and he had a ciggie dangling from his lips as he swayed slightly in the doorway.

'Harry!' Annie chided, standing up. 'Have you been on the sauce?'

'Can't a man have a drink?' he said crossly, glaring at her. He turned his back on her and stalked away to the bedroom, pulling the door shut behind him.

Annie sat back down. His evening paper lay folded in its usual place on the table, waiting for him, but he didn't return. She sighed to herself and heated up some stew on the stove, taking him in a plate of it as a peace offering.

He was lying on the bed, fully clothed and with his shoes still on, staring at the ceiling.

'I'm sorry,' she began, going to his side and putting the plate down on the bedside table. 'You're working so hard, I didn't mean to say you couldn't go for a drink. Of course you can.'

He looked up at her and in an instant, his eyes filled with tears and then he started to sob, his shoulders heaving as his face crumpled. 'I'm sorry, I'm sorry!'

'Harry,' said Annie, reaching out to him. 'What's wrong?'

He sat up, grasping her waist, and pulled her to him, burying his face in her apron. 'I just wanted to forget, just for one night. That's not too much to ask, is it?'

Carefully, she laid her hands on his back and started to stroke downwards, just as she did with the baby when she was crying. 'What is it?' she said. 'What is it you want to forget?'

'Everything,' he replied, turning away from her.

*

It was pitch black when Harry sat bolt upright in bed, his eyes wide open, and screamed. Annie shook him. 'Harry! Harry! It's all right, it's just a dream.'

'I'm sorry,' he said, lying back down. 'I'm sorry.'

He turned over on his side, facing the wall, as he always did. Annie reached out to touch him, but he brushed her hand aside. 'Leave me be now, Kitty. What's done is done.'

Annie felt tears sting her eyes.

'My name's Annie,' she whispered into the blackness enveloping her. 'I'm Annie. And I'm your wife.'

8

Kitty

Newcastle upon Tyne, May 1916

The white feather lay on the mahogany table in the dining room as the clock marked time on the mantelpiece.

Harry was sitting there in his waistcoat and shirt-sleeves, with his head in his hands.

'Where did that come from?' said Kitty, panic rising in her voice. She unbuttoned her jacket and ran to his side.

Harry looked up at her, his eyes as grey as slate. 'I went for a quick pint in the Bigg Market after work and a woman came up to me in the pub and pressed it into my hands. 'She asked me why I wasn't in uniform, when her son was already away fighting.'

'But that's ridiculous!' said Kitty, giving her thick, auburn hair a shake as she unpinned it, letting it fall to her shoulders; she hated having to be so buttoned up for work. She sat down beside her brother. 'She should mind her own business. You aren't going to take any notice of a stranger, are you?'

Harry sucked in a breath. 'I don't see that I have a choice, Kit. I'm bound to be drafted at some point. I'm nineteen now, I'm old enough to fight. She's right.'

Ever since the Military Service Act had been passed a couple of months ago, Kitty had known in her heart of hearts that her little brother would have to go away to war. Wherever she went, there were posters of Lord Kitchener pointing his finger, saying 'Your Country Needs You!' You couldn't pass a shop window or get on a tram without seeing a bill urging young men to 'Enlist Now!' Lord Kitchener and his unrelenting gaze seemed to be seeking out Harry. And now, at last, he'd found him.

'But it's different for us because Dad isn't here,' said Kitty. 'We need your wage. It's not practical for you to go away. Mum'll have to go back to doing extra hours teaching and you know she's got a weak heart, and with her rheumatism it could kill her.'

Harry was working as an apprentice engineer at Hawthorn Leslie, one of the big shipbuilding firms, and he was learning how to build the diesel pumps for the engines which powered the ships, which were such a major part of Tyneside, with black smoke belching from their funnels as they headed out to sea. Just as the River Tyne ran through the heart of the city, shipbuilding was the lifeblood of the economy and it made Kitty proud that her brother was a part of that.

Mum and Kitty didn't involve him in the running of the house, but the price of food had rocketed in recent months. They weren't struggling to put food on the table like some folks, but they were already feeling the effects of the war on the household purse strings. Bread was getting very expensive and she and Mum had both noticed that all their essentials – meat, cheese, flour, eggs and sugar – had gone up by tuppence a pound, sometimes more. People were becoming anxious and that had even spilled over into unrest when one shopkeeper had pulled down his blinds at noon and locked the door, saying he'd run out of food. A crowd had gathered and hammered on his window, shouting abuse. Of course, the papers had just put it down to people losing their nerve, faced with the anxiety of war, but there were days when the queues were simply ridiculous and you couldn't get basics like sugar for love nor money anywhere in the city.

Kitty's words came gushing out, but Harry only shook his head, his jet-black hair flopping forwards as he did so.

'There's shame enough on this family without me adding to it by being called a coward. I'm not scared to go to the front,' he said, scuffing his feet on the worn patch of carpet under his chair.

'But *I'm* scared,' said Kitty. 'I'm scared for you and I'm scared about what it'll do to Mum if you don't come back. It will destroy her, Harry!' She stood up and walked over to the window, where the aspidistra was wilting slightly in its yellow ornamental pot.

She read the local papers, the *Northern Echo*, the *Newcastle Journal* and the *Evening Chronicle*, and she'd followed the reports of how our Tommies were giving the Hun a good hiding. But she couldn't help noticing that the list of the fallen seemed to get longer by the day. And, what's more, she had no intention of her little brother's name appearing there.

She hesitated for a moment and then spun around to face him. He was staring into space, thinking, as the clock ticked slowly towards the end of the hour, while the two china dogs at either end of the mantelpiece stood guard.

There was fire in her eyes as she spoke. 'What do we care what other people think of us, Harry? Haven't we been through enough? Don't speak to me of shame! I won't have it. I'm not ashamed. Dad told us never to be ashamed, to look people in the eye and hold our heads high. I'm not ashamed for you to be alive. Don't be such a fool.'

Harry's mouth pressed itself into a thin line and he rose to leave, his fingers gripping the green leather back of the dining room chair. 'I care what other people think of us, Kitty. I've had more than five years of it. I thought it would get better, but at least when I was a boy I could raise my fists and fight, even if they beat the living daylights out of me. It's worse now, in some ways, people talking behind our backs or giving us sideways glances.

'This is my chance to bring some honour back to the family. My mind's made up and there's no changing it. I'm joining up first thing in the morning.'

Mum went into a frenzy of cleaning after Harry broke the news that he was going to volunteer, just as she had the night they'd said goodbye to Dad for the last time. Kitty tried to get her to stop, to rest and have something to eat after her long day teaching at the primary school, but she wouldn't hear of it.

'We can't have the place looking like a slum, Kitty. What will the neighbours think?' she said, frantically polishing the dining table. 'And I'm sure people will want to pop in for tea soon to ask how Harry is getting on in the army, won't they?'

It was Mum's dearest wish to have people to visit, but no one ever stopped by. Mum said it was because they'd moved from the smarter side of Jesmond, with its leafy streets and grander houses, to Simonside Terrace in Heaton, which was that little bit more working class. They'd had to economize now there were just the three of them paying the bills, so it was further for friends to come. Kitty knew different. Nobody wanted to be seen darkening their door any more.

Mum's cloth worked its way over the remnants of the life they'd led before: the piano, the glass-fronted bookcase, the tallboy with all their silver cutlery in it and the walnut kissing seat which had come from Dad's side of the family. They'd been gentlemen farmers only a few generations back, Freemen of the city of Alnwick, before they'd moved closer to Newcastle to set up a flourishing farming and butchery business and that was the life that Dad had been born into. But he had other ideas and trained as a ship owner's clerk instead, which hadn't gone down too well with his father, by all accounts.

The family had blamed it all on a wild streak from the French side of the family – Dad's mother, Zelina, was from the Champagne region, and she'd been a governess for one of the wealthy shipbuilding families in Sunderland. Dad only had the haziest of memories of her because she'd died in childbirth when he was just three but everyone who'd known her said she was a spirited woman, determined and outspoken, making her views known in an accent which was a curious mix of English overlaid with Gallic, and a distinct hint of Geordie.

Dad's job had changed quite a bit when Kitty was growing up but that hadn't affected their home life at first. He'd become a secretary to one of the colliery companies, but he helped broker a takeover deal which had made him redundant, even though he got a decent pay-off. Then he came into some money from a wealthy relative in France, and that's when everything changed.

By the time Kitty was fifteen, leaving school and starting secretarial college, they'd moved to their home in Lily Avenue thanks to his inheritance. Dad's head was full of big ideas to use his inheritance to make even more money as a speculator in the coalfields, with one eye on where the next pit shafts might be sunk, so that he'd earn yet another big commission.

Mum seemed worried by it all because Dad was spending more time away at the races, where he'd place bets on behalf of wealthy coal merchants. Kitty realized, from the hushed conversations she'd overheard between her parents, that being a bookie was illegal and he was sailing close to the wind, but Mum did her best to shield Kitty and Harry from her concerns.

There were big losses but there were big wins too, and then he'd really celebrate. Mum could only laugh when one evening he came home three sheets to the wind, clutching a massive, ornate glass bottle filled with coloured water that he'd bought from the chemist's shop, thinking it was perfume. 'I just want to give my darling wife a lovely present,' he slurred, swaying slightly as she took it from him and placed it on the mantelpiece. Kitty and Harry were shooed away into the scullery while she helped him out of his new winter coat with its astrakhan collar and he fell asleep in the armchair by the fireside for a while. Later that evening, Kitty heard Mum helping Dad find his way up the stairs and into bed.

Dad was a bit shamefaced at breakfast and Mum seemed to enjoy teasing him, raising an eyebrow when Harry asked about the new glass ornament, filled with garish pink liquid, which loomed large over the table.

But what followed only a few months later was no laughing matter. Kitty had gone over and over it all in her mind. Could the people he was dealing with at the races, in Birmingham and York and Newcastle, have been to blame somehow? She was clutching at straws but sometimes she'd lie awake, staring at the ceiling, willing the hands of the clock to run backwards, so that she could say or do something that might change what had happened.

The chimes rang out in the parlour. Kitty glanced at the silver fob-watch that Dad had bought her for the last Christmas they'd had together, before their lives were turned upside down. It had been a Sunday tea-time ritual for Dad to take the clock down from the mantelpiece to wind it. Harry was supposed to do it now, as the man of the house, but he kept forgetting – at least, that was his excuse. It was running slow again. Kitty knew that once

Harry had joined up that task would fall to her because Mum wouldn't be able to bear it; it reminded her too much of the quiet Sunday evenings they used to enjoy together, reading, playing the piano or a round of bridge.

It was dark outside now and the house was filled with the overpowering smell of furniture polish. Every piece of wood shone from Mum's efforts and she had collapsed in her favourite chair in the parlour. Kitty brought her a cup of cocoa and sat at her feet, just as she used to do when she was a girl.

'Must he leave us?' said Mum. She reached for the cocoa but her hands seemed almost frozen with rheumatism after all the cleaning, and she winced in pain.

Kitty lifted the cup to her mother's lips and she took a sip and then Kitty started to rub some life back into Mum's swollen fingers.

'Yes,' said Kitty, who could almost hear the sound of boots marching in time through the city streets, as hundreds of young men like Harry headed off to war. 'He must.'

Mum dressed in black the next morning as all three of them left the house. She and Kitty were taking Harry to swear his oath of allegiance to the King. Her long skirt swept the ground as they walked, arm in arm, to the tram stop to take them the two miles from Heaton into the city. She was still a fine figure of a woman, with her waist nipped in by her corset, which she insisted on wearing every day, and she had a quiet dignity about her which commanded the respect of her pupils at school.

Kitty couldn't be doing with all that whalebone and lacing, mind you. She wore her skirt shorter, so that her ankles and her woollen stockings were just visible, and she preferred a longer, looser belted jacket to go with her sailor-collar blouse, so that she could get through a day's work without feeling faint. She'd been a shorthand typist and secretary for a firm of accountants in the city for the last few years. It was steady work, boring really, but at least she didn't have to spend long hours in a factory or stand around in a shop trying to sell things to those silly, flighty women who made a career of acquiring fripperies. They dressed in gauzes and silks, trussed up in their corsets, waving their gloved hands at whatever took their fancy. Despite all that, they had nothing between their ears.

The three of them climbed aboard the No.11 tram with a huge Bovril advert emblazoned on the front and, of course, Lord Kitchener plastered on the back. Mum sat next to Harry, clasping his hand, and Kitty sat behind them, rocking gently from side to side with the movement of the tram as it clattered over the cobbles and against the metal rails. It took them down Jesmond Road, through the leafy suburb and past the cemetery and the park, where they'd spent so many happy hours when they were younger – when they were still a real family.

Kitty would have traded places with her brother, if only she could, so that Mum wouldn't have to lose him. She should have been born a boy; that's what Dad used to say when she was kicking up her petticoats to run about in Jesmond Dene with Harry when they were bairns. Dad hadn't minded; in fact, he'd encouraged her. He always laughed when she and Harry played rough and tumble, his hazel eyes shining with delight. But there were limits, like the time Harry tied her to a tree in the back garden with her skipping rope and cut a lump out of her fringe in a game that got out of hand. Dad had thrashed him for that, even though she'd begged him not to.

As a schoolteacher and a working woman, Mum had encouraged her to have her own thoughts and never to be afraid to speak her mind. She was friends with Mrs Harrison Bell, who'd been a primary school teacher in Heaton, and when she became a leading light of the Newcastle and District Women's Suffrage Committee, Mum went along to her meetings at Fenwick's Drawing Room Cafe.

'Off to your tea and cake chinwag again?' Dad would tease Mum, who'd roll her eyes at him and bang the front door shut. Kitty was just turning sixteen when she was allowed to go along to those gatherings for the first time and she listened, transfixed, as Mrs Harrison Bell – who looked like she wouldn't say boo to a goose with her little round glasses and warm expression – expounded her views on women's emancipation with zeal, to an eager audience.

Before long, the Newcastle suffragettes had moved from the tea room of the department store and church halls to the streets. Mum and Kitty went along to listen to the speakers and to march alongside well-to-do women, wearing sashes of green, white and purple, the colours that Mrs Pankhurst wore; they signified purple for dignity, white for purity and green for hope – Kitty had learned that off by heart.

What's more, there was a group of young women, not much older than Kitty, who were in favour of direct action to force the men in power to listen.

'Making a nuisance of themselves' Dad had called it. Mum wasn't in favour of that either and she made it clear to Kitty why: 'Breaking the law is never the right thing to do. We are law-abiding people, Catherine. You must never forget that. We can't win this battle by getting into trouble with the police. It's about calm and reasoned argument and political change.'

But there was a spark in their eyes which ignited something in Kitty. She sewed her own little rosette to wear at meetings and on marches, but she had to pin that on her lapel when Dad wasn't looking, or he wouldn't be best pleased; in fact, he'd make her take it off.

Kitty began to idolize the suffragettes who carried placards and wouldn't be shouted down by the Bigg Market thugs. Instead, they resolutely insisted that they should have a voice and rights at the ballot box, the same as men, and when it didn't happen, they were prepared to take matters into their own hands.

Dad had put his foot down after the Battle of Newcastle in 1909. That was what the papers had called it, after suffragettes broke windows all over the town and one even took an axe to a barrier in Percy Street. The city had never seen anything like it. Lady Lytton, who was so posh she spoke like she had a mouth full of plums, chucked a stone at Chancellor Lloyd George's car and got sent to prison, along with ten other women that Kitty had come to know so well. There were hunger strikes, and force feeding, and, in Lily Avenue, the most almighty row between Mum and Dad.

Raised voices were not something Kitty was used to. Yes, Mum might get cross when Dad had spent too much money betting on the horses or when he'd come home one over the eight after a big win, but that was about the extent of it. Until that cold night in January of 1910, just a few months before he went away for good, that is. Her parents were having a late supper together in the dining room and Kitty was upstairs in bed when she heard them rowing.

'You cannot let her go near those bloody women again!' he yelled. 'I will not have my daughter involved with criminals, do you hear me?'

'Please, Jack, don't be so angry with me,' Mum sobbed and then Kitty heard Dad's murmured apologies and no more was said of it. Kitty just wasn't allowed to go to meetings any more. After he left, she did, of course, because he was no longer there to stop her. Besides, she felt so full of rage that he'd gone, it was good to channel that anger into doing something positive.

She was only too happy when the pavilion at Heaton Park got burned down shortly before the war and she didn't feel a shred of remorse about the attempt to set fire to Heaton station. In fact, it was a shame when the stationmaster smelled burning and found the large cardboard box filled with tins of oil, rags and a candle in one of the ladies' lavatories because the whole timber structure would surely have gone up in flames. Not that she knew anything about it at the time, of course, but that is just what she read in the papers.

Once, she had even wanted to throw a brick through a police station window, like the suffragettes, but she'd thought better of it. Yet she could have done it. Just knowing that was enough to get her through the days in which her dreams were reduced to keystrokes at her typewriter, her ambitions boxed and filed away in buff-coloured envelopes. She still wanted more. She couldn't help it, even if she was a woman; she was a woman with ideas and Mrs Harrison Bell, Lady Lytton, the Pankhursts and all the rest had fanned the flames of something in her and they would not be quenched. A little ember was still burning inside her. Kitty knew it could never be snuffed out, not even by this war.

The tram trundled on past the big houses, where the grocer's van was delivering to servants. There'd been plenty of talk about the wealthiest in the city stockpiling food despite the higher prices, and while shopkeepers might close their doors and say they'd run out of eggs and flour, there always seemed to be plenty for the better-offs, Kitty had noticed that much.

Approaching the city, the buildings grew taller, blackened from years of smoke and dirt and soot. Coal and steel were the lifeblood of Newcastle but there was something elegant about it too, with the neatly laid-out gardens of Eldon Square and the imposing statue of Earl Grey at its heart, towering high above the bustling shopping streets below. They got off the tram and walked down

Grainger Street to the town hall, where a crowd of young men had gathered as a recruiting officer waded through them, armed with a clipboard and pencil.

'Now then, lads, we'll have you sworn in in groups of ten,' he said, his moustache bristling as he ushered the first lot inside to take the oath. 'And you will then report to barracks in the morning.'

Mum clutched Harry's arm. 'Are you sure you want to do this, son?'

He turned and kissed her on the cheek. 'Of course,' he said. 'It's my duty.'

Harry joined the Royal Field Artillery and his first month was spent dressed in a Kitchener Blue standby uniform of the scratchiest serge, doing his basic training on the Town Moor in Jesmond.

Half of the moor had been dug up by miners who were practising their trench-digging skills and the other half was used to drill the new recruits. He was given leave every Sunday and came home to tea, to a hero's welcome from Mum, even though he was yet to see a shot fired in anger.

Mum always made him his favourite bread and butter pudding, even if it meant she went without during the week to have enough leftovers. She poured him endless cups of tea and drank in every last detail of his life as a gunner.

He was based at No.1 Depot on Barrack Road and had quarters in a temporary hut at St James's Park, the football ground across the way. The horses that would be used to pull the guns into battle were stabled underneath the stadium and Harry couldn't hide his love for the animals and how he'd learned to ride them. There was a sense of their training being a bit like an extended holiday with the boy scouts for the new recruits. Many of them were around Harry's age and they found humour where they could.

'We had to fix bayonets and attack sacks stuffed with straw yesterday,' he laughed, through mouthfuls of pudding. 'I just sort of growled at them to keep the drill sergeant happy, but you've never seen 'owt so daft as a horde of us charging across the moor screaming our heads off.'

He travelled to the shooting range in Ponteland to learn how to load shells and fire them from the eighteen-pound guns and howitzers. 'It took seven men to move the big gun into position and, oh good Lord, the noise of the shells when they exploded. My ears are still ringing,' he said. All the fresh air and exercise seemed to have turned him into a man, and he had muscled arms from all the heavy lifting. Kitty thought he looked more handsome than ever.

But she knew that his time in Newcastle could not go on forever and so it came as no surprise one Sunday afternoon in late June when he turned up in a smart new uniform and announced excitedly that he would be leaving for France in the morning, where he was to join the 55th Lancashire Regiment of the Royal Field Artillery.

Mum and Kitty met him on the platform at Newcastle Central Station to say their farewells, amid a seething mass of khaki and weeping women. So many young men were leaving. Families were losing husbands, sons, brothers and cousins, all travelling on to an uncertain future on the fields of France and Flanders.

'No tears,' said Harry, hugging Kitty tightly as she handed him a little parcel containing chocolate, biscuits, tobacco, some warm socks she'd knitted and some tins of corned beef. 'Promise me.'

'I promise,' said Kitty, who despite not wanting him to leave, felt so much pride in what he was doing. She'd come to accept it over the past few weeks and she was determined to keep positive. He would survive because she was willing him to.

'Well, *I* won't promise not to cry,' said Mum, clutching him to her. 'So just you come back safely to me, Harry.' And she sobbed on his chest until it was time for him to go and join the other volunteers.

The carriage door slammed shut and the last Kitty saw of her brother was his hand, still waving goodbye from the window through the steam blowing down the line, as the train took him away from Newcastle and off to war.

9

Kitty

Newcastle upon Tyne,
September 1916

'It's a man's work, on a man's wage, so do you think you're up to the job?'

The editor of the *Shipbuilder* peered over his half-moon spectacles as Kitty stood, hands clasped in front of her, in the dusty office which was strewn with paper and stuffed to the gunnels with leather-bound copies of his publication. He must have been forty, perhaps, and he dressed in tweeds with a little handkerchief neatly folded in his breast pocket, but he had a boyish look about him.

'I do,' she said, looking him straight in the eye while trying not to tread on the plan of an ocean-going liner which was laid out on the floor. 'I'm a fast learner and I have excellent shorthand and typing skills . . .'

'I'm not looking for a secretary,' he muttered under his breath. 'But I suppose you're the best of a bad lot. I've lost so many men to this blasted conflict in the last six months it's a wonder I haven't got my own mother on the payroll.'

'I'm not afraid of long hours and hard work,' she said, ignoring his put-down.

'Not got a boyfriend away at the front, then?' he said, stuffing some tobacco in his pipe and patting his waistcoat in search of some matches. Kitty spotted the box he was looking for, hidden underneath some documents at the edge of his green leather-topped desk. She handed it to him.

'No, I certainly have not,' she said indignantly, glaring at him. 'I've no time to waste on affairs of the heart. I'm a working woman, with bills to pay. I help support my mother, and my brother is away in France with the Royal Field Artillery.'

'All right, all right,' he said, striking a match and putting it to his pipe. 'It's only fair of me to ask, you see, because the last thing I need is to spend months training you up only for you to run away up the aisle at the first opportunity or get yourself in the family way.'

'Well, that sort of thing definitely doesn't apply to me,' said Kitty. The very idea was patently absurd. She had no time for romantic dalliances.

'How old are you?'

'I will be twenty-four later this month.'

'Hmm,' he gazed at her thoughtfully. 'You're leaving it a bit late to get married anyway, aren't you? So, I suppose I'm minded to believe you.' He put down his pipe and rapped his fingers lightly on the desk. 'Remind me of your name again?'

'Catherine, but everyone calls me Kitty.'

'Well, I can assure you that in my office, you will be

known by your Christian name, Catherine,' he said with a laugh. She looked at the floor. It had been a mistake to tell him her pet name – it made her sound silly and girlish.

'All right, Catherine, you can start on Monday. Eight thirty sharp, and on deadline days you'll be working until the journal is put to bed, do you understand? We are a monthly publication and we have the highest standards of accuracy. Our readership includes the captains not just of ships, but of industry.'

'Yes, sir,' said Kitty. 'I won't let you down.'

'Very well,' he said, returning to a sheaf of papers on his blotting pad. He dipped the nib of his pen in a pot of ink and began to write. She stood there, not knowing whether the interview was at an end. He glanced up. 'Still here? You can run along now. I don't need any help with my editorial.'

'Yes, of course,' she stammered. 'I will see you first thing on Monday!' She practically skipped out of his office and into a bigger room, which was filled with middle-aged men in varying states of decay. A portly, grey-haired gentleman was quietly snoozing at his desk in the corner, while another, skinny with a bald pate, was frantically scribbling some notes. A third man, gangly, with a squint, was leaning back in his chair, idly blowing smoke rings into the air which was already blue with the fug of tobacco.

None of this mattered to Kitty. The words 'a man's work on a man's wage' were ringing in her ears. She emerged onto the street, her heart pounding with excitement. She had done it. She had got herself a proper job.

Somewhere in France
17th September 1916

My dearest Kitty,

I am writing to you from my dug-out at the front. We face a tough road ahead to crack the Hun's defences, but I have every faith that we will do it, and so must you. I'm wearing the red rose of Lancaster on my uniform with pride and we have been training for this moment, so please do not worry.

I hope you are both in good health. Please tell Mum not to fuss too much around the house and to rest when she can. Well done to you on the subediting job! I always knew you were clever, Kit, but imagine how proud Dad would be. Next thing we know, you'll be running the country. Just don't expect me to salute you next time we meet!

We've had an awful lot of rain, which makes life a misery because the trenches fill with water and then we're up to our necks in mud, rolling around in it like cattle in the fields. Mum would have a fit if she saw the state of me, all clarty. The horses find it tough-going when it's like this, but they are as brave as the men. I ride up front driving the big guns into position, on a black stallion called Domino. He's a fine animal, stands more than seventeen hands high and has smart white socks. His best mate is Top Hat, black as the ace of spades but with a white blaze down his nose, so he

*looks like he should be going for a night out on the
tiles at the Assembly Rooms. I swear those two
spend time plotting what jinks they're going to get
up to next when we come to get them in the gun
harness. And Domino's got a memory like an
elephant. When the sergeant slapped him round the
chops, he waited for his moment and kicked him
up the rear! The sly devil. I had to laugh. Sergeant
didn't see the funny side, though.*

*Well, Kit, I'll close now. We're back on it bright
and early, giving the Hun a pounding with our
shells to help our brave boys break through the
German lines. I'm sending all my love to you and
Mum.*

Godspeed,
Harry xxx

Kitty stuffed the letter into her jacket pocket and
returned to the work in front of her before her boss
could spot what she was doing. She'd only just had time
to skim over it on the tram on the way in this morning
and it wasn't enough to read his words once. She wanted
to pore over it, again and again, especially now he was
at the front. She'd heard about people getting a letter
from their loved one in the morning only to have a telegram from the War Office in the afternoon, bringing them
bad news.

'What's that you've got there, Catherine?'

She hadn't even realized that the editor was lurking
over her shoulder. Honestly, she'd learned the hard way

over the last few weeks, it was as if he had eyes in the back of his head and the ability to appear and disappear, like the Scarlet Pimpernel.

'Nothing,' she lied, blushing and returning to her type-writer. She started tapping out the details of the ships docking over the past week – their tonnage and freight.

He touched her lightly on the shoulder, which was unexpected, and she turned and found herself gazing up into his eyes, which were so green and reminded Kitty of an agate brooch that her mother wore.

'Is it a letter from your brother?' He gave her such a look of concern that it was pointless lying to him.

'Yes.' She pulled the crumpled paper from her jacket pocket. 'It is.'

'It's fine to take time to read it,' he said softly. 'I know it must be terribly hard to have family away fighting. He's a brave lad, your brother, by all accounts.'

'Do you have anyone over in France, Mr Philpott?' She'd asked the question before she could stop herself. She only hoped he wouldn't find it impertinent.

'No,' he replied. 'I've never married so there are no Philpott minors; there's just myself and my mother these days.' He ran his hands through his wavy hair, which was dark brown, like a chestnut. 'I'm always here to talk, if you need to share the burden.'

'I see,' said Kitty, who wasn't sure she wanted to know any more about Mr Philpott's family circumstances or share anything more than proofreading duties with him. 'That's very kind of you.'

He gave her a little smile and turned on his heel to go

back to his office, which was half-glazed so that he could keep an eye on what his staff were up to. He never closed the door so that he could eavesdrop too; well, probably. He wasn't a bad boss, though. She was still pondering how old he was; he had a calm air of authority like older gentlemen, but there was a sort of bounce to his step, which made him seem younger. Not that any of that mattered one jot to Kitty.

He expected the highest standards, but he gave praise where it was due. He'd never raised his voice to her, as he did with the other staff, particularly Gerald, the portly chief sub-editor, who was renowned for his long lunches and had once fallen asleep under his desk. But Kitty didn't want to feel that she was being treated any differently just because she was a woman.

She worked every bit as hard as the men, if not harder, and was only too happy to proofread late into the evening, even when she was so tired that she was squinting. The blokes all grumbled about staying late these days because the pubs stopped serving after nine p.m., due to the wartime restrictions on alcohol. More often than not, Kitty would volunteer to stay behind with Mr Philpott, to painstakingly pick their way through page after page of small print about ships, checking for errors, while everyone else trooped off for a well-earned pint. Mr Philpott would light his pipe, put it down, mislay it and she would find it for him. Then he'd pat about his waistcoat for his matches and it would fall to Kitty to find those as well, just as she had done the first time they met. Not that she dwelled too much on that occasion. It had been a memorable and happy day because she'd got herself a proper job – man's work.

The light was fading as she left the office, and the first chill of autumn was making itself felt on the evening air. She pulled her coat around her and glanced upwards to spot Mr Philpott at the window. He gave her a little nod and she smiled up at him, more out of politeness than anything else.

For some reason, she couldn't get the image of Mr Philpott out of her head as she wandered up Percy Street towards Grey's Monument to board the tram home. In the end, to banish him, she started humming a nursery rhyme that Dad used to sing to her when she sat on his knee as a little girl – 'This is the way the ladies ride, trit-trot, trit-trot' – and she thought about Harry astride Domino, hauling the heavy guns to the front, the rattle of the metal wheels on the French roads and then the deafening roar of shelling and explosions as the horses sank in the thick mud of the battlefield, struggling with their load; then the shouts of the soldiers and the screams of the injured. It was an awful thought but she'd overheard the sub-editors talking about the shocking truth of battle, and wounded soldiers seemed to be everywhere in Newcastle these days, dressed in their blue hospital uniforms, with their distinctive scarlet ties. Their missing limbs and terrible scars were proof enough of the horror of war. And they were the lucky ones.

She didn't have much time for God, not after what had happened to her father, because although she'd prayed so hard, God hadn't helped. Now, for Harry's sake, she was

prepared to turn to Him once more and as she waited for
the tram she offered up a silent prayer to keep Harry safe.
In her mind's eye she saw her brother loading the shells
and taking cover as the gun recoiled and they exploded on
their target, the air thick with smoke and shrapnel.

The tram screeched to a halt in front of her and she
boarded. She paid a penny fare, not to the conductor, but
to a conductress. So many women were working on the
buses and the trams now, it had become commonplace,
even though such a thing would have been unthinkable
before the war. She'd even seen women dressed in police
uniforms patrolling the city streets. The suffragettes had
ceased their campaigning at the outbreak of war, at the
behest of their leader, Mrs Pankhurst, but no one could
have imagined that the loss of life on the Western Front
would lead to such a change of opinion towards women
doing men's jobs.

Women had proved themselves, in the most terrible of
circumstances, but the question in the back of Kitty's
mind was what would happen once the war was over?
Everyone wanted that moment to come and it seemed
wrong to talk about the future of the female workforce
once men returned from the trenches, but Kitty was
thinking about it because she didn't want to go back to
being just a shorthand typist again. She was enjoying her
job so much.

And then, just like that, despite her best efforts, she was
back to thinking of that damned Mr Philpott again, with
his eyes as green as agate.

*

Kitty wrote often to Harry, filling him in on the most mundane details of her daily life, and she'd taken to embroidering things for him, just little keepsakes, to stop herself going mad with worry. But it was nearly a fortnight before she received another letter from him and her hands were shaking with excitement as she opened it.

Somewhere in France
29th September 1916

Dearest Kitty,

Your prayers have been answered and I am safely back from my spell at the front. Came back with fleas all over me, worse than the neighbour's cat! Next time, please mention that to the Good Lord Almighty and ask him to send hot water and Borax. Thanks so much for the baccy and the chocolate. A real treat and keeping my spirits up. The embroidered handkerchiefs are lovely – Top Hat and Domino are honoured that you have captured their likenesses so beautifully. I always knew you were a dab hand with the needle and thread, Kit, but they are so special to me. I can imagine you in the parlour working away on them. And they're just what I need to keep my runny nose at bay!

We're on a respite now for a week, which means lots of drills and checking over the guns plus a rest for the horses before we move on – Flanders most likely but we won't know for certain for a few days yet. Domino is in good spirits. Top Hat showed

signs of lameness, but he's had a poultice and is
doing much better. Tough as old boots, just like me.
Talking of which, I'd love some more woollen socks
if you can persuade Mum to knit me some to match
the ones you sent. We have a hell of a job getting
things dry.

Godspeed. I'm sorry I haven't asked how your
work is going, Kit, silly of me. I do hope you have
got those men in the office marching to your tune
by now!

Yours, lice-ridden but with love,
Harry xxx

He wrote letters to Mum too, of course, and that meant the pleasure of hearing from him was doubled, because he managed to report different things to them both. He was delighted to hear that Mum had been keeping so busy with charitable work to help the war effort and passed on his good wishes to her new acquaintances, the Misses Dalton – a pair of spinsters who were pillars of the local church, and helped to organize a voluntary fund for the military hospitals in the city.

The Misses Dalton had even come round for tea one day last week, which had left Mum in a state of high excitement. She'd dusted off her best china and used all the sugar and dried fruit in the pantry to make a cake for them.

With their lace collars, starched bosoms and rustling silk skirts, they reminded Kitty of Queen Mary herself, but in duplicate, and they were quite scandalized when they heard from Mum that Kitty was working in an office as a sub-editor.

'An office full of men! How extraordinary!' they chorused.

The next time they came calling, they peered at Kitty through their pince-nez spectacles as if she were a curiosity at a funfair. Kitty knew how much it meant to Mum to have their company, so she was always polite, answering all their questions about her work, which seemed to impress them more with every passing week.

'You are so very modern, Kitty,' they'd say, as Mum poured the tea. 'But aren't there any fine-looking journalists in the office who might catch the eye of a lovely girl such as yourself?'

Kitty shook her head and they listened intently as she told them all about Mr Philpott and his many editorials about important subjects in the shipping world, which were very widely read among the powers that be, not only in Newcastle but also in London. Rumour had it that the Prime Minister himself was an avid reader of his column. So, it was perfectly clear to everyone that, with her workload, she had no time for romance. That was just for giddy girls, not working women.

A particular concern of Mr Philpott's was the sinking of so many ships that had been built on Tyneside, particularly after the Battle of Jutland back in the summer. The whole city felt their loss, because the shipyards were part of the lifeblood of the community and everyone poured their hopes for victory into them, for the war effort. The incessant hammering of the rivets into iron and steel rang out along the Tyne from Newcastle all the way to the

North Sea and when a ship was sunk, it was like losing a member of the family.

A further menace was the German submarines sinking British merchant vessels, which only made food shortages worse, particularly after the potato crop had failed earlier in the year. Doctors had even seen cases of scurvy amongst the poorest children. The Misses Dalton had already helped set up a soup kitchen for the needy in the church hall, but they were planning to do more. Mum wanted to help but Kitty was worried that they barely had enough to feed themselves some days. Mum spent long hours queuing to get vegetables and fruit, often only to find that they had all sold out by the time it was her turn to be served. A decent cut of meat was hard to come by and everyone knew that the baker was adding sawdust and Lord knows what else to the bread to make it go further. The submarine blockades had stopped grain being imported and with so many men and horses away at the front, farms were struggling to keep pace with demand.

The hunger didn't bother Kitty; she'd focus on her work, the words and proofreading. Besides, just being around Mr Philpott in the office seemed to take the edge off her appetite most days.

They struggled on through Christmas and New Year, feeling guilty for opening their presents in the comfort of their home while Harry was in the trenches. And whatever hardships they faced in Newcastle paled into insignificance next to what Harry was going through, as his letters showed that winter.

Somewhere in Flanders
February 1917

Ghastly few days. The brigade has suffered much but we are not broken, Kit. Top Hat and Domino, fine animals, showed their strength and bravery under a heavy artillery barrage from the Hun and are now having a well-earned rest.

It's freezing cold here, snow on the ground. We do what we can in our dug-outs with straw and firewood to make them cosy. Our rations of bully beef are not enough to feed a fly so I'm grateful for the extras, Kit, and though we get our tot of rum and a smear of axle grease on our biscuits, it's nothing like the parlour at home. How I miss you all. I have waking dreams, Kit, of Simonside Terrace and even on the darkest nights when I cannot sleep, Lily Avenue, as it was, the four of us, with Dad and his betting slips and Mum fussing around making steak and kidney puddings. It brings me such comfort. I could reach out and touch you all.

I am your loving brother, Kitty, and tell Mum she can hold her head high in Newcastle because everything I am doing here is not only for our country but for our family name.

Harry xxx

10

Harry

Cambrai, France,
30th November 1917

Artillery barrage to be put down in support of infantry operations today on GILLEMONT FARM and the KNOLL at Honnecourt, following smoke shell bombardment.

At ten minutes before zero, smoke shells will be fired from 4.5 Howitzers into the trenches to encourage the enemy to put gas masks on, if the wind is favourable.

The battalion will form up in NO MAN'S LAND about 300 yards from our positions and attack with four companies in line. The infantry will advance at ZERO. ZERO will be 06.20 a.m. Heavy artillery barrage to be put down at 06.30 a.m.

Harassing fire by a few 18-pounders will take place at the same time and on the same targets as given above for the 4.5 Howitzers, with due regard for the safety of our own troops.

Zero plus ten to zero plus twenty, 3 rounds per gun per minute.

Zero plus twenty to zero plus twenty-five, 2 rounds per gun per minute.

Zero plus twenty-five – CEASE FIRE.

Two guns will move in a creeping barrage to assist the defensive barrage. Every platoon will be issued with SOS signals and observation posts will be held in the craters to watch for these and repeat them.

Machine guns will bring indirect fire on the ground and be held in reserve when the SOS goes up, to assist the defensive barrage.

Watches will be synchronized by an officer from the heavy artillery batteries.

The village of EPEHY is to be held at all costs.

ACKNOWLEDGE

After the sea of mud at the Somme, the chalky French soil of Cambrai came as a relief, but the bitter winter wind that whipped across the desolate landscape offered little comfort and the pain of the biting cold rendered Harry and his pals dumb in their dug-outs.

There were those who jabbered incessantly through the night in the grip of trench fever, which many saw as a fate worse than taking a German bullet. There was one who sang 'Blaydon Races' at the top of his lungs at all hours until the sergeant had him taken away because no one got any rest. It was never the most obvious candidates who went doolally; not the quiet, shy ones, but the most chatty and cheerful, the ones who'd not be out of place getting lairy after a few pints in the Bigg Market back home.

Harry had resolved early on to keep his own counsel. People seemed to respect that.

As the brigade made ready for battle at first light, they were enveloped in a thick and freezing fog, heavier than the early morning fret on the Tyne. At the head of the column, Harry could only hear the shouts of the gunners as they attached the harnesses at the rear and made ready the ammunition wagon. The horses always got a bit skittish before zero hour, stamping their hooves in readiness, great clouds of condensation rising from their nostrils. But Domino stood stock-still, waiting for Harry to give the order to move off.

They were stretched thinly along the front, it had to be said, with the whole division defending about thirteen thousand yards of trenches and fortified posts, supported by just two brigades of field artillery.

Harry climbed up into the saddle, settled his feet into the stirrups and touched the packet of letters from Kitty that he kept in his breast pocket for good luck. They were wrapped in a handkerchief she'd embroidered for him, of the horse with a white blaze down his nose. Poor old Top Hat. Harry had made sure he didn't suffer in the end. Top Hat had broken his leg falling down a shell hole on the Ypres Salient. Harry had pulled out his gun, patted the horse's muzzle, said his farewells, and fired a good clean shot between the animal's ears, to put him out of his misery.

He hadn't the heart to tell Kitty. She lived for all the tales about Top Hat and Domino, their bravery under fire, what they got up to when the battle was over and how they gave the sergeant gyp. Of course, Harry was acting sergeant now, a German sniper had seen to that a few months back, but he didn't tell Kitty or Mum that either because they'd only worry about him. Harry had to admit, it gave him something to think about too, keeping all those stories going for his sister, recreating battles in which the horses were heroes and the men lived to fight another day.

It was true that Domino was a diamond and Harry would never be happy going into battle without him. He'd heard about it from other brigades, when the lead driver had lost his best animal and then their luck changed. As long as Domino was with him, he'd get through it. He reached down and gave him a little pat on his flank, just as he always did before they set off.

So many pals of the 55th had perished in the mud of the Somme and Ypres; Flers-Courcelette, Morval, the Menin Road Ridge, Passchendaele. They were just foreign names to folks back home but to him they were a living nightmare, of men drowning in a sea of mud, the screams of the dying, the sky blackened by smoke from the endless artillery barrages and the air thick with the stench of death and cordite. The gas, oh God, the mustard gas; the poor sods who'd been blinded, their eyes covered with thick bandages, feeling their way, hands on each other's shoulders, the burning pain etched on their faces. He'd rather die, like his mate Robbo, who had his head blown clean off his shoulders by an enemy mortar, than face that agony.

Harry knew the desperation of hurling himself into a

freezing, muddy trench at nightfall to take cover from enemy machine gunfire; the horror of opening his eyes at first light, the rain pattering on his face, to find he was sleeping with men who would never wake and the rats were already at work, gnawing at their fingers. The sight and smell of the dead rotting in flooded shell holes haunted his dreams. So, there was no shame in lying to his family. He was doing a job that would make them proud, even if he couldn't tell them the half of it.

Word had reached the brigade that after the first tank assault on Cambrai last week, church bells had rung out back in Blighty, but everyone here knew that the powers that be were just looking through rose-tinted spectacles. The Boche was dug in hard and little ground had been gained. Tanks had got stuck in the canal and one had even busted up the bridge that the troops needed to use to get across to attack enemy positions. Newfangled machinery was a wondrous thing in battle, but only when it worked. Yes, horses were old-fashioned but as far as Harry and his men were concerned, they were bloody effective war machines and more reliable than tanks.

Harry had learned to blot out the deafening din of exploding ordnance, but the sheer scale of the enemy's artillery barrage that morning made his ears ring to the point where he could no longer form a sentence. Up ahead, a small copse of trees was being felled by a relentless shower of mortars from the Hun lines, blowing everything to splinters with a roar and whoosh, punctuated by the staccato fire of British Lewis machine guns in response. Suddenly, through the smoke and shrapnel, wave after wave of enemy soldiers came charging down Villers Ridge, firing on every living creature in their path. Seconds later, another sound joined the battle. Enemy aeroplanes buzzed low, strafing lines of men in khaki beneath them. Harry watched his fellow Tommies drop like skittles, as still more coal-scuttle helmets and grey uniforms appeared on the ridge and it seemed the front would be overrun by Germans in moments.

The 55th had been given their orders, to hold the position at all costs, so the gun was rolled forward to provide the creeping barrage of supporting fire which would force the Hun back or at least make them dive for cover. The ground was hard, frozen solid, which made the going easier, as Harry gave Domino a little nudge to walk him on. They couldn't have gone more than twenty yards when someone yelled, 'Incoming!' and the gun, horses and men were blown ten feet in the air in a blinding flash of white light.

Snow was falling when Harry came to and the battlefield was eerily quiet.

A searing pain in his abdomen nailed him to the spot. He inhaled sharply, hearing himself rasp. Glancing down, he saw blood oozing through his khakis, underneath his ribs, and the shock of it made him want to scream. He wriggled his toes, relieved to find both legs still attached, but he was stuck fast, buried deep in the earth from the blast. He tried to move, to pull himself free, but his strength was draining away; the effort provoked a gush of blood, which spread downwards, spilling out over his trousers. Instinctively, he fumbled in his top pocket and pulled out the bundle of Kitty's letters, holding them to the wound to try to stem the flow. For an instant, he was floating high above himself, looking down at his broken body as his blood seeped crimson through Kitty's needlework and drenched her words. Then he was back in the shell hole, as the snow started to form a blanket over him.

Turning his head to the side, he felt warmth on his face, and heard an unmistakable whinny. It was Domino, bloodied, but still alive lying next to him. A deep gash on the horse's belly had exposed the muscle underneath which was twitching in a nest of red sinews. Domino's back legs lay at crazy angles, his rump half covered by earth. The animal's eyes rolled in a silent agony.

'It's all right, boy, we'll be all right,' Harry murmured, his hands closing fast around the letters. They lay there together, Domino's breath mingling with his own. And then the blackness enveloped them.

A shot rang out. 'I've put him out of his misery, poor blighter. Shame to see such a fine animal end up like that. I used to ride them on my dad's farm when I was a boy. He'd weep to see what we do to them over here.'

'Another goner here! Come on, mate, let's get you back where we can give you a decent burial at least.'

Harry tried to scream but he could make no sound. His fingers were frozen solid, he was unable to move. He felt himself being pulled from his grave in the shell hole and covered with a tarpaulin as he was carried away.

11

Kitty

Newcastle upon Tyne, December 1917

Mum held the telegram between trembling fingers, her mouth gaping in shock.

Kitty rushed to her side and snatched it from her, sinking to her knees on the red tiles of the hallway floor.

Deeply regret to inform you that your son, Acting
Sgt RFA 149044, has been reported missing.

Mum let out a wail loud enough to wake the dead. 'Not my boy! Oh, dear God, not him, please!'

The world seemed to be spinning around them and they clung to each other for comfort, sobbing.

Ever since Harry had left for the front more than a year ago, they'd been living in fear of this moment. Now it had happened, nothing could prepare them for it, nothing could help them through it. They were like so many families who received one of the dreaded War

Office telegrams saying that a soldier had disappeared in battle.

They were caught in the no man's land of despair, clinging to the faint hope that their loved one could be a prisoner behind enemy lines but haunted by the reality that he may have perished on the fields of France and Flanders.

Mum was poleaxed by the news, unable to eat or speak, and she took to her bed, while the Misses Dalton tended to her. Every postal delivery over the coming days brought fresh agony: the terror that a buff-coloured envelope would bring the cold certainty of death in battle.

Kitty had to go out to work. She couldn't afford to lose her job, and so each day she made the journey down into the city on the tram, past the long lines of women queuing for food outside the shops. A gloom seemed to hang over Newcastle after three years at war. People were hungry, tired and working all the hours that God sent in the munitions factories, with no end to the conflict in sight. Every day brought more battle-damaged ships back to the Tyne for repair, and the remaining men of Newcastle got to work, patching them up and sending them off to sea again.

At her desk at the *Shipbuilder*, Kitty tried to focus, to lose herself in the intricate details of her work, truly she did, but instead she found herself gazing out of the office window and drifting off up the grey waters of the Tyne until it reached the sea. She floated on, around the coast and past the White Cliffs of Dover, washing up on the beaches of France. She picked her way through the ruins of bombed-out French villages to the battlefields. Harry was leading the gun column, so smart in his uniform, astride Domino, with Top Hat trotting along beside them and the rest of the horses following. She ran alongside her brother but just couldn't keep up. Before she knew what was happening, a shout went up – 'Over the top, boys!' – and khaki-clad Tommies clambered out of the trenches into no man's land, guns at the ready. The rat-a-tat of machine guns rang out as the Germans did their worst, and the soldiers fell to their knees in the mud, which seemed to swallow them whole. Kitty called out to Harry but he couldn't hear her, and he rode on with Domino and Top Hat, until he was consumed by the fog of war, shells exploding in his wake.

The clatter of her fingers on the typewriter keyboard brought her back to reality, her face wet with tears. Mr Philpott was standing beside her.

'Catherine,' he began gently. 'Come into my office for a moment.' He offered her his arm and she leaned on him for support, because her legs were giving way beneath her.

'Sit down, please.' He motioned to the chair in front of his desk and she settled herself, wiping her eyes on her sleeve for a moment, because she couldn't remember for the life of her what she had done with her handkerchief.

He opened the ornate cigarette box on the edge of his desk. It was decorated in the Chinese style, with two fat, orange koi carp swimming in opposite directions to each other. He offered it to her and she shook her head.

'Is it Harry?'

'Yes,' she cried, covering her face with her hands. 'He's missing. Nobody knows what's happened to him. Forgive me . . .'

He rushed to her side and put his arm around her.

'Don't apologize, Kitty, please,' he said. 'You shouldn't be at work today. You must go home to be with your mother.'

'But you need me here, and I need my wages or we won't be able to eat,' she said, barely registering the fact that he'd called her by her pet name. She stared at the floor with shame that she'd had to talk about money so openly in front of him.

'I won't dock your pay, you need to have some time to . . .' He stopped himself and they looked at each other. They both knew in that instant that the word on his lips was 'grieve'.

The bitter wind of a Newcastle winter howled through the back alleys by the Quayside and whipped up the cobbled streets towards the city centre. As she made her way back to work, Kitty wandered along the quay, her hair billowing out behind her. She'd taken a few days off to recover her composure but the dread of waiting for the post each day with little else to occupy her but Mum's sadness was more than she could bear. She'd always found it easier to just try to get on with life as best she could. She used to love coming down to the quay with Harry after Dad had gone, to show him sailing ships with their tall masts, so they could lose themselves in the hustle and bustle of it all. Once they were nearly knocked flying by a drift of pigs being herded along to the market and laughed themselves silly about it for days.

Wherever she went in the city, she was reminded of her brother. They'd grown up darting on and off trams together, visiting the central library, walking with Mum to the fish market. It didn't seem possible that she'd never see him again, but she knew life had to go on, somehow.

Back in the offices of the *Shipbuilder*, the room fell silent as she walked in and Gerald, the chief sub-editor, was the nicest he'd ever been, even bringing her a cup of tea, which he plonked down a bit heavily, sloshing some on her neatly typed copy and prompting a flurry of apologies. After a few hours, things returned to normal – which was a relief, actually – and Mr Philpott had started calling her 'Catherine' again, like he always did. There were a few quiet moments when she caught him glancing over at her from his office, checking that she was all right, but other than that, it was business as usual.

Mum had bought them both a little pendant badge that so many war widows wore nowadays. It cost a shilling and was in the shape of a silver heart, with one word engraved on it: 'sacrifice'. She'd pinned it to Kitty's lapel before she'd left the house, but Kitty didn't need to wear a badge to show the sacrifice that Harry had made; she felt it, deep in her own heart.

Christmas was fast approaching and after work, she made time to wander through the Central Arcade. They barely had the will to celebrate, with Harry missing, but Kitty wanted to do something to mark the day at least. The Central Arcade was one of her favourite places, with its magnificent barrel-vaulted roof and mosaic flooring, and shopkeepers had done their best to make it festive, despite the war, putting up holly, ivy and ribbons along their frontages. It was nice to see other people enjoying the festivities and Kitty took some comfort in that. People liked to gather in there, to peer at the things they couldn't afford to buy, mostly, and to take shelter from the elements, especially on a really chilly winter's day. Kitty had been saving hard to buy some new ribbon from the milliner so that she could smarten up Mum's felt hat for her for Christmas. It was a small gift, a token really, and she also bought a couple of yards of lace to add some detail to one of Mum's blouses as a special surprise.

She was still clutching her brown paper bag of Christmas treats as she came through the front door of their home in Simonside Terrace, stamping her feet to bring some life back into them after the freezing walk from the tram stop. Glancing down, she spotted a letter lying on the doormat. She picked it up, her heart pounding, and tore open the envelope.

The handwriting was not Harry's, but his words washed over her, bringing with them a great tidal wave of relief.

My dearest darling Mum and Kitty,

I am asking the nurse to write this for me. I'm weak from a bullet wound but hope to be entrained soon to return to Newcastle where you can see for yourself that I am still your loving son and brother.

I don't remember much about the past few weeks, as I have been so sick with sepsis, but I am now at the British Red Cross hospital in Calais and doing much better.

I was one of the few from my brigade to make it back alive. I was shot and lay in a shell hole with Domino for days before I was found. I'm sad to say, Kitty, the old boy didn't make it but the fact he was there with me helped keep me going, so he was loyal to the last.

It was snowing hard and I froze, which stopped the bleeding, so the doctors say; that and the fact that the German bullet passed clean through me. They thought I was dead when they took me off the battlefield. I sat bolt upright in the morgue and that gave the stretcher bearers a fright. It is, as the doctor said, nothing short of a miracle that I'm here. Life has given me a second chance.

I can only imagine how worried you both must have been but please don't fret any more because I am safe now.

I will write to you again soon and cannot wait to see you back in Blighty.

Sending you both all my love,

Harry xxx

Kitty clasped the letter to her and shouted up the stairs, 'Mum! Come quickly! It's a miracle – Harry's alive!'

Her mother stood at the top of the stairs, her hair hanging loose and her eyes red from crying. She steadied herself with one hand against the wall as she made her way down towards Kitty, shaking her head in disbelief that after so much bad news, the impossible had happened. 'Can it be true?'

Kitty ran to her, waving the letter triumphantly. 'Yes! It's him! Our Harry's coming home to us!'

They hugged each other and Kitty felt the warmth of her mother's embrace, her breath in her hair mingling with tears of joy and relief. They would be a family again.

It was like the sun had come out again in Kitty's world and the years seemed to fall away from Mum, who was so happy she was even singing in the scullery in the mornings, like she used to when Dad was alive. Knowing that Harry was safe and would soon be on his way home was the best Christmas present they could ever have wished for.

Even the sleet and the snow of Christmas Eve couldn't dampen Kitty's spirits and she decided to go to a service at St Nicholas's Cathedral, to give thanks that Harry had been spared. Mum and Dad had got married there and she and Harry had been christened in the cathedral too, so it seemed the right place to be. It was a landmark for all Geordies, with its spire visible for miles across the city.

Mr Philpott had asked if he might accompany her and she couldn't find a reason to say no, especially after he'd been so kind to her when Harry was missing in action. After locking the office door for the Christmas holidays as all the other sub-editors trooped off to the pub, they muffled themselves up against the cold and set off together.

Snow started to fall, deadening the sound of their feet on the cobbles and dusting the blackened buildings so they looked as if they'd been coated with icing sugar.

Mr Philpott wanted to go over every last detail of how Harry had survived a German bullet and come back from the dead. It wasn't often that anyone got such good news from the front, so the story had done the rounds of the office and Mr Philpott agreed it would probably be the talk of the Bigg Market by now.

The cathedral was lit by candles and already packed to the rafters with the well-to-do folk from Jesmond, with the ladies swathed in fur. Kitty didn't have anything as posh, of course, but she was wearing a lovely new scarf that Mum had knitted for her and a beret too, in blue wool; she'd been allowed to open her present early on account of the filthy weather, to keep her from catching cold.

Mr Philpott sat next to her in the pew and they had a whispered conversation about their plans for Christmas Day. A hush fell over the cathedral as the Bishop of Newcastle, in his golden robes and mitre, led the service. Looking around her in the candlelight, as the choirboys sang 'Silent Night', Kitty couldn't help wondering how many people had lost a loved one in the conflict. She felt lucky, blessed even, for Harry to have been given a second chance, by some small miracle, which she would never understand but always be grateful for.

After the carols, just as she was preparing to say goodbye to Mr Philpott on the cathedral steps, he put his hand in his pocket and produced a little gift, beautifully wrapped with a red ribbon. She was frozen for a moment, as the wind whipped the snow into a flurry, catching in her hair and making her shiver beneath her thin woollen coat.

'I'd like you to have this,' he said.

Kitty was flabbergasted. 'That's too kind. I'm afraid I haven't got you anything . . .'

'Catherine, there's no need for you to buy me a present. Just seeing you open this will be gift enough for me.'

She was blushing as scarlet as the bow around the little box, but she untied it with fumbling fingers and opened it to find a stunning emerald ring inside, nestling in a velvet case.

'It's beautiful!' she gasped. 'I couldn't possibly accept this, Mr Philpott. It's too expensive for a start.' She tried to hand it back, but he covered her hands with his own and held them for a moment.

'Please, call me Charles. I want you to have it. You see, I was hoping you might accept it, as a token of my affection,' he said.

She gazed up at him and found genuine warmth in his eyes, which seemed to make her heart flutter.

He got down on one knee, in the freezing snow, as people around them looked on in amazement. 'The thing is, Kitty, I'm in love with you and I want you to be my wife.'

Kitty kept the ring hidden in the drawer of her bedside table and told no one.

She was so blindsided by the proposal that she'd told

him she needed time to think. She couldn't quite believe that the editor, the man who she'd worked with day after day, wanted to marry her.

It was all too confusing. She loved her job and she liked Mr Philpott. In fact, if she were being honest with herself, she was very fond of him indeed. He was clever and handsome, in his way. Was she in love with him? She wasn't sure of that but perhaps she could come to love him. A lot of people did that in marriages. She'd overheard Mum talking to the Misses Dalton about women who'd 'made the best of it' and then found they'd fallen head over heels in love once they'd set up home and had children.

But if she married, he'd be bound to ask more about her family and then the truth about her father might come out. That fear hung over her like a black cloud. It had just been the three of them – Mum, Harry and Kitty – for so long and only they understood how it felt to be part of their family, the shame they carried. Sharing that secret with someone who said he loved her just didn't seem possible because once he knew the truth, he would surely change his mind.

And in any case, if she got married, she would have to give up work, which she enjoyed so much. Mum relied on her wage too. It wouldn't be fair for her to go and get married and start having children to care for. Who would look after her mother?

'Kitty, love?' Mum's voice carried up the hallway. 'What on earth are you doing up there all alone? It's Christmas Day! Come and lay the table, the Misses Dalton will be calling around later and I need to get things ready for them.'

With Harry safe, Mum wanted to have a proper celebration and she'd been steaming a beautiful pudding all morning to accompany the goose she'd managed to buy at the butcher's. But Kitty seemed to have lost her appetite entirely.

'I'll be there in just a moment,' she shouted.

She sighed to herself and put the sparkling emerald back in its box and shut the drawer.

On New Year's Day, Mum and Kitty travelled to Armstrong College, which had been requisitioned to house the 1st Northern General Hospital, to be reunited with Harry. Nurses in starched white uniforms and caps, with black and red capelets around their shoulders, were coming and going from the red-brick building as they approached.

Mum clasped Kitty's arm for support.

'Do you think we will recognize him?' she said.

'Of course we will,' said Kitty. 'He's our Harry.'

They entered a big hall which was filled with beds as far as the eye could see, so there must have been more than forty wounded soldiers recuperating in there. A couple of men with their legs missing below the knee sat at a felt-covered table in the middle of the room, playing cards. There were bandaged arms and patched eyes, and the nurses seemed to glide along, tucking in a bedsheet here and there, telling some to rest and others to try to get up and walk about.

Kitty spotted him first, propped up on a pillow at the end of one of the rows, nearest to the fireplace. Mum rushed along the highly polished floor, which reeked of disinfectant, letting out a squeal of delight – much to the annoyance of the nurses, who tutted their disapproval. Harry was thinner than they'd ever seen him, but when he smiled, his whole face lit up.

'Two visitors at a time only, please,' said a nurse, who appeared to have rolled silently to the bedside, as if she were on castors. 'And please be mindful that there are some very sick men in here who need quiet and rest.'

Mum ignored her and bent down to kiss Harry's cheek, running her hand across his forehead. Her son had come back from the dead and she wasn't going to stand on ceremony for Florence Nightingale or anyone else for that matter.

Kitty sat on a wooden stool at his side and clasped his hand. 'It's so good to see you. How are you feeling?'

Harry laughed, and he was the same Harry that she'd always known and loved. 'Well, it's better than being in the trenches, I can tell you.' He shifted uncomfortably and put his hand to his belly. 'I'm still in a lot of pain. Doctors say the scar isn't healing too well yet, so I'll be in here for a while before I'm allowed home. But I'm doing better than some, so we must be grateful for that.'

Another soldier, who looked little more than a boy himself, was sitting on a bed clutching his knees, rocking back and forth. 'He's been like that for hours,' said Harry, lowering his voice. 'Nurses tell him to stop, but he can't. I've seen it before – the war does terrible things to a man's mind.'

Kitty felt her brother's fingers start to tremble. 'The dead have it easy, Kitty, the dead have it easy.'

Mum recoiled in shock. 'Don't upset yourself, now, Harry, what's done is done.' She used to say that to both of them when Dad left, to help them get through the long and lonely nights.

He looked up at his mother, anguish etched on his features.

'I want to come home with you, because every night, when the lights go out, we're all back there at the front, every last one of us in here,' he said, gripping Kitty's fingers. 'There's no escape.' Fat, salty tears rolled down his face and soaked his nightshirt. 'Please let me come home!'

The nurse reappeared and freed Kitty's hand from her brother's grasp. 'Come along, Harry, I think you need to let your mam and your sister be getting on now. They can come again tomorrow, when you're feeling better, but the doctors will need to see you soon.' She leaned down and put his arms under the covers, tucking them in tightly as if he were a child.

Mum was struck dumb and looked over to Kitty.

'Well, let's do what the nurse says, Harry, because we want you to get better and then you can come home,' Kitty said, kissing him on the cheek.

His grey eyes searched her face and she smiled at him reassuringly. 'Don't worry. We will certainly be back tomorrow. And the day after that, and the one after that too. We will come every day until you are well enough to come home. We won't leave you. Ever.'

Her words seemed to make him relax and he closed his eyes. Kitty took Mum by the arm to escort her back out of the ward. The ward sister was waiting for them by the doorway and she walked with them down the long corridor. 'It will take time, but you must understand that his wounds are mental as well as physical. It's best not to talk about the past, but to concentrate on the future, on happy and familiar things. Do you understand?'

Mum nodded. Kitty understood perfectly. She knew what she had to do.

Kitty carefully placed the ring, still in its box, on top of a pile of papers at the front of Mr Philpott's desk. A look of hurt flickered across his face and he leaned back in his chair.

'Do you have something you want to say to me, Kitty?'

'I wanted to thank you for your very kind offer, but I can't accept it because I have my family to think about. My brother needs me now, more than ever.'

His voice fell to a whisper. 'I can provide for all of you, if you'll let me. Your mother and brother would be welcome to move in with us, in Jesmond. We have room—'

'You're very kind,' said Kitty, 'but we are quite set in our ways.'

'I could wait, Kitty. If you think you could grow fond of me . . .'

Outside on the Tyne, a ship was sliding down the slipway into the murky waters below. Nothing could stop it now. It had been set free from its moorings and there was only one way forward.

'I am fond of you, Mr Philpott,' she said. 'Very fond.' She ignored the awful sinking feeling in her chest as she spoke the words. 'But I also need this job and I'm not about to give it up for you, or any man for that matter.'

She leaned forward and pushed the ring box towards him. It sat there, in the no man's land between the edge of his desk and his blotting pad.

'I will always be grateful to you, especially for the kindness you have shown me, but I have to put my family first,' she said.

'Kitty—' he began.

'And do please call me Catherine. I like that at work.'

He picked up the ring box and put it in his drawer, watching her as she turned and walked out of his office.

Kitty settled herself down at her typewriter, inserted a fresh sheet of paper into the mechanism, and began to tap away, writing up the tonnage, freight and specifications of the ships in this month's edition.

With every keystroke, she determined that things would go back to the way they had been before the war. Harry would get better, she would see to it, and then it would be just the three of them.

Kitty, Harry and Mum.

12

Annie

Acton, October 1942

'And what in God's name are you wearing, my girl?'

As Bill's voice carried up the hallway at Grove Road, Mum and Annie peered around the scullery door to see what all the fuss was about.

Elsie was standing by the front door, ready to go out to work at the munitions factory, dressed in a pair of blue dungarees, with a headscarf knotted around her head.

'You can't go out looking like that!' cried Bill. 'People'll think you are a blooming communist!'

'Dad,' said Elsie, with her hands on her hips. 'Dungarees are utility workwear. All the girls are wearing them these days. They are practical, comfortable and stylish. The War Office says so.' She turned on her heel and slammed the front door shut.

'Well,' said Bill, muttering to himself as he made his way into the scullery for a reviving cup of tea. 'I haven't seen anything like it in all my born days . . .'

'Oh, don't be so hard on her,' said Mum, popping little

Anita into a high chair for some porridge while Annie cradled her youngest, John, who was coming up to three months old now. 'She's working hard down that factory and I think she looks lovely.' What's more, Elsie was bringing in two pounds and five shillings a week and although she kept some for herself, she was generous with it, putting more than half into the old tea caddy which served as a household kitty.

'Looks like a bleeding fella in those overalls, if you ask me,' said Bill, chewing on a crust of toast. Mum tutted at him.

'I don't think there's any mistaking Elsie for a bloke,' Annie laughed. Her youngest sister had blossomed into an extraordinarily good-looking young woman and you only had to walk up Churchfield Road beside her to see heads turning.

The government had passed an order which meant all single women aged nineteen to thirty had to register for war work. A lot of married women were helping out in the factories too, even if it was just in the canteens, and Annie had started to get itchy feet staying at home all day. She just felt she should be helping the war effort, especially since George was now over in North Africa fighting.

He'd taken part in the successful attack on the German-held fortress of Tobruk with the Eighth Army, but luckily was already in Egypt when it was taken back by the German commander Rommel earlier in the summer. That defeat was a crushing blow to morale, with so many soldiers taken prisoner. George sent postcards for Anita, just as he promised he would, and letters for Mum which didn't say very much other than that it was blooming hot and the flies were purgatory. He was proud to be one of Field Marshall Montgomery's Desert Rats and said that they should not give up hope of winning the war.

Annie confided in Mum about her plans, who rolled her eyes at the very thought of Annie leaving the children and going out to work. 'Oh, you're worse than your friend Esther! I saw her down on the High Street doing a flag day to raise money for War Weapons Week. It's all well and good but who's looking after her kids? They'll be getting up to no good without their mother to keep an eye on them, you mark my words.'

It was true, Esther was always out volunteering but her children seemed perfectly well mannered and her eldest, Leonard, was out of London at the weekends with the Scouts and he was always helping out down at the Women's Voluntary Service, lugging bags of clothing donations about or setting out chairs for meetings in the church hall. Annie couldn't help thinking Mum was still a bit cross about Elsie commandeering half her cooking pots to give to Esther for scrap metal drives; she'd taken to hiding her best stockpot in the pantry every time Esther set foot in the house.

'I don't know,' said Annie, wiping the baby's mouth with the edge of a tea towel. 'I just feel I could do a bit more, if you could help out with the kids a bit? Or I could always put them in a nursery. There's a new one opening down on the High Street so that mothers can go out to work.'

'Oh, over my dead body will my grandchildren go into

a nursery!' Mum cried, snatching John from Annie's arms. 'How could you even suggest it? Look at his little face! As long as there's breath in my body, I will help out, of course I will. But it just seems daft to volunteer when you've got so much on, Annie. What will Harry say?'

'Oh, he'll be fine about it, I'm sure,' said Annie, going over towards the sink to wash up. She turned away so that Mum wouldn't see the sadness in her eyes. Harry didn't seem to say much to her these days. He was exhausted by the factory shifts and his ARP duties, but his nightmares had been getting worse and Annie found he preferred sleeping in a rocking chair in the kitchen whenever they were at home. He'd tell her that he hadn't wanted to disturb her by coming to bed, but it had put a distance between them and with every day that passed, the gap was growing wider. She could feel it.

'Well, Ivy's got a little one and she doesn't feel the need to go out working,' said Mum matter-of-factly. That was true but even having Charlie on a different continent fighting with the army wouldn't stop her being under his thumb. If the truth be told, they were all a bit wary about what exactly was going on behind closed doors. Mum and Annie talked about it a lot, in hushed tones, when they were making do and mending in the scullery. Ivy hadn't said anything about it and they didn't want to pry, but she was slimmer now than before she'd had her baby and Mum couldn't persuade her to eat so much as a fairy cake, even as a special treat, because 'Charlie wouldn't like it.'

Now Mum was giving Annie one of her concerned looks, the type she normally reserved for Ivy.

'Love, is everything all right indoors?' Mum said, laying a hand gently on Annie's shoulder.

'Of course it is! Why wouldn't it be?' she said airily. Annie didn't want to tell her mum about it. It wasn't as if they were having problems, it was just that Harry seemed quite affected by everything he'd seen in the Blitz, that's all. 'I just want to do my bit for the country, like everybody else.'

'Well, if it means that much to you, Annie, of course I can take the babies for you during the day, but you need to think carefully about it before you start offering too much work-wise. You've only got one pair of hands.'

Annie nodded and gave Mum a little smile.

She understood what her mum was getting at, but at least if she had some war work to keep her occupied, it might help Harry see that they were both in this together. She'd hoped that having another baby would bring them closer but they were both so tired and worried about the way the war was going, it hadn't turned out that way. He was more distant than ever and she didn't want to grumble about that because it wasn't her way, but she wanted him to talk to her about things more. Some nights, she'd lie there on her own and wonder if this was what the rest of her life was going to be like. It was like living with a stranger. If she could get a job, perhaps then he might see her differently. That might encourage him to share whatever was on his mind.

'Why don't you invite your sister, Kitty, down here for a visit?' said Annie brightly the next morning, as she mixed up some powdered eggs for Harry's breakfast.

Harry kept his head buried in last night's *Evening News*. 'Annie, pet, there's a war on and she's looking after my mother, who's not been in the best of health. She can't just leave her, you know. Newcastle is a long way away.'

'Well, I know that,' said Annie, whisking some milk in to try to make the mixture look as appetizing as possible – which was no mean feat with powdered egg. 'I just thought it might be nice for her to see the children and perhaps it might lift your mood a bit.'

Harry flicked the newspaper closed and glared at her.

'What's wrong with my mood? Not to your liking, is it?'

'Don't be like that, Harry,' said Annie, laying some toast in front of him. The floorboards above creaked as their neighbours came into their kitchen upstairs. She lowered her voice because she didn't want the embarrassment of people overhearing their private conversations. 'It's just that you haven't been yourself lately, with all the air raids, and I thought maybe it might help to talk to Kitty. From what you say she's a—'

'She's a very forceful woman, our Kitty,' Harry cut in. 'Opinionated. You might not get on with her.'

'But she's family!' said Annie, throwing up her hands in exasperation. 'I have had your kids and I haven't even met her.'

'Well, we've got Herr Hitler to thank for that, haven't we?' said Harry, picking up his newspaper again. He spoke to the pages in front of him, rather than looking her in the eye. 'Kitty would start meddling in our affairs. She'd want the bairns out of London and living up there in Newcastle with her, you mark my words.'

'What?' said Annie. 'She couldn't come down here and take my children; I was only suggesting that she could come and visit.'

'Oh, you just watch her. She's a force of nature. She'd persuade you to it, Annie. Trust me, she's my sister and I have known her all my life. She's got a man's brain in her head and she won't take no for an answer. You know she's cleverer than I am. She can outwit anyone, our Kitty can.'

'But—'

'Just leave it, will you?' he said, getting up and grabbing his coat and flat cap. 'She's not coming down here and we are not going up there and that's the end of the matter. Now, I'm going out.'

Annie turned around just in time to see the eggs burning in the pan on the stove. As she scraped them into the bin, something inside her snapped.

She didn't need his permission and she wasn't going to ask it, not after the way he spoke to her this morning.

Annie stood at the gates of Acton Works with her handbag on her arm and her heart in her mouth as she watched a steady stream of women walking in and out, nattering to each other as they went.

She didn't dare turn up at C.A.V., the factory where Harry worked, because word would get around to him straight away. At least this way, she stood a chance of signing up for a war job and then it would be too late for him to do anything about it.

As she made her way up to the entrance, a fella on a bicycle wobbled past and gave her a low wolf whistle. She

Beezy Marsh

buttoned her coat and strengthened her resolve. Another bloke in a pair of overalls, carrying a ladder, stopped and asked her if she needed to find the way to the canteen.

'No,' she said politely, 'I'm here to see the manager. I want to volunteer.'

'Righto,' he said, gesturing through a set of double doors.

It was a vast space, stretching as far as the eye could see. There were railway carriages being built down at one end and the noise of machines on the shop floor was a bit overwhelming. Women clad in the same dungarees that Elsie wore were working away on the heavy machinery, turning lathes, finishing off complicated bits of metal-work.

Annie found her way to the manager's office in the corner, taking in the nameplate on the door – Mr D. Pritchard – and tapped lightly.

A grey-haired gentleman with eyebrows like two black caterpillars looked up at her as she entered. He had a kind of warmth to his face and he broke into a smile. 'Well, what can we do for you today?'

Annie cleared her throat because for some reason there appeared to be a frog sitting in it at that very moment. 'I've come to volunteer for some war work. I've got experience of working as a machine hand, but that was down at C.A.V. a while back, with the diesel engines. People say I have got a good eye for detail. I can sew as well, if you need some help with upholstery in the carriages you're making.' She knew she was gabbling but she couldn't help herself. Her nerves had got the better of her.

'Well, that all sounds wonderful! I'm sure we can make good use of you,' he said.

He sucked in a breath and sat back in his chair for a moment, flashing her a perfect set of white teeth. Annie couldn't help thinking he was a bit like one of those ventriloquist's dummies she'd seen down at the varieties at the Chiswick Empire. There was something relentlessly cheery about him, although that wasn't necessarily a bad thing, with all the doom and gloom of the war.

He extended a hand to her. 'I'm Mr Pritchard, but you can call me Dennis. And you are?'

'Annie,' she said. 'I should tell you, I can only really do three shifts a week at the moment because I have little ones at home, but my mum will be minding them for me.'

'That's fine,' he said. 'You can see how you get on. What about your husband; away with the forces, is he?'

'No,' said Annie. 'He's working down at C.A.V. and does nights with the ARP too.'

He flicked some imaginary dust from his trouser leg before glancing up at her. 'And does he mind that you're coming out to work?'

'No, not at all,' Annie said, clasping her handbag a little more tightly. 'He feels it's my patriotic duty.'

'Does he? Good fella. Well, you can start on Monday morning then.'

'You've gone and done what?'

Harry's eyes were molten with anger.

'Harry, please, keep your voice down. You'll wake the

children and the neighbours will hear us rowing. You know I don't like a fuss.'

'Well, you should have thought twice before going to volunteer like that! Who's going to be running the house and looking after the bairns?'

'I will, and Mum will help me with the children,' said Annie, smoothing her hands down over her apron. She rarely argued with Harry and his words cut her like a knife, but she had signed up for war work now and there was no going back, they both knew that. 'It's only three shifts a week but it will bring more money in and at least I can hold my head up and say I'm doing my bit. Plenty of women are helping. Even Vera is in the ARP.'

'Well, not for much longer the way things are looking,' said Harry matter-of-factly.

'What do you mean?' asked Annie.

Harry sighed and ran his hands through his hair. 'There's a lot of talk about food going missing from the canteen and people think Vera's behind it.'

Annie swallowed hard. She remembered what Bessie had told her about Vera hanging around with Herbie, the local spiv. She couldn't help but wonder if it had been more than gossip, after all.

'Has anyone got any evidence?'

'Not yet,' said Harry. 'But if they do, she'll be out on her ear and if she's profiting from it by selling things on, that could be very serious indeed.'

'But she's a good worker, isn't she?' said Annie, desperate to stick up for her friend.

'Fearless,' said Harry, standing up and pulling on the

black woollen jacket of his air-raid warden uniform. 'There'll be incendiary bombs raining down on us and Vera won't shirk from her duties. I've seen her stick two fingers up to the sky as they're coming down. She's cut from a different cloth, that girl.'

Annie smiled to herself. 'That sounds like Vera, all right. Do you want me to try to have a word?'

'Be my guest,' said Harry. He pulled her to him. 'Look, Annie, I didn't mean to lose my temper, but I just wish you'd discussed getting a job with me first, that's all. I wouldn't have stood in your way, you know.'

She gazed up at him as his eyes searched her face.

'Are you happy, Annie?'

'I don't think any of us are happy at the moment, with the war and everything,' said Annie, shrugging her shoulders. 'I feel happier knowing I can do my bit, but you and the children are my priority, you mustn't doubt that.'

He leaned forward and kissed her, their first proper kiss in what seemed like forever. She buttoned up his jacket for him and he put his tin hat on his head, ready to go out for the night watch. He did look handsome.

'I know I'm not always easy to live with, Annie, but I do love you and the bairns, don't ever forget that,' he said.

He smiled at her and gave a little wave, just as he always did when he was going out with the ARP, and as she watched his back departing, Annie realized that she was crying.

A hush fell over the Acton Works canteen as the BBC announcer's voice carried over the airwaves: '*This is Godfrey Talbot reporting in the desert. It's been a cold night, a night when a man takes every opportunity to lie as snug as he can in his foxhole in the sand.*

'*I watched as hundreds of guns opened up, launching thousands of shells, a demon racket, which shook the ground. All the sky was alive with flashes and with that and the moon, there wasn't much darkness.*

'*Infantry and sappers were at work, fighting bravely; they are engaging now, we await more news . . .*'

Knives and forks clattered onto plates and spam fritters were left untouched as everyone crowded around the wireless.

'*The tanks are moving now and each tank as it goes past churns up a great cloud of dust and sand . . .*'

'My brother's over there,' whispered Annie to Mavis, who worked shifts on the lathe with her. Acton was so far from El Alamein, but she wanted to reach through the wireless and dig through the sand with her bare hands until she could touch George, just to know that he was safe.

She felt someone touch her lightly on her shoulder and spun around to find herself gazing up at Dennis, the foreman.

When he smiled, it was as if he was spreading happiness as wide as the grin on his face. Everyone liked him. It wasn't just that he was a fair boss, he was a decent bloke with it and his door was always open to anyone who needed to chat.

Annie loved being there, the whole camaraderie of the shop floor, listening to *Music While You Work* and singing along to her favourites, 'The Lambeth Walk' and

'We'll Meet Again' and 'Run Rabbit Run'. When they were all pulling together, it made her feel invincible. Every shell case that was turned, every rivet that was hammered in, everything helped to fight the Nazis and she was part of it.

'Now, now, don't get worried. I read the paper this morning and they were saying that Monty's got Rommel on the run! His tanks are shot to pieces. It's the best news we've had in ages,' said Dennis.

The assembled crowd gave a little cheer at that.

'So, let's eat up and get back to it, shall we?'

He gave Annie a wink and it seemed in that moment that the war would go their way and a light in her world shone a little brighter.

13

Annie

Acton, May 1943

'Well, she ain't welcome in the air-raid shelter no more, I'll tell you that for nothing!'

Bessie sat like a mother hen at her kitchen table, with little Anita at her feet on the bare floorboards, babbling away to herself, and baby John snoozing in her arms, as she shared the news of Vera's disgrace. Anita picked up a big brass button from the box Bessie had given her to play with and held it between her chubby little fingers. 'Button!'

Bessie always made such a fuss of the kids when Annie brought them round to Soapsud Island for a visit.

'Ooh, that's a lovely one, chicken, yes!' said Bessie, taking the button from her. 'Can you find me another?' She lowered her voice and turned to Annie. 'I told you that Vera had been on the rob and it was going to catch up with her. Well, now it has. That good-for-nothing Herbie's due up in front of the beak and she's lucky she's not going with him.

'And she got chucked out of her rooms in Stirling Road an' all. Lady downstairs said there were so many men in uniform going up and down the staircase it was like an escalator at Piccadilly Circus. And some of them were *Americans* too!' Vera had got herself rooms near her mother's so that she could have some space but still be on hand to help and now even that had gone terribly wrong. Annie's heart sank.

American soldiers had been causing quite a stir around town and a whole bunch of them were stationed up the road at Park Royal. Elsie had been out dancing with a few at the Hammersmith Palais on Saturday afternoons and had come back with some fancy new dance steps and a pair of nylons. Mum seemed pleased because it meant Elsie would stop pinching her gravy browning, which she'd been slapping on her legs because she'd run out of clothing coupons for new stockings.

The Yanks were always flush with luxuries and very generous too, so it was no surprise that Vera had been entertaining half the US army, but it didn't seem fair to judge her too harshly because of it. The filching of food from the ARP canteen was another matter, of course. That was unforgivable when so many people were struggling to get by on rations.

Annie had tried to warn Vera that the ARP supervisors were watching her and told her that if she was stealing anything, she should stop, but Vera had just shrugged her shoulders, taken a drag of her ciggie and said, 'Don't know what you are talking about there, Annie.'

The final straw came last week, when three tins of corned beef had gone missing the night she was washing up in the canteen and although she swore blind that she'd had nothing to do with it, the chief warden had given Vera her marching orders.

A few days later, Herbie had an unscheduled visit from the boys in blue, who had uncovered his stash of black-market goods, including his petrol tank hidden behind the garden wall. He was due up in court for profiteering. There was no proof that Vera had been involved but that didn't matter to Bessie or any of the Soapsud Island women. She'd been seen often enough in his company for people to talk.

Now it seemed the world was out to get Vera and all the hatred and suspicion people had been harbouring for the last few years came pouring out. Her landlady didn't want to be tarred with the same brush, so she'd taken it as an excuse to get shot of her.

'So, where is she going to live?' said Annie.

'Can't say I care two figs to be honest,' said Bessie sniffily. 'But I heard she's got herself a job behind the bar in The Gladstone. That's her natural habitat if you ask me. She'll find it makes her line of work a bit easier, I dare say.'

Annie knew that what Bessie was saying was true, but it didn't make hearing her friend being talked about in that way any more palatable and Annie certainly wasn't going to join in.

'Well, I'd better be getting back,' said Annie, giving her a tight little smile.

'Do you have to go so soon?' said Bessie, her face falling. 'It's just, you know I love seeing the little ones.' She gave John a hug.

Bessie didn't have any other family, so Annie relented

and stayed a while longer. As she sipped her scalding hot tea, she had the germ of an idea to bring Vera and Bessie closer together again, to heal the rift. 'I'm thinking of going up to the open-air concert at Springfield Park tomorrow. Why don't you come with us?' Music in the park was just one way the council tried to keep people's spirits up.

Bessie beamed at her. 'I'd love to. It'll do me good to get out and about.' She put her hand inside the pocket of her apron. 'I almost forgot, you'd better take these.' She pulled out a pair of knitted bootees in blue wool. 'I made them for the baby.'

'They're beautiful, Bessie,' said Annie. 'You shouldn't have.'

'I unpicked one of my old shawls. I don't have much need for it, so thought it would be more use for the baby than me.'

That was the Bessie who Annie knew and loved, the woman who would give the clothes off her own back to help, not the bitter gossip who seemed to love spreading the dirt about Vera, who she'd once counted as a friend.

As Annie pushed the pram up Acton Lane, with John tucked up inside and Anita sitting on the front with her legs dangling between the handles, she could only wonder about how much this war had changed their community and whether things could ever be the same again.

The days when it wasn't respectable for a woman to go into a public house on her own had passed since the war began. Some of the older folk might raise an eyebrow, but pubs were doing a roaring trade, with single girls nipping in after their factory shifts. More people than ever took solace in a drink and the inevitable knees-up that the end of the night would bring, and many drinkers even ignored the air-raid sirens and stayed put. Most would move away from the windows because of the risk of flying glass from a bomb blast but they showed determination to enjoy their free time and many saw it as a way of sticking two fingers up to Hitler.

Annie dropped the children round to her mum's and headed back down Acton Lane towards The Gladstone pub on Park Road. It had a bit of a reputation as a rough place, a real spit-and-sawdust establishment, but Annie had grown up round these parts so that didn't put her off.

A couple of old geezers glanced up as she pushed open the door and walked in. The air was redolent with the stench of stale tobacco and the floorboards nearest to the bar were sticky from pints of beer being sloshed about. Vera was hard at work, her dirty blonde curls shaking as she polished glasses with a tea towel that had seen better days.

Annie stepped over a little heap of sawdust full of cigarette ends and waved at Vera, who greeted her, dead-eyed. 'Hello, Annie, come to gloat?'

'That's no way to treat a friend,' Annie chided. 'I've come to see how you are getting on.'

Vera shrugged her shoulders. 'I didn't mean to be off-hand, it's just I don't have many people who want to pass the time of day with me any more.'

'Well, I was wondering if you might like to come to the

concert tomorrow up at Springfield Park, with me and the kids?'

'Sounds nice,' said Vera. 'Fancy a drink?'

Annie didn't have time to respond because Vera was already pouring a couple of large sherries.

'Won't the landlord mind?'

'Nah, he's permanently pickled and, in any case, he knows I'm a good worker, so I'm allowed to have a few bevvies on the house,' she said, giving Annie a little wink.

Annie took the glass and had a teeny sip, out of politeness more than anything else.

Vera leaned forward and smiled, flashing her yellowing teeth. 'I know you tried to warn me to watch my back at the ARP, but I swear I never nicked anything that night. Don't matter now in any case. They'll have to manage without me, won't they?'

'Well, it's their loss,' said Annie. 'Harry says you were good at your job. Where are you staying these days?'

'Have you been listening to gossip about me, Annie?' said Vera, her eyes narrowing to slits.

'No, I just heard you weren't round at Stirling Road when I went looking for you,' Annie lied.

Vera paused for a moment and took a large slug of her drink before wiping her mouth on her blouse sleeve and continuing: 'Got a room up the road from an old couple. They don't seem to mind me 'cos I'm helping with the rent so that's all they care about.' She itched a row of bites up her arm as she spoke. 'Bed bugs are troubling me something rotten, though. I expect the fresh air tomorrow'll do me good.'

As Annie was leaving Vera shouted out across the bar, 'And I bet there'll be some handsome GIs there too, won't there?'

She was the same old Vera all right.

Hundreds of people flocked to Springfield Park for the concert on a bright and sunny early summer's afternoon when the blossom was still on the trees. If it hadn't been for the absence of so many of the menfolk between the ages of eighteen and forty, it would have been like any other show before the war.

Dozens of little heads were bobbing about in front of the Punch and Judy show, which was festooned with Union Jack bunting. Mum and Ivy sat with the children, who were mesmerized by it all. They'd been promised a magician and a clown later on too, which was a real treat.

Esther had organized some stalls to raise more money for the war effort and people were chucking balls at tin cans which had been painted to look like Hitler, for a penny a shot. Three in a row got you a ha'penny back. Her boy Leonard and some of his friends had glued a few cans to the posts, of course, but nobody minded really. It was all a bit of fun.

Music seemed to make life more bearable for everyone and people were already tapping their feet to the pianist up on the bandstand, who was tickling the ivories for all she was worth.

Strolling among the crowds, standing a head taller than most of the Londoners, were a whole bunch of American GIs in their sand-coloured uniforms. They cut a swathe through the girls and appeared to be towing half the snotty-nosed urchins from Stirling Road in their wake, who were badgering them, 'Got any gum, chum?'

Annie had spent ages helping Elsie get her hair just right, carefully rolling up the sides and pinning it, and sorting out a bit of lift at the front too, just like Vera Lynn. She had also reworked an old blouse for Elsie, creating the fashionable leg-of-mutton puffed shoulders that she was after, and Elsie had nipped in her waist with a belt to set off her best printed cotton skirt, which had already seen a few summers but still looked pretty.

'I bet Joan's got something new to wear,' Elsie had confided. 'I don't know how she does it on the ration.'

'Oh, don't be daft,' said Annie. 'You'll both look lovely.'

But Joan had pulled out all the stops. Her honey-blonde hair was pinned behind one ear, with the rest falling in loose waves, so that she appeared to be coyly peeking out from a shimmering golden curtain. Her cotton dress was covered with little roses, with a belt made from the same material showing off her impossibly tiny waist. She'd always been tall and slim, but the war work seemed to have honed her figure so when she sashayed across the park to greet them, she looked like a film star.

Elsie's face fell for a moment, but she wasn't down-hearted for long, because the Pioneer Corps Orchestra struck up a tune and a very handsome American soldier asked her to dance. As Elsie trotted off, Annie spied Bessie trudging across the park; she was a martyr to her varicose veins from all the years of standing on the cold, wet floors in the laundries of Soapsud Island.

Annie waved and pointed to a couple of empty deck-chairs near the bandstand and Bessie gratefully sank into one, like a deflating balloon. 'Ooh, that walk up Acton Lane nearly did for me but I'm glad I made it. Is Harry coming along? Haven't seen him in ages.'

'No, he's on a shift today,' said Annie. Harry hadn't shown the least bit of interest in having any fun with her or the children, but she didn't want to dwell on it.

'How's he taking the fact that you're a working woman, then?'

Annie hesitated for a moment.

'Come on,' said Bessie. 'You can tell me; a problem shared and all that . . .'

'I can't say he's happy about it but it's giving us extra money and we might be able to think about getting a bigger flat so that the children can have their own room. Might give us a bit more peace and quiet, which would be nice,' said Annie. That was about as far as she would go in telling Bessie that there were any problems between her and her man. Bessie got the message, because she nodded sagely.

'Well, he should look on the bright side, then, shouldn't he?' said a voice from over her shoulder.

Annie turned around to find Vera smiling down at her. 'Mind if I join you two?'

Bessie's face set like stone. 'I was just leaving.'

'Wait!' said Annie. 'Don't go. Why don't you stay and chat with me and Vera for a while?'

'Can't say I like the company in the park any more,' said Bessie, sticking her nose in the air and pulling her cardigan around her ample bosom. 'I'll see you with the children another time, Annie.'

'Oh, suit yourself!' said Vera, folding her arms and glaring at Bessie.

Bessie heaved herself back out of the deckchair and shuffled off across the park before Annie could stop her.

Vera sat down, muttering, 'Miserable old cow,' but she'd barely exchanged two words with Annie before she was off again, like a rat up a drainpipe, in pursuit of a skinny-looking GI who was standing a bit forlornly watching his comrades manhandling Elsie, Joan and every good-looking girl in the borough around the grass in time to the music, in a blur of beige uniforms and swirling skirts. The soldier clapped eyes on Vera and pulled out a smoke from the packet in his top pocket. Vera leaned in close as he lit it for her and the pair of them strolled off arm in arm and that was that.

Annie was just about to get up and go back to the Punch and Judy show, where the children were screeching 'Oh no he doesn't' at the top of their voices, when her boss, Dennis, appeared in front of her, grinning from ear to ear.

'I hate to see you looking so lonely,' he said, offering her his hand. 'Care to dance?'

'Where's Mrs Pritchard?' said Annie, glancing around.

'She died before the war,' said Dennis, smiling resolutely. Even when talking about the loss of his wife, his chirpiness was relentless. He laughed. 'Looking on the bright side, I get to dance with you without her interfering.'

Before she knew what was happening, Dennis was leading her up to join the waltz. Planting one hand around her waist, they began to dance, with Dennis spinning her enthusiastically, forwards and backwards, until she felt quite dizzy. His arms were rigid and strong, and she kept bumping into his knees, but he carried on regardless, flashing a rictus grin. 'Having fun?'

Dennis was leaning in close, so that his bushy eyebrows almost tickled her cheek, when Annie caught sight of Harry by the bandstand, watching her with a look of disbelief on his face.

'I'm sorry!' she cried, freeing herself from Dennis's grasp. 'I've got to go!' Annie pushed her way frantically through the crowd of dancers but by the time she reached the bandstand, Harry was nowhere to be seen.

Harry didn't pop round to Grove Road that tea time before his ARP shift and Annie sank into a misery as she plunged her hands into the suds in the sink to wash up. She couldn't tell anyone what was wrong, she was just too ashamed. What on earth had she been thinking, dancing with Dennis like that? She hadn't really wanted to and the look on Harry's face had said it all.

Elsie, meanwhile, was giddy with happiness, still twirling around the scullery, stopping only to blow the most ginormous pink bubble with her American gum.

'For the love of God, girl,' said Bill, nearly jumping out of his chair as she popped it. 'You are like a cow chewing the cud. Spit that out, will you?'

'Oh, spoilsport,' said Elsie, dodging a swipe from the back of his hand. 'Josh gave it to me and we're going dancing at the Hammersmith Palais next week!'

Bill rolled his eyes and Mum tutted at him. 'Oh, leave her be, it's nice that she's got a fella. Where's he from, Elsie?'

'Ohio,' she said. 'He's going to bring some photos of his farm to show me.'

Bill flicked open the *Evening News* and grumbled, 'Oh, I bet he is.'

The familiar wail of the air-raid siren cut through the evening air and normal household life came to an abrupt halt; gripes were forgotten as Annie and Mum ran upstairs to grab the kids and bring them down to the Anderson shelter. It was only just getting dark, because of double British Summer Time, but there was a chill in the air, and Annie wrapped John in a shawl to keep him snug in the top bunk next to Anita, who was still half asleep.

Elsie brought a candle in on a dish and covered it with a flower pot and they all settled down to wait for the all-clear, as they had done so many times before. Before long the barrage of the ack-acks over at Gunnersbury started up, making deafening cracks and bangs, and then there was an almighty explosion. Annie stifled a scream as the whole ground shook and the children woke up, crying in fear. The picture of the King was dislodged from its nail and Bill only just caught it before it fell on the floor.

Mum started praying quietly: 'The Lord is my shepherd, he makes me lie down in green pastures . . .' and the sickening thud of bombs dropping nearby went on for what seemed like an eternity.

Elsie started to cry and squeezed Annie's hand. 'Please don't land here, please not here . . .'

They sat there by the dim light of their candle, more terrified than they'd ever been, dreading what they'd find when the all-clear sounded. Annie's mouth had gone dry and her heart was pounding as she thought about Harry. Mum caught the look in her eye and leaned over to her. 'He'll be fine, you'll see.'

Her mum always had such a way of calming her. It sounded as if the world outside was ending but Mum gave her courage.

It was well past midnight by the time they were able to leave the air-raid shelter, and Annie ran down to the end of Grove Road to see what had happened. A thick, black pall of smoke was rising over Acton Lane and people were rushing up and down the High Street bringing news of the bombing.

She stopped a firewatcher, his face black with soot, who told her, 'Park Road North's badly hit. The Gladstone pub's gone, the dairy's flattened and half the street with it. Best get yourself home and count yourself lucky.'

Annie didn't sleep a wink that night and got up at first light to head down to Soapsud Island to see what she could do to help. Water jetted up in the air from broken pipes and the acrid smell of burning caught in the back of her throat as she turned into Park Road North. The dairy that used to stand on the corner of the street had been razed to the ground and all the shops along Park Road had been reduced to a pile of rubble, along with the pub where she'd had a drink with Vera only a few days ago.

The row of terraced houses opposite now had a gaping hole in the middle of it, as if a giant had come and stepped on people's homes, reducing them to chunks of plaster and matchsticks. Air-raid wardens were digging through the rubble with their bare hands, shouting, 'Is anybody there?' but there was no reply, only an eerie silence.

The whole neighbourhood was struck dumb with shock. Women stood around in little clumps, dressed in their housecoats and curlers, huddling together for comfort, and Bessie was among them, beside Vera's mum, Mrs O'Reilly, who had a small child clinging to her arm.

When the last stretcher was carried out, Annie knew it was Vera. A blanket had been thrown over her, half covering her face and reaching just to her thighs, but the headful of dirty blonde curls and mottled legs spotted with rows of blackening bed-bug bites confirmed the worst.

Mrs O'Reilly let out a sickening wail and sank to her knees as Bessie cried, 'Oh my Gawd, Vera!'

The housewives' murmurs filled Annie's ears. 'She weren't using the shelters no more, you know?', 'Poor soul, that Vera', 'What a way to go, she deserved better.'

Bessie took off her shawl and struggled down onto the ground to kneel beside Vera's body. With shaking fingers, she adjusted the hem of Vera's nightie, pulling it downwards for decency's sake, before gently placing her shawl over Vera's naked legs and tucking it in under her feet, as if she were trying to keep her warm. Mrs O'Reilly had to be held back by the ARP to stop her from hurling herself onto the battered remains of her daughter.

'Bloody German swines, they've killed her!' said an old man, shaking his fist at the rubble.

'They'll never win!' said one of the housewives, as the assembled crowd nodded in agreement. 'Rule Britannia!'

Annie went over to Bessie and helped her up.

'We've all killed her, haven't we?' said Bessie, her shoulders sagging as she turned to go back to her flat, the cat and her life in Stirling Road.

Annie was lying in the dark, pretending to be asleep, when Harry finally came home and got into bed that night.

She felt his arms slip around her waist and he pulled her close. 'I won't lose you, Annie.'

Annie rolled over and felt his lips brush hers and they clung to each other for a moment.

'I'm sorry about the dance,' she began. 'It meant nothing to me.'

'I've been a fool to neglect you,' he said. 'The war is no excuse. It's just easier to shut things out, the memories, what I've done. There are things a woman shouldn't have to hear, but please understand that I can't bear to lose you, Annie. You're the love of my life.'

She ran a finger down his cheek and kissed his face, which was wet with tears.

'Vera died,' she whispered. 'She was killed in that blast. I saw her brought out of the rubble on a stretcher. So, talk to me, Harry, please. I can't change the past, but we've all suffered terrible losses in this war. I'm here for you, but you've got to tell me what happened to you.'

In the black of the night, she felt his shoulders start to shake.

'I'll try, Annie, but God knows, I want to forget most of it.'

14

Ethel

Newcastle upon Tyne, June 1923

She'd been saving up for ages to buy a new hat for the Hoppings fair and now Da wouldn't let her go. Ethel dried her tears and pressed her ear to the bare floorboards in her bedroom as Mam did her best to persuade him otherwise, downstairs in the scullery.

'She's a good lass, she's been working so hard, it doesn't seem right that she should miss out when all the others from the shop are making a day of it.'

A fist thumped the table. 'It's the wrong sort of place for her, all those hawkers, freak shows and fortune telling. It's ungodly!'

'Nathan, please,' said Mam. 'She knows right from wrong and it's run by the Temperance Society so there'll be no one supping pints there and she won't be tempted to do anything daft, I know it.' There was some murmuring and then Ethel heard the sound of footsteps coming up the stairs, so she leaped onto her bed, picked up her Bible and pretended to read.

The bedroom door creaked open and her father stood in front of her, his thumbs tucked into the thick leather belt around his middle, his moustache twitching a bit. He was tall and striking, with high cheekbones and clear blue eyes, which seemed to pierce her. 'All right, pet, you can go but there's to be no funny business or you'll feel the back of my hand, do you hear? A whip for the horse, a bridle for the donkey and a rod for the back of fools, so says the Lord.'

'Amen,' said Ethel, running into his arms. She listened to his heart beating through the rough wool of his waistcoat. 'Thanks, Da.' He'd always held her like this, ever since she was a little girl, but even though she was nineteen now and many lasses her age were already married, Ethel still loved to feel his arms around her. He was protecting her from the world outside, keeping her safe, she knew that.

'You're precious to me,' he said, as he stroked her hair. 'I just want the best for you, that's all.'

The next morning, all the talk on the haberdashery counter at Fenwick's department store was about the trip to the Hoppings. Even Miss Simpson, her snooty supervisor, was in a better mood than usual, rather than stalking about the shop floor with a face like she was sucking on a lemon.

Ethel hung on to every word of the chatter because she'd never been allowed anywhere near the fair before. It was the biggest social event of the year in Newcastle, when everyone could enjoy the spectacle and let off steam, but her mate Ada reckoned this year wouldn't be as good as in the past. The Hoppings used to be held on the Town Moor but nowadays the powers that be had shifted it to Jesmond Vale, which meant it was a bit smaller, with fewer rides.

'Oh, you should have seen it before the war!' Ada cried. 'It was packed as far as the eye could see, the moor was heavin'.' Of course, there was always the possibility that Ada was trying to show off that she'd been loads of times, to get one up on Ethel; as they were friends, she was prepared to let Ada have her moment.

Legend had it that a gypsy curse meant it always rained on the Hoppings, which dampened the atmosphere. 'Let's hope it's not ploating down later,' said Ada, with a laugh. 'Me hair will gan all frizzy and I'll bet there'll be loads of canny lads there.'

Miss Simpson decided she'd had enough gossiping. 'Come along, girls,' she said, pulling open a drawer full of cotton reels beneath the glass-topped counter. 'This lot needs sorting out before opening time. We must remember our standards; this is Fenwick's, jewel of the North, not Paddy's Market, Ada.'

Ada shot her a filthy glance. Everyone knew that Newcastle's flea market was full of bargains and there was no shame in shopping there. Ordinary folk couldn't afford the likes of Fenwick's fancy goods.

Miss Simpson really stuck the boot in. 'And, Ada, please address the customers politely today, like Ethel does. We're not in the collieries now.'

Poor Ada, it wasn't her fault she had the broadest accent imaginable. Her dad was a miner and she was full of pit-yacking talk – 'hoy that here hinny', 'creels and clarts' and even worse sayings that made Miss Simpson blanch. The living end was when she once exclaimed, 'Hadaway an' shite,' when Ethel had told her how much a particularly posh lady had just spent on an order of silk; Ada had almost got the sack for that.

Ethel made a point of trying to better herself. She was just a girl from the terraces of Benwell, so it wasn't a case of putting on airs and graces, but she tried to live up to what her father wanted her to be. For as long as she could remember, she'd practised reading aloud from the Bible on Sunday evenings and he'd corrected her, occasionally rapping her across her knuckles with a wooden ruler if she struggled with long words. It had stood her in good stead because she'd learned to speak clearly. She could slip into Geordie slang like Ada, because she'd grown up playing out in the back alleys, but these days she tried to copy the soft, lilting tones of the well-to-do women she served as a shop girl, day in and day out.

She loved her job, being surrounded by so much colour and finery; the excitement of new bolts of material arriving weekly, in rich shades and textures. Ethel didn't mind sorting through buttons or threads and she had a good eye for colour, Miss Simpson said so, which meant she could help people choose and customers liked that. Every season brought new dress patterns and Ethel studied them, feeling a little well of excitement inside her, because she would buy one for herself, and with her work discount she'd usually be able to get an offcut or two to make a new blouse or a summer dress. Mam was very handy with a needle and thread and she'd always made beautiful things for her, ever since she was a bairn, so Ethel had help with the sewing if she needed it.

Mam popped in to see her once, bursting with pride that her daughter wasn't working in a factory, but serving behind a counter in the finest department store in the city instead. And Da, well, it went without saying that he was over the moon. He told everyone at his work down at the grocery wholesalers, where he was a clerk, that his daughter was working in Fenwick's, and of course it was repeated in the church, where he was a lay preacher.

Da always said she was a bright spark, his jewel. It was true, Ethel looked different to the girls in her street and that did set her apart. They dressed in lumpen shoes, shapeless pinafores and heavy coats, but her clothes were cut from a finer cloth and her dresses made at home by her mam in the latest styles. She was fine-boned, small and slight whereas some of the lasses had legs like pit ponies. She'd had her blonde hair cut into a fashionable wavy bob, which drew envious glances. Da had belted her for that, because he liked her to wear it long, but it had been worth it.

Ada had promised to loan her some lipstick for later and Ethel was planning to nip to the make-up counter in her lunch break to get one of the girls to pencil in her eyebrows, to make them frame her face a bit more, because she was very fair. The only thing she didn't much care for were her teeth, which were a bit crooked at the front, but that was the way God had made them and so there wasn't much she could do about it.

*

The hours seemed to drag by until closing time, when there was a stampede for the doors and all the shop girls met up at the tram stop to take them to Jesmond.

Once they were on board, a whole gang of them started singing and Ethel found herself caught up in the excitement of it all, tapping her feet in time. 'Oh, me lads, you should've seen us gannin, gannin along the Scotswood Road, with all the people standing. There were lots of lads and lasses there and all with smiling faces, gannin along the Scotswood Road, to see the Blaydon Races!'

Nobody minded about the racket, they knew that they were all high as kites because of the Hoppings.

All the shop girls were wearing beige nylon stockings rather than the boring black ones that working-class lasses wore, and some had rolled them down just below the knee, which was a bit of a daring fashion, because that meant you liked to dance. Ada had rolled hers and so while they were sitting at the back of the tram, Ethel did the same. She felt a little thrill as she did so, because she was more sheltered than most girls her age. Other lasses who were nineteen went out dancing sometimes with lads they liked but she was never allowed.

They linked arms as they strolled along into Jesmond Vale, which had transformed from a peaceful, rural place, a spot for quiet family picnics, into a brash, bustling, noisy world of roundabouts, shuggy boats, sideshows, garish awnings and endless possibilities for fun. Black smoke and soot belched out from tall chimneys at the side of each ride, so that the punters didn't get their clothes all covered in smuts. Towering above it all, painted in the boldest red and white stripes, was a helter-skelter and the shrieks of people whizzing down it could be heard across the fairground.

The music of the steam-driven carousels was belting out and schoolboys had taken off their shoes and socks and were mucking about on the weir, which sloped gently from an old millpond nearby. Once they'd spent all their ha'pennies most bairns made their own fun in the water or just darting about around the stalls, occasionally getting a clip around the ear, but they didn't seem to mind.

A crowd of blokes had gathered outside a boxing booth and several were taking off their caps and rolling up their sleeves, ready to fight the champions who were lined up, bare-chested, showing off their muscles. A couple of clowns worked the crowd, trying to encourage volunteers to step forward. It was a sad fact that since the war, most of the contenders were still wet behind the ears or looked like they were too old to go more than a round before being knocked out.

Ada wanted to buy a toffee apple, but Ethel was more interested in the sideshows which were offering everything from the Wonders of the East and the Mysterious Zano, to a living leprechaun and a lion-faced lady, so she wandered off while Ada queued up for her treat.

Ethel joined a small crowd in front of a stall promising a flea circus, 'The Smallest Show on Earth', with a high wire, chariots no bigger than a farthing and even weights for them to lift.

'Come on, step right up! Don't be shy, only a ha'penny a turn,' said the stallholder, who was dressed in the full circus ringmaster garb of top hat and tails.

'Where d'you get your fleas from?' said a man who was standing next to her.

'Steelworkers' socks,' said the ringmaster. 'Well, we did find quite a few good ones in a house in Gateshead too, I can't lie.'

A ripple of laughter washed over the assembled punters and as Ethel giggled, the man turned to her and said, 'That's a bonny smile you've got there.'

She blushed.

He seemed quite a bit older than her but there was a light in his eyes and his mouth curled slightly at the corners as he spoke, which made him look boyish. 'Can I buy you a ticket for the show?'

Ethel wrinkled her nose. 'I'd rather go on the scenic railway,' she said, pointing to the gaudily painted, undulating ride across the way which had carriages shaped like motor cars. She'd been dying to go on that – it would probably be the nearest thing she'd ever get to sitting in a real one. Ada had chatted about it incessantly; she said it was the best fun ever. Well, now Ethel was going to go one up on her, by going on it with a fella!

He smiled.

'My pleasure,' he said, doffing his flat cap to reveal hair as black as coal.

'I'm Ethel,' she said, pushing her hat back on her head a bit, so that he could see her face better.

'Nice to meet you, Ethel,' he replied, as she gazed into his grey eyes – he was rather handsome. 'I'm Harry.'

Ethel selected the shiniest car, painted bottle green with red leather seats and brass fittings. There were three rows of seats in each carriage, but she took the front one to get the best view, smoothing her skirt down over her knees so that the tops of her rolled stockings were not visible – she didn't want him to get the wrong impression. He climbed in next to her and paid their fare to a gent in a bowler hat as a steam organ pumped out a tuneless version of the 'Can-Can'.

Ethel grinned at him and murmured, 'Thanks.' She'd never had anyone buy anything for her other than her mam and da.

'So, what's the best thing about the Hoppings so far?' said Harry.

'Well, I've only just got here but I'd have to say, the company's grand,' Ethel replied, batting her eyelashes at him, just as she'd seen some of the other girls at work do. That felt good.

The ride set off and as it spun faster, Ethel started to giggle. It was such a strange sensation, going up and down the slope. Her insides had turned to jelly.

'That's quite an infectious laugh you've got there, Ethel,' said Harry. 'Is it catching?'

It was true, her da always said she could brighten up any room with it. She clung to the edge of the car windscreen, as the shouts and whoops of the bairns in the car behind filled the air.

'I'm not sure,' she said. 'But my head's spinning!'

After the ride they wandered off together towards the shuggy boats, but Ethel caught sight of Ada heading towards her with a face like thunder, so she pulled Harry into the bioscope to see some moving pictures. She was enjoying his company too much to share him with her friend.

As the lights went down and the screen flickered to life, Harry slipped his hand into hers and she didn't try to stop him. In fact, she quite liked it.

By the time he got her home to Normanton Terrace, Ethel had found out quite a lot about Harry. He'd been lucky enough to survive the war and he had an easy manner about him, so it seemed as if they'd known each other forever as they sauntered along. He was softly spoken and not a show-off like so many of the fellas she'd seen at work. Perhaps it was because he was a bit older than her, six years to be precise, but that made him all the more attractive to Ethel. He was a perfect gentleman and he didn't even try to kiss her; not like some of the gobby delivery boys that Ada had told her all about, with their wandering hands in unexpected places.

Harry was educated and clever; he was working as an engineer, which would be sure to find favour with her da because that was a job with good prospects.

Ethel hadn't ever been allowed to walk out with anyone before – her da wouldn't hear of it – but Harry had promised to come around and ask his permission, man to man. That was something that her father would respect, she was sure of it.

But until then, she made sure that Harry dropped her off at the top of her street, just in case anyone saw them together, because if they did and Da found out, she knew she'd be for it.

The following Saturday afternoon, there was a knock at the front door, and Harry was standing there, cap in hand, when her da answered.

Ethel hovered at the top of the stairs, listening to the murmured conversation, before Da turned to her, with a look approaching hurt in his eyes, and said, 'You'd better get down here. And tell your mam to put the kettle on.'

Harry smiled up at Ethel, as if this was the most normal thing in the world, to just stroll into her home and talk to her father. Her insides were churning but there was something about Harry that was so reassuring, she felt almost compelled to be near him.

Da showed Harry through into the kitchen. He wasn't about to welcome him into their front room, that much was clear, and Mam shot Ethel a concerned glance as the two men sat down at the table.

Mam hurriedly swept some breadcrumbs away with a dishcloth and filled the kettle, before disappearing into the pantry with Ethel hot on her heels.

'So, what are your intentions towards my daughter?'

Ethel peered through a crack in the pantry door as Da sat, with his long legs splayed out in front of him, and eyed Harry across the kitchen table.

Harry opened his mouth to speak but a football clattered against the back gate, where the lads were playing in the alley, and Da got up and yelled across the yard, 'Pack it in or I'll come out there and give you all a hiding!'

He sat back down and returned his gaze to Harry, who smiled and said, 'I'd like to take her out from time to time. Afternoon tea, a walk in the park, dancing perhaps . . .'

'Oh, I don't know about that,' said Da, as Ethel pretended to busy herself in the pantry with Mam, who gave her arm a little squeeze. 'Our Ethel, she's well brought up, not like the lasses you get from Jarrow, you know. Where'd you meet my daughter, tell me that, now, won't you?'

'At the Hoppings,' said Harry.

'My point exactly. She's never been there before and she won't be going again. Wrong sort of place for my daughter.' He balled his hand into a fist and held it in mid-air for a split second, as if he were about to bang it on the table, but Harry just raised an eyebrow, and Da thought better of it.

'She seems like a very sensible girl and I respect that,' said Harry, leaning forward to make his point. 'She knows her own mind and that's because you're a family with standards, but I wasn't suggesting we go out alone. I'd be bringing my older sister. She's a journalist, works for the *Shipbuilder* – she's a senior sub-editor. So, you see, it would all be respectable.'

Da stroked his moustache for a moment and gave a little nod, as if he were ruminating on this piece of information and was quietly impressed. 'And you live over Heaton way?'

'Yes,' said Harry. 'I'm an engineer at Hawthorn Leslie and my mother's well known as a local school teacher.'

Ethel brought the tea loaf she'd made earlier out of the pantry and started to slice some onto their best china plates.

As Mam handed a piece of cake to Harry, Ethel couldn't help noticing that her mother's hands were shaking. Ethel brought the teapot over to the table and Da let it brew for what seemed like forever before he pushed a mug towards Harry, poured him some and said, 'Well, all right then. She can go out from time to time. But no funny business, mind, or you'll be hearing from me.'

15

Ethel

Newcastle upon Tyne, January 1924

It was such a grand place, with its chandelier, arched alcoves and polished wooden floor, that Ethel felt like a princess as she twirled around in Harry's arms. The room was so elegant, with high ceilings and ornate plasterwork, it was like the inside of a palace.

Ethel knew, from the ladies who came to the haberdashery counter at Fenwick's, that a dance at the Assembly Rooms was the place to be seen in Newcastle. She'd never have dreamed that she might one day get to dance in the footsteps of all those rich folk, who arrived in their furs and fine jewels. Harry must have saved up for ages to afford it and that only made her feel more special.

Mam had worked her fingers to the bone to get her beautiful dress ready on time. It wasn't silk like the dresses of the wealthy ladies but that didn't matter one bit. Hers was in gold-coloured rayon but it had been cut to the latest pattern from Fenwick's, with a dropped waist, fluted hem and scooped neck.

Luckily for her, Da had been out at the football when she left the house, or he'd have sent her back upstairs to change.

'You look lovely,' said Harry, as the orchestra struck up another tune and the pace quickened into a foxtrot. Ethel was light on her toes and although she'd never had lessons, she was a natural on the dance floor.

'Why doesn't Kitty get up and dance?' whispered Ethel in Harry's ear.

His sister was sitting at their table having another one of her long chats with Mr Philpott, her editor from the newspaper.

'Oh, she's enjoying herself fine,' said Harry. 'She's not one for showing off and socializing, our Kitty.'

For the life of her, Ethel couldn't fathom that relationship out. Kitty and Mr Philpott seemed to spend a lot of time in each other's company, but she'd once made the mistake of asking if they were walking out together and Kitty had shot her a look that could have curdled milk. Ethel had only once heard Kitty call him by his first name, Charles, in all the times they'd been out together as a foursome, and he called her Catherine rather than her pet name.

Yet there were little signs of tenderness between them: he'd brush some hair out of her face when he thought no one was watching or touch her gently on the arm as they spoke. Once Ethel had caught them holding hands in the parlour at Harry's house but that left them both incredibly flustered.

'Are you worn out with all this dancing yet?' asked Harry, as he pulled her closer to him. She felt her heartbeat quicken. There was something about him that just made her go weak at the knees. Her friend Ada at work reckoned it must be love.

The music stopped, and the band leader held up his hands and called for 'a bit of hush'.

He flicked his tailcoat as he addressed the crowd. 'There's a very special announcement to make, so if we could all just clear the dance floor for a minute.'

A murmur ran through the crowd as people edged their way back to their seats.

Ethel was just heading to their table when Harry caught her by the hand.

'Wait,' he said.

Suddenly, they were the only couple on the dance floor and all eyes were on them.

He got down on one knee and pulled out a ring from the pocket of his waistcoat.

Ethel gasped. It was the most beautiful thing she'd ever seen: a huge sapphire set on a gold band and it sparkled in the light. The room started to spin before her eyes.

'I love you, Ethel,' he said. 'Will you marry me?'

'You're ganna be a blushing bride!'

Ada picked up a yard of lace and threw it over her head as a makeshift veil, as she gallivanted around in the storeroom at Fenwick's. 'Now, show us that sparkler on yer finger again, I cannae believe it!'

All the shop girls put their heads together as Ethel held

out her hand to show them the beautiful sapphire engagement ring that Harry had given her. 'Gan on, tell us again how he popped the question,' said Ada, peering around the door in case their snooty supervisor, Miss Simpson, was on the prowl.

'I was so surprised I think I nearly fainted,' Ethel giggled. 'Of course, I said "yes" and then we had a dance, just us two, with everyone cheering and clapping. It's like a dream come true.' Well, most folks clapped and cheered, but Kitty had sat there, with her handbag perched on her lap and a face like a wet weekend. Ethel wasn't sure why, but she just got the feeling that Kitty thought she wasn't good enough for Harry.

'Oh, don't be daft,' Harry would whisper whenever Kitty shot Ethel one of her reproving looks. 'She's just got her head full of ship specifications, that's all. She carries a lot of responsibility, our Kitty does. You mustn't hold it against her.'

No matter how hard Ethel tried to chat to Kitty, about anything from the weather to the latest bolts of cloth she'd been selling on the haberdashery counter at Fenwick's, Kitty just seemed bored by it. Harry's mam was a different kettle of fish. She was kind, a bit nervous perhaps, but she'd welcomed Ethel into their home, which was so posh, it had polished wood furniture and fancy antiques and paintings on the wall. The only picture Ethel had in her house was one of Jesus on the cross and that hung in the kitchen and, to be honest, she hated it because it always reminded her, for some reason, of her mother just quietly putting up with Da's moods, day after day.

There was a bond between Harry and Kitty, something that Ethel couldn't quite fathom. They seemed to know what the other one was thinking and were very protective of each other. All that would change as soon as she got married, Ethel was quite sure of that. She was Harry's jewel now. He had told her so when he'd slipped the engagement ring on her finger.

The excitement of Mam making her wedding dress seemed to lighten the atmosphere at home and even Da was whistling to himself as he sat on the netty in the back yard these days.

He'd given his permission for Harry to propose, as she was not yet twenty-one. It seemed like a miracle had happened, because not only had Da said 'yes', but he seemed genuinely happy for them. He was a lot less moody when Harry was around. Maybe it was just being able to talk man to man, but Harry liked a good chinwag and Da spent ages talking about politics with him. Harry was a very clever man, Ethel was certain of that.

He'd read loads of books about communism and all sorts of other things that Ethel wasn't remotely interested in. Not only that, he'd got himself quite involved in the union at work and was always going off for meetings. Some of that was just an excuse to nip to the pub for a sly pint because Da was teetotal and wouldn't approve of that. But Harry had his ear because he'd fought in the trenches during the Great War and Da respected that. He never wanted to talk about what he had done over there in France and Ethel had seen enough wounded soldiers around the city, just quietly getting on with their lives, to know that this was simply the way things were. Nobody wanted to look back to that time. A whole generation had been wiped out and, as Ada told her ruefully the other day, there were so few fellas, Ethel should count her lucky stars to be walking up the aisle with one.

Harry had wanted them to live over in Heaton, at his mother's house, but Da wouldn't hear of it.

'You'll live here, Harry!' he said, thumping his fist on the table. 'Surely you can see it makes sense? Ethel will want to be near her mam when there's the patter of tiny feet, won't you, pet?'

Ethel hadn't really thought about it, to be honest, but she knew it was best to keep the peace, for everybody's sake, so she nodded in agreement. Harry caught the look in her eye.

'If that's what Ethel wants, then that's what we'll do,' he said.

'Well, that's settled then,' said Da, taking a slurp of his tea which was as brown as boot polish. 'You can have our room, we'll get a bed for the front room and then the grandbairns can have Ethel's old room. One happy family!'

Mam gave them all a weak smile. Da had Ethel's family life all planned out. Ethel caught her mother's eye for a split second but said nothing. It was better for all of them if she went along with his plans. She just wanted to be happy, that's all, and nothing was going to spoil her big day.

A wedding date had been set for April and all the shop

girls at Fenwick's shared in the excitement of how Ethel's dress was coming along. Da had given her a couple of pounds that he'd been saving up for this day since she was born, so that she could look every bit as beautiful as one of the film stars at the talkies; Da let her go out courting properly with Harry now, with barely a word said about it.

For her big day, she'd got herself a pair of cream satin shoes and the dress would be made of yards of cream silk that she'd bought from Fenwick's. The excitement of cutting that bolt of cloth and feeling the softness of it between her fingers was like nothing else. Miss Simpson wrapped it for her, personally, and wished her the very best of luck.

The biggest surprise came on her last day at the shop, when Ada, who was going to be her bridesmaid, and the others presented her with some lace and trimmings that they'd all chipped in to buy on their tea break.

'Your life's ganna change now, Ethel, you'll be a married woman. It's like a dream come true.'

As she rang the last customer's shopping through the till that afternoon, Ethel glanced around the shop floor. It had been the only real excitement in her world until now but she was moving on to bigger and better things. Being married to Harry was going to give her everything she needed now and more, she felt certain of that.

Her veil hung almost to the floor and was held in place by a garland of white roses.

Mam had made the dress with a stunning square neckline

and there was a tiered drop waist edged with lace which was set off by her train. Benwell had never seen anything like it and an excited crowd of kids bobbed about by her front door as the wedding car arrived. Da had pulled out all the stops and even spent some of their health insurance money to make sure everything was perfect.

As they stood in the hallway, Da lifted her veil, put his hands on her shoulders and looked deep into her eyes. 'I am so proud of you. Promise me you will honour and respect him as much as you do me and the good Lord himself.'

Ethel's voice quavered a bit as she made her vow. 'I will.'

16

Ethel

Newcastle upon Tyne, May 1926

The General Strike was the biggest walkout the country had ever seen.

Harry had left his work at Hawthorn Leslie early with the other union men from the street, to gather in the city centre and try to persuade scabs not to drive any trams or trains.

'Don't worry, pet,' he'd told Ethel, kissing the baby tenderly on the cheek before he left. 'Nothing bad's going to happen. We're all sensible people. We just want to make a point to the blacklegs that this will all be over more quickly if they join us. You'll be fine to go up the shops later.'

He seemed relaxed enough, but she couldn't help noticing his jaw had set firmly, as if he were quite determined that this cause was worth fighting for. What's more, she'd overheard Da and Harry discussing the emergency powers that the police had been given to arrest anyone who looked like a troublemaker for the duration of the strike.

The shipyards, the factories and stations were all deserted as thousands of men downed tools to stand shoulder to shoulder with the miners, who'd been locked out of the pits in a dispute over their pay.

'Just be careful, won't you?' she said, ignoring the sinking feeling in the pit of her stomach.

Little William was coming up to a year old now and he was the apple of Harry's eye. He had Harry's jet-black hair and grey eyes and such a sweet smile. Da doted on him and was often to be found proudly dandling him on his knee on the front step and praising every sound that escaped the child's lips, as if he were holding the future prime minister in his arms.

'Oh, he's bright as a button!' he'd cry, clapping his hands as William held a bobbin between his chubby fingers. 'Look at that!'

Mam could barely keep her hands off the baby either and she carried him around on her hip until Da would tell her to hand the bairn over. 'It's not good for a boy to spend so much time tied to his grandma's apron strings,' he'd say with a laugh. 'You want your grandad, don't you, little man?'

The whole house had come alive thanks to William, who'd already brought so much happiness to them in his short life. Of course, it was hard work having a bairn, but Mam helped with all the washing: boiling the copper, washing the nappies and the baby's clothes and running them through the mangle before hanging them on the line in the back yard.

As Ethel left the house, all the other housewives were

nattering to each other on their doorsteps. She liked to pass the time of day with them, especially having a brew when William was asleep in his pram outside, but she knew they viewed her with suspicion. She'd worked at Fenwick's, her husband was a union shop steward and her sister-in-law was a journalist. Their family was a cut above in the pecking order of such a close-knit community.

It's not that she minded too much, she'd always been set apart from the rest by her father growing up, but it did mean she was often last to hear about the gossip. The thing she secretly missed was the excitement of working in the department store: knowing what all the fashions were, seeing all the posh ladies dolled up. It made her feel part of a bigger world, away from Benwell with its greasy cobbles and grim rows of terraces with their 'backs' full of screaming bairns. The city had so much more to offer, if only she could grasp it. Now she had her hands full with the little one, there wasn't much chance of that. Ada had promised they wouldn't be strangers, but they'd seen less and less of each other and every time they got together Ethel felt a little stab of jealousy that her friend was still enjoying her dancing days.

William slept peacefully in his pram as she hurried along the Westgate Road to get to the grocer's shop before all the food ran out. Mam had bustled out of their terraced house earlier, to go to the butcher's for the same reason. At least if they split up, they'd have more chance of getting something in for their supper.

As she rounded the corner of the Westgate Road to go

up to the shops on Grainger Street, she couldn't help noticing that the clatter of daily life had disappeared. But it had been replaced by another sound – of men shouting; it was a real din and it was getting closer.

'One Out! All Out!' and 'Not a penny off the pay! Not a second on the day!'

She quickened her pace as dozens of men in flat caps hove into view, waving home-made placards with the messages 'MUST THE MINERS STARVE?' and 'DEFEND THE WORKERS'. The metal studs on the soles of their boots struck at the cobbles as they approached, seeming to swell their numbers. There were women among them too, with pinched faces, drab shawls pulled tightly around their shoulders. Ethel knew they were the poorest in the city because some of them had clogs on their feet. They were the dockers' wives, the kind who had to live by the dozen in a two-up, two-down; whose kids went without shoes all summer and who relied on handouts from the Poor Law to put food on their table.

Out of nowhere, a line of bobbies appeared behind her, at the bottom of Grainger Street, walking slowly in front of a bus with their batons raised. Ethel could see the driver; he was a young lad – he couldn't have been much more than eighteen. But he was posh, with a neatly cut suit and his hair parted and slicked down to one side. He had the same look about him as all the wealthy blokes she'd served in Fenwick's, except he was white with fear.

A murmur ran through the crowd of strikers and before Ethel knew what was happening, a few of them had broken away from the main group and were running down the hill towards her. Some of the men at the front of the crowd shouted, 'Good order! Keep good order!' but their pleas fell on deaf ears. The dockers' wives followed, the struggle of their daily lives plain for all to see as they screamed, 'Scab! Scab!'

As one of them passed Ethel, she stopped, turned to her and gently said, 'Go home, pet.'

But it was too late.

Shopkeepers the length of the street yanked down their blinds and locked their doors. Ethel heaved the pram into the nearest doorway and hammered on the glass for all she was worth, tears streaming down her face. 'Please, let me in! I've a bairn with me!'

There was no reply. William woke up and started to cry.

Ethel turned and watched in horror as the two sides met in a tangle of fists and the sickening thud of baton strikes. Placards were splintered. The bus was surrounded, and the strikers started to rock it from side to side. Hatred burned in the women's eyes as they pulled stones from their aprons and lobbed them at the policemen and the bus. As they hit their targets, the sound of shattering glass brought a cheer from the crowd.

A policeman staggered forward, towards Ethel, clutching his nose, which was spurting blood. It spilled onto the blue serge of his tunic with its shiny buttons before splashing onto the cobbles at his feet. A split second later, horses came cantering down the road as mounted bobbies joined the fray, cutting through the strikers like a knife through butter. Men fell, women screamed, and people ran in all directions.

It was over as quickly as it had begun. Ethel waited for the last of the shouts to die away before pulling the pram back into the deserted street with shaking hands, and hurrying home to the safety of Normanton Terrace.

'What in God's name were you thinking?'

Anger blazed in Da's eyes and he raised his hand to slap her but thought better of it. She'd never heard him take the Lord's name in vain, not in all her born days.

'Leave her be!' cried Mam, putting her arms around Ethel's shoulders, which were still shaking. 'Can't you see she's had a terrible shock?'

'You should have stayed home, Ethel; you can't risk my grandson like that.'

Harry appeared in the doorway, his face ashen, and said quietly, 'He's our son, Nathan. Don't talk to Ethel like that.'

He went to Ethel's side. 'Are you all right, pet? Were you or the baby hurt?'

'N-no,' she stammered. 'We're fine. A bit shaken, that's all.' Tears spilled down her cheeks. 'Oh, Harry, it was terrible, I was so scared. There was a fist fight and blood and everything.'

She felt the beating of his heart as he pulled her to him. 'You're safe now. It's best if you stay home. Things are getting ugly and we don't know how long it's going to go on.'

Ethel glanced up and saw Da glaring at her, the colour rising in his cheeks. Then he looked away, stalked out into the yard and banged the netty door shut behind him. Ethel felt sick to the pit of her stomach about what Da might do but Harry held her tightly and whispered, 'Don't be scared, pet, I will handle him. You're safe now.'

Harry sat at the kitchen table reading the strikers' news-paper, *The British Worker*.

> At Newcastle the stoppage is complete! Reports to the HQ of the Northumberland miners show a staunch determination to stand fast. Good order prevails.

> Middlesbrough is a dead town. Thirty thousand iron and steel workers are out. Tram and bus services have ceased. The railway station is closed. At Sunderland the stoppage of the railways, trams and buses is complete and the docks stand idle.

The strike had been going on for five full days and the government had even sent a warship to Newcastle. It loomed large and grey over the Tyne, like an unwelcome visitor. There had also been scuffles down at the docks where the authorities wanted to unload supplies of food under armed guard.

Next to Harry's steaming mug of tea on the table sat the government's official newspaper, *The Gazette*. He picked it up, tutted, and put it back down again.

Ethel hated it when he got round to reading *The Gazette* because it put him in a very bad mood indeed. The word was that the government had even dropped a load of copies on the collieries by aeroplane; miners were using them as firelighters.

'It's all nonsense, pet,' he said, peering at her over the top of the paper. 'The government says it's an attack on the constitution, but it isn't. It's a lawful strike, not a revolution.'

Da and he weren't seeing eye to eye any more because Da had decided that the strikers should listen to the Prime Minister, Stanley Baldwin, and go back to work. Things were getting out of hand, with strikers chaining lorries to the railways in Middlesbrough to stop the trains running. People involved with the *British Worker* in London had been arrested by the police.

'All this law-breaking doesn't sit well with me, Harry,' said Da, wandering in from the back yard.

'The unions want good order, the police have been heavy-handed with the strikers,' Harry countered. 'And milk supplies are getting through. No one wants to stop people having food, there's no question of that.'

Ethel couldn't help wondering whether Da's sudden change of heart about the strike had something to do with Harry standing up to him the other day, though.

Da threw up his hands and went back out through the yard and across the road to the allotment. He seemed to be spending more time in his shed there than he did in the house. Mam didn't seem to mind, in any case.

Harry got up and the chair screeched on the tiled floor. He pulled on his jacket. 'I'm off for a union meeting, I'll see you later. Kiss the boy for me.' And with that, he was gone.

Ethel knew that meant he was going to meet some work colleagues down the pub. Beer was still available despite the shortages of food, and men liked a pint, didn't they?

*

One afternoon a couple of days later, Ethel had just put William down for a nap when there was a knock at the door.

She came down the hallway and opened it to find Kitty standing there, glancing nervously up and down the street. A few women were peering out of their windows to see who this stranger was; it wasn't often that you got well-heeled women down their way.

'Not at work today?' said Ethel, who was rather wrong-footed by her sister-in-law turning up on her doorstep. She hadn't called round once since the wedding.

'No,' said Kitty. 'I had a terrible headache, so I've taken a few days off. Mr Philpott understands.'

'Would you like to come in?' said Ethel, hastily pulling off her apron to make herself a bit more presentable.

'I can't stop,' said Kitty. 'But I need you to give these to Harry.'

She opened her handbag and pulled out a sheaf of printed pamphlets.

'Where did you get these?' said Ethel, as she read '*British Worker, Official Strike News Bulletin*' and emblazoned above it in bold type 'NEWCASTLE EDITION'. Across the bottom of the front page was written, '*Pass this on, or post this up.*'

'I found them lying around in the street,' said Kitty airily. 'I thought Harry might like to read them. Now, I must be getting on. And Ethel' – she laid a gloved hand on Ethel's arm – 'best not to say to anyone that I was here. Do you understand?'

Ethel's mouth fell open. 'Yes, Kitty,' she said.

Ethel understood perfectly.

Union men were being arrested for speaking out and Harry told her the authorities would get more heavy-handed now, especially because some strikers had derailed the Flying Scotsman as it was coming in to Newcastle. There were more than three hundred people on board at the time. Thankfully no one was hurt but the engine and several carriages went right off the rails and tipped over. Ethel had seen the picture in *The Gazette*. Da had used it as further evidence that the strike had lost its way and was now calling the whole protest 'sinful'.

Ethel watched Kitty picking her way over the greasy cobbles, back to whatever it was she'd been doing on her day off sick. Although they didn't get on, Ethel had to admit, Harry's sister was cut from a different cloth.

On the afternoon of the ninth day of the strike, Harry came trudging down the road, his hands in his pockets and his cap pulled low.

Ethel was just pushing William in the pram, to get him to drop off, and she rushed up to meet him. 'What's wrong, pet?'

'We've had word from the Trades Union Council,' he said, staring straight ahead. 'Our leaders have met the Prime Minister and told him that the General Strike is to be called off unconditionally, from tomorrow.'

'But what about the miners?' Ethel gasped.

'They're still out but the TUC is saying everything's in place to sort their pay. They've sold us out.'

'Well, perhaps it's for the best,' she said, laying a hand

on his shoulder as they walked on together. 'Everyone tried. There's no shame in that.'

Ethel was relieved that things would be getting back to normal at last. She hated not being able to take William into the city to go to the shops and having to worry about where their food was coming from, not to mention fearing that Harry would get hurt or arrested every time he left the house.

He turned to her, his cheeks hollow and tears brimming in his eyes. 'That's not the worst of it. The government says that there's nothing they can do to force the factories to take the strikers back.'

'Well, they can't sack everyone,' said Ethel. 'The whole city's been out.'

'You're right, they can't, but they can sack the union men they see as troublemakers, to make sure it doesn't happen again,' said Harry. 'I've lost my job.'

17

Ethel

Clapham, March 1929

Ethel was jolted awake by the sound of Mam coughing through the thin bedroom wall.

She rubbed her eyes and swung her legs out of the bed, feeling the chill of the linoleum under her feet as she wandered over to the window. Pulling back the curtains, she saw that the street was shrouded in a thick, yellow mist.

It was another pea-souper; no wonder Mam's chest was bad.

Newcastle was full of soot and smuts and there were many mornings when the fret on the Tyne hung so low you could barely see a hand in front of your face, but the air down here was so full of fumes that some days the whole city struggled to draw breath.

They'd been in London for over a year now, but she still had so many things to get used to and she didn't like to trouble Harry with it because, well, he hadn't quite been himself since the General Strike.

For the first week after he was sacked, he lay in bed, just staring at the ceiling. He wouldn't wash or shave; Da said it wasn't right for a man to let himself go like that. He wouldn't eat with the rest of them, so Ethel had to bring him his meals on a tray which she'd leave outside the bedroom door. Then, every night when she came to bed, he'd get up, go out and walk the streets for hours. Sometimes, when he finally came home, Ethel would hear him pacing up and down in the scullery, muttering to himself.

Da had tried to talk to Harry, to make him see sense, but they'd nearly come to blows before Ma begged them to stop it. She didn't like to dwell on his odd behaviour. Harry never spoke of it in any case so it was all forgotten.

Everything started looking up again from the moment that Harry and a few of the other lads from the factory got together and went off to London in search of work. He lived away for about a year, sending his wages home to Ethel. She thought she'd find that very hard but when he left, it was like a black cloud over their house had lifted. His moods had weighed on her and his strange behaviour and nightmares, well, they hadn't really been getting any better either. Ethel loved Harry, of course she did, but with him gone, she could focus on the baby, and Mam and Da were so supportive of her, she even found time to go out and see Ada on a few occasions, which was nice. She wrote telling Harry of every little snippet about William that she could think of and he wrote back to her, long letters – too long, he had such a way with words! – promising her that he carried her in his heart every day.

Before she knew what was happening, twelve months had gone by and then he wrote that he'd found some lodgings and she and William should come and join him.

Ethel hid the letter in the pocket of her apron for a few days before she broached the subject with Da.

'You're not leaving us and going down to London on your own!' he cried, slamming his hand on the table, sending Mam scurrying off into the pantry.

It had been ages since he'd lost his temper like this. His eyes were alive with rage and spittle formed in the corners of his mouth, which had twisted itself into a snarl. 'I won't let him break up our family, Ethel. It isn't right!'

'But, Da,' she pleaded, sitting down opposite him and clasping his hands. 'I'm his wife, he has every right to ask me and the bairn to go down to London to live with him, surely you can see that.'

Da looked away for a moment and then exhaled heavily. 'All right, of course, I know you are right. It's just, you have been so much happier lately and the boy is blossoming here with us all to help. How about we all go to London together? It can be a fresh start for everyone. I'll get myself a job, we can help you with the rent.'

Mam stuck her head around the pantry door. She had blanched from the shock of Da shouting but the colour was slowly returning to her cheeks.

'What do you think, Mam?' said Ethel kindly. 'Would you like to come to London?'

Mam's voice was so quiet, she was almost whispering. 'I'll be very happy to come and live with you and do whatever your da thinks is best.'

Da leaned back in his chair and beamed at Ethel. 'Well, that's decided, then. You'd better write to that husband of yours and tell him to find a place big enough for all of us!'

Within a few weeks, they'd sold off all their furniture and packed everything up, lock, stock and barrel, and moved to London. True to his word, Da had wasted no time in getting himself a job, at the grocer's up on Clapham High Street, so they never ran short of fruit or veg and William was all the better for it. Harry hadn't minded them all coming down; if anything, he seemed happy because Ethel found it easier to settle in with her folks under the same roof.

Ethel peered out of the window, wringing her hands together to get some warmth into them as she watched the shadowy shape of a man making his way up the street carrying a long pole. It was the knocker up; he tapped on the windows to get folks up for their shift at one of the many factories up the road in Battersea. Their whole side of town was given over to industry of one sort or another and if the wind was blowing in the wrong direction, you knew about it. The stench from the tanneries was enough to turn your stomach.

But Ethel knew that they had much to be grateful for. Harry was working at the cardboard-box factory and they had food on their table. It was soul-destroying work, being a machine hand and making those boxes day in and day out, but he did it to keep the family afloat. There were many whose husbands had given themselves over to drinking or gambling because of the despair of the dole queue and whole families had ended up in the workhouse or living hand to mouth, relying on the parish for help, and all the shame that brought with it. However strangely he'd behaved, Harry had never put her through that and he lavished all the love that a father should on his son.

He was forever tinkering away in the back yard with William, hammering some wheels onto a plank of wood to give the boy a cart to ride up the street on with the other kids, or carving him a little sailing boat to take up to the pond on Clapham Common.

William was growing up to be a healthy little lad, sturdy and strong – although Da couldn't quite get over the fact that his grandson now spoke with a Cockney accent instead of a Geordie lilt. It was just Ma who was a worry, really. The move hadn't suited her at all and she was getting very picky with her eating, so her clothes seemed to hang off her and her apron strings went twice around her waist.

Harry was still snoring softly, facing the wall with his back turned to her, as he always did. Ethel knew better than to try to get near him in the night because it brought on the terrors. He'd wake the bairn with his screaming and half the neighbourhood too. The nightmares had started the moment he lost his job and no matter how hard she tried, he wouldn't talk to her about them. She'd seen the sideways glances from the neighbours after his worst ones. He sounded like he was being murdered and then he'd weep, and she'd try to console him, but he'd just brush her off and grunt, 'What's done is done.'

It was scary, seeing a grown man crying like that, and she knew from the looks Mam and Da exchanged that it wasn't something they approved of. Ethel sighed. Harry wasn't the man she'd married six years ago. He'd changed, and not for the better.

'No rest for the wicked!'

Ethel smiled at Doreen, the woman from over the road who was on her hands and knees on her front step, scrubbing for dear life. It wasn't yet nine o'clock, but she was already hard at work with carbolic soap and a stiff brush, to get it gleaming.

'I've got to do mine later,' Ethel replied, tucking her pile of dirty linen under one arm and giving her a wave as she made her way up to the communal laundry. She liked it up there, it was a chance to get out of the house while Mam looked after William and chat with the other mothers. It had taken a while for some of them to accept her and they still laughed about the first time she'd gone in on washday and they could barely understand a word she said.

She'd only asked where the mangle was and one of the women had looked up from her washtub, wiped some sweat from her brow and said, 'Sorry, love, I didn't catch that, are you foreign?'

It was the same in the shops, too, so she'd tried to change the way she spoke, to fit in with them. Whatever the differences in their accents, they were just hard-working folk and they meant well.

On the corner of Edgeley Road, a gaggle of little kids were poking at a dead rat in the gutter, its eyes glazed and its tongue bloated and sticking out of its mouth. 'It's as big as Missus Anderson's cat!' one cried.

Ethel shuddered. The long-tails made their nests over

on the railway line which ran along the back of their yards and she lived in fear of one getting into the house.

The rhythmic clatter of the trains going by was just a part of the daily cacophony of noise in their neighbourhood. There was a constant round of comings and goings, from the muffin man who rang his bell on Sundays, to the delighted squeals of stampeding kids, to the tallyman, the milkman and the coal merchants. Once a week the rag and bone man would wend his way past their front doors on his filthy cart, pulled by a scrawny old piebald nag, shouting for 'old iron!' as he headed towards Clapham High Street. William wanted to feed that horse, like the other bairns, but Ethel wouldn't let him, in case he caught something nasty from it.

As she hurried by, one of the kids picked up the rat and swung it by its tail. It landed, with a splat, at her feet and she screeched and dropped her washing as they scarpered.

She was just tutting to herself and picking up her bundle of bedsheets, which were now covered in filth, when a fella crossed the road to help her. Before she knew what was happening, he'd picked up half the linen and was handing it to her. 'Those cheeky little blighters! Are you all right?'

'I'm fine, honestly,' she said.

There was a roundness to his features, from his glasses to the shape of his face, which reminded Ethel of one of her favourite schoolteachers back in Benwell. It was silly, really, but it made him seem familiar and as he helped her to her feet, she beamed at him and said, 'I'm Ethel, by the way. I live just a few doors down.'

He held out his hand to her and she shook it. 'Len,' he said, with a laugh. 'At your service, Ethel.'

He paused for a split second and then caught sight of the wedding band on her finger. 'Well, I'd best be off. I'm late for work.'

As he walked off, whistling to himself, there was a jauntiness to his stride, a real spring in his step, and that made Ethel smile more than she had done in a long time.

Going for a night out at the talkies with Harry down at the Majestic on Clapham High Street was the highlight of Ethel's week but he didn't seem to share her enthusiasm for the cinema any more. He stood glumly in the queue beside her, his hands thrust deep into his pockets and a muscle twitching in his cheek.

'Is everything all right, Harry?' she said gently.

'Oh, stop going on at me!' he replied roughly, pulling away. 'There's nowt wrong with me, I'm just tired, that's all.'

Ethel felt tears sting her eyes. He couldn't have hurt her any more if he'd slapped her. No matter how hard she tried, she just couldn't seem to get close to Harry. It was like being with a dancing partner who kept treading on her toes. She was sure he wasn't doing it deliberately, but it didn't make it any less painful.

A couple in the queue behind them started whispering to each other and she overheard the words 'lovers' tiff' and felt colour rising in her cheeks.

It was a relief when they got into the auditorium and she could lose herself in the fantasy of her surroundings, with the beautiful balconies and ornate plasterwork in white and gold, making it seem like a palace. As the lights went down and the film started, she sought out Harry's hand and gave it a little squeeze. Her heart sank when there was no response, but she wasn't going to let him spoil her night out watching *Cupid in Clover*.

She loved romances but that wasn't the only reason she enjoyed coming to the flicks. She studied the actresses and the way they spoke, with their perfect red mouths rounding over their lines. She'd copy them at home, when no one was around, to improve the way she spoke. Little by little, she was changing her accent and it was true she probably sounded a bit posher than most in her street.

Sitting there in the dark, she was fascinated by the smouldering glances that the leading ladies gave and the way they laughed, or cried, or gazed shyly up from under their lashes. This was how they got what they wanted; it worked for them on screen, so why not for her too? She didn't want to be plain little Ethel from Benwell any more.

Before Ethel knew what was happening, tears had started to roll, silently, down her face. She wiped them away. Harry seemed to have grown tired of her and Ethel had grown tired of herself, in any case. She needed to be someone new; someone fun and exciting, someone who Harry would want to hold in bed at night and talk to, like he used to. The city was full of possibilities; the world around her was changing fast, with electric lights and motor cars everywhere.

Now she was in London, perhaps she would change too.

*

Politics was the only thing that Harry was remotely interested in over the coming months and when a general election was called in May, he was cock-a-hoop about it.

He spent hours poring over *The Evening News*, devouring every last dreary detail of how Prime Minister Stanley Baldwin faced a growing threat from the Labour Party.

'The common man will have his say at the ballot box, you mark my words,' he said, glancing up from his paper. 'And the common woman too, Ethel. You'll be able to vote for the first time!'

Ethel feigned interest but really, she wasn't that bothered about having the vote. Besides, politics had brought their family nothing but trouble; she still hadn't forgotten all the upheaval caused by the General Strike when Harry had lost his job. All women aged twenty-one to twenty-nine were going to be able to go to the polls for the first time and the whole thing had been nicknamed the 'Flapper Election' after the dancing girls. Ethel would have given her eyeteeth to be a flapper girl, out on the town up in the West End, dressed in her glad rags. Instead, she had a steak and kidney pie to attend to and was feeling more like a drudge with every passing day.

She served it up for the three of them because Da was out at a church meeting. Mam took hers and ate it on her lap, sitting by the fire she'd lit earlier. It wasn't cold at all, but she'd been complaining of a chill and her cough wasn't getting any better. In the fading light of the late afternoon, Ethel couldn't help noticing how drawn Mam was looking as she sat there picking at her food. What's more, her skin had a definite yellow tinge to it.

'Mam,' said Ethel, popping some boiled greens on Harry's plate. 'Do you think you might go and see a doctor about that cough of yours?'

Mam shook her head. 'Oh no, pet. There's no need for that. I'm just a bit under the weather. And anyway, it costs too much. I'd rather you save the money in case William gets sick.'

'You've not been right for a while now,' Ethel said.

'It's probably just the change of water down here,' said Mam. 'Plays havoc with your digestion. It'll be better soon, you'll see.'

But it didn't get better and by the time the autumn came around, Mam had taken to her bed. Every day brought some new agony: pains in her side, aches in her hips, and she was wincing in agony and barely had the energy to feed herself. Ethel went to the butcher's and got some beef bones to make a broth for her, to try to nurse her back to health.

Eventually, after Da insisted, Mam agreed to see a doctor. Ethel wasn't sure who to go to, so after consulting Doreen, the lady opposite, she went to fetch the doctor who was widely thought of as the kindest, and not too expensive either.

Dr Perkins was a small, slight man, balding, with tufts of greying hair at either side of his head, giving him the appearance of an owl. Ethel had only seen a doctor once in her life – for scarlet fever as a young girl – and she remembered a giant of a man with a booming voice and big hands, so this little fella, with his voice almost a whisper, was a turn-up for the books.

While Da and Harry stayed downstairs in the scullery, Ethel held Mam's hand as the doctor examined her. When he pulled up her nightgown, Ethel was shocked to see Mam's ribs, but lower down, beneath her belly button, she was all swollen.

The doctor prodded at her and she winced.

'What's wrong with me?' said Mam, anxiety etched on her features.

'I think you are just very tired and need plenty of bed rest. Have you been doing too much around the house?'

'No, not any more than usual,' she said, groaning as she tried to pull herself up onto her elbows.

'Well, in my experience, every woman works twice as hard as the man because she is constantly attending to everyone's needs. Sometimes it's nature's way of saying you need to slow down a bit. Your daughter here seems to be easing the load. She'll look after you.'

He packed up his stethoscope and made his way downstairs to the scullery.

Da leaped to his feet as he entered.

'No need,' said the doctor, motioning for him to sit back down. Ethel followed him into the room and shut the door behind her. 'Are you her husband?'

Da nodded.

'It goes without saying that your wife is very sick,' said the doctor. 'I am fairly certain that she is in the advanced stages of womb cancer and there is little that can be done for her.'

18

Ethel

Clapham, November 1929

The low mumble of Da saying his prayers resonated through the house.

He sat at Mam's bedside morning, noon and night, reading from the Bible, heaping blessings on her in the hope that she might get better. Ethel couldn't bear it, watching her wasting away day after day. Word got around the street that her mam was very sick, and women started plating up meals, dropping off cakes, and inviting Ethel in for a cup of tea or taking William off her hands for a few hours. It was wonderful to have their support because Harry wasn't much help; he kept making excuses to be out of the house with union work or extra shifts. Da muttered, within earshot, that he was about as much use to Ethel as a chocolate fireguard.

Doreen from over the road was a real boon because she'd heard about doctors cutting out tumours. There was a woman around the corner who'd been cured of cancer that way, so she said. With that in mind, Ethel decided to make an appointment to see Dr Perkins, to find out more and see if he could help get Mam to see an expert at the hospital. It would cost her money to be seen – nothing came free – but it would be worth it to help her mother.

The surgery was a few streets away, just off Clapham Manor Street, and Ethel scurried along nervously, as if the weight of the world was on her shoulders. When she got there, the people sitting in his waiting room were a pitiful sight and half of them looked underfed. Skinny bairns with dark circles under their eyes played listlessly on the floor while their mothers shushed squalling babies on their laps. Wizened old folk dozed, their hunched shoulders and gnarled hands proof enough of the many years of hard graft they'd put in to make ends meet.

No one wanted to be here, not least because seeing the doctor meant they'd be robbing Peter to pay Paul. Either the tallyman, the rent man or the milkman would have to put their dues on tick for a week or so. Although it had to be said, this doctor was more reasonable than most and he'd often let you pay him off at a shilling a week, which was why his waiting room was so full.

After waiting for more than an hour in the crowded room, which was fetid with the smell of so many bodies in damp and dirty clothing packed tightly together, it was Ethel's turn.

The doctor listened intently but when she asked about the operation, he shook his head and said, 'She's riddled with disease, I'm afraid, so the cancer is inoperable. The kindest thing is to just look after her at home but if she needs to, we can bring her to hospital so she can have morphia.'

'She won't want to leave us and be in the hospital!' Ethel cried. 'We're her family.'

'That's my point exactly,' he said, polishing his glasses. 'Leaving home only distresses people in their final weeks. Give her all the tender loving care you can, that is my best advice to you. Cherish the time you have left with her and try to ease her worries by telling her she is going to recover.'

'You want me to lie to my own mother?' said Ethel incredulously.

'No. I'm just telling you to think of what is kindest for her,' said the doctor, with a reassuring smile.

But as Mam lay in bed day after day, growing weaker, her skin yellowing like old wallpaper, she guessed the truth.

One cold December morning, when you could see your own breath inside the house and there was ice on the inside of the windowpane, she clasped at Ethel's hand with bony fingers and said, 'I'm dying, aren't I, pet?'

Ethel looked away for a moment, feeling the sharpness of the lie she was about to tell stabbing at her heart. She smiled and then rearranged Mam's pillows to make her more comfortable.

'No, Mam, the doctors just say you need plenty of rest and by the spring, you'll feel a lot brighter,' she said. 'You've just been doing too much, that's all.'

The terrible struggle of Mam's last days would live with Ethel forever.

Cancer had no respect for the weak, the kind and the gentle. It ripped through Mam's body, causing her such pain that even to hold Ethel's hand was agony by the end. Hours passed in a blur of pained cries and visits from the vicar, punctuated by cups of tea.

Ethel slept in a chair by Mam's bedside, as Da had long since decamped to the front room, where he paced nightly and read aloud from the Bible. Anger welled in Ethel's stomach about Harry keeping himself to himself so much. It was as if he couldn't bear to face any of it, beyond asking 'How's your mam doing today?' Like Da said, in times of crisis, he was as much use as a chocolate fireguard.

It was a mercy when Mam slipped into unconsciousness but now her every breath came as a terrible rattle which would stop alarmingly and then start up again. Ethel began to pray, guiltily, for Mam's release from suffering. She stared at the cross on the wall above the bed for hours on end, willing Jesus to do something.

Eventually, after three long days, Mam finally slipped from the room with a sigh, her body just skin and bone.

She'd given most of herself to Da in this life, and in death, the disease had taken what was left of her.

It was such a waste.

Ethel wept.

Later that night, after Ethel had washed and laid out her mother's body in a clean nightdress, just as she would have wanted, Harry did his best to comfort her.

'Your mam was a lovely woman,' he said, hugging her

tightly to him in bed. 'But death is just a part of life. We've all lost people. She's at peace now.'

He turned his face to the wall.

She wanted to feel his arms around her, for him to hold her, like he used to when they lived in Newcastle and the baby was due. He'd stroke her belly and whisper in her ear that he'd always love her, and he'd be there for her. Their whispered conversations in the pitch black of the night in that little terraced house in Benwell had been their own secret world.

Now all she had was her grief and the back of his pyjamas for comfort.

With just a week to go before Christmas, Harry announced that he intended to go and visit his family back in Newcastle to spend the holiday with them.

He was always scribbling letters to that sister of his and Ethel couldn't help thinking that Kitty had probably demanded to see him, but she was his wife and she needed him here in her time of mourning. Mam had barely been cold in her grave for a month.

'Well, you can go but I don't want to. This is our home now,' she said.

'Don't be like that, pet,' he said. 'I need to go and see my mother too, I haven't been back for over two years now and Kitty said Mum had a bit of a funny turn the other week. I thought I'd take William with me. Mum and Kitty are asking after him and they would love to see how big he's grown.'

'Suit yourself, but I'm staying put,' said Ethel.

He took a step backwards, as if she'd struck him.

'But, Ethel, I thought you'd want to come with me!'

'Well,' she said, tilting her chin a little at him so she almost smirked, 'you thought wrong. I am not going and that is that.'

He reached out to her but she brushed him away. 'No, Harry,' she said. 'My mind is made up. I need to be here for Da.' He shrugged his shoulders, as if he would never understand women, and walked out of the scullery.

Ethel busied herself with her basket full of ironing for a moment. Her heart was pounding. She'd stood up for herself for once. That was certainly part of the reason she wanted to stay behind, to make sure Da was all right, out of a sense of duty to him, but also she was so fed up with Harry and the way he had treated her she'd be damned if she was going to sip tea in his posh parlour in Simonside Terrace, with all its fancy antiques, while that snooty sister of his looked down her nose at her. No. She was staying here, and anyway, Doreen and the other women in her street were planning a little knees-up in the pub around the corner, so if he was going off to Newcastle without her, she'd go down the boozer to keep her spirits up.

Da had been out in the back yard cleaning William's boots but the door was ajar, and once Harry had left the room, he came in and laid a hand on Ethel's shoulder.

He looked down at her with affection, just as he used to when she was a girl. 'You've done the right thing, pet. Our family belongs down here now, not back up in Newcastle.'

*

On Christmas Eve, despite Da's disapproving looks, she spent ages with her hair in curlers and popped on some lipstick and powder. She practised a look in the mirror, like the film stars did, before giving herself a slow smile. 'You deserve to have some fun, Ethel,' she said to her reflection.

Ethel linked arms with Doreen as they tottered off to the Manor Arms, around the corner on Clapham Manor Street. 'Is Harry not coming along later?' said Doreen, pulling her mink stole around her shoulders. Doreen's husband was a butcher and, with all the extra business over Christmas, he was flush with cash.

Ethel eyed it enviously. There was no chance Harry could afford to buy her anything so fancy on his wages.

'He's gone home to his mother,' she said, picking at her nails. 'Not that I mind too much.'

Doreen gave her a little nudge and giggled. 'Well, you know what they say, while the cat's away . . .'

The noise from the pub could be heard from the top of the road and as they drew nearer the sound of songs being hammered out on the piano carried through the cold night air. Ethel felt a little frisson of excitement as they pushed through the doors and heads turned to look in her direction. Right on cue, she gave a shy smile, just like the actress in *Cupid in Clover*, as they made their way to the bar.

The girls from their street were tucked into a corner and were already a few sherries ahead of them by the look of it. Ethel ordered a port and lemon for herself and one for Doreen but when she came to pay for them, she felt a hand on her shoulder and a voice said, 'I'll get these, ladies.'

She spun around and came face to face with Len, the bloke who'd helped her when she'd dropped her washing. 'I was hoping we'd bump into each other again,' he said. 'Where's your fella? I can't believe he would let a lovely lady such as yourself go out on your own.'

'Well, she's not on her own, because she's with me,' said Doreen, with a laugh. 'But I'm beginning to feel all green and hairy, rather like a gooseberry, so I'll just be over in the corner. Wave if you need me, Ethel!' And with that, she trotted off to join the others, leaving Ethel at the bar with her admirer.

Len coloured up a bit.

'Oh, don't mind her, she's only joking,' said Ethel, fiddling with her hair and forgetting all about trying to act like a film star. 'What about you? Don't you have someone waiting at home for you?'

'No,' he said, looking rather crestfallen. 'I lost my wife a couple of years ago, so I'm on my own now.'

'I'm so sorry,' she said. 'I didn't mean to intrude . . .'

'Not at all,' he said. 'It's been hard coming to terms with it, but life goes on.'

She hesitated for a moment, taking a sip of her drink before adding, 'I know it's not the same thing, but I lost my mam only a few weeks back to cancer. I don't think there's ever a good time to lose someone dear, is there?'

In the middle of the shrieks of laughter as the women from her street gave an impromptu performance of 'Knees Up Mother Brown', Ethel found herself pouring her heart out to Len about Mam falling ill and the doctor telling her not to reveal the truth to her about the cancer. He was just so easy to talk to and, what's more, he was genuinely interested in her.

Just before midnight, the landlord shouted, 'Christmas lock-in!' and everyone cheered because that meant the drink would keep flowing for those lucky enough to be inside.

The pianist started to play a song that Ethel hadn't heard before, but she tapped her feet along in time and the words seemed so funny, she had to laugh: 'Birds do it, bees do it, even educated fleas do it . . .'

'Would you care to dance, Ethel?' said Len, offering her his hand. A few couples were already shuffling their way around together in each other's arms, in drunken clinches.

So right there, in front of the bar on the carpet that was so claggy with beer that your shoes stuck to it, Ethel and Len waltzed together, as the clock struck midnight on Christmas Eve.

And the whole pub joined in on the chorus, 'Let's do it, let's fall in love!'

As the last of the revellers staggered out of the pub and into the street, Ethel was still at Len's side.

'Do you fancy a nightcap at my place?' he whispered.

Ethel nodded. Da would be snoring his head off in bed by now in any case, so she might as well be hung for a sheep as a lamb and stay out a bit later. And as for Harry, well, he'd chosen to go away for Christmas, so she didn't give him a second thought.

They waited until the others had rounded the corner

before falling into step with each other and heading up the road, in the other direction, to Len's street.

It was a bit icy, and so Len put his arm around her protectively, to steady her as they went, with only the sound of their footsteps and the faint hiss of the gas jets in the street lamps filling the night air.

They turned into Elmhurst Road and paused for a minute outside his front door while he fumbled for his key.

He stepped inside and as she was crossing the threshold, he turned and pulled her to him.

'Welcome home, Ethel,' he said.

19

Ethel

Clapham, January 1930

Harry was a changed man after his visit to see Kitty and his mum in Newcastle.

He came back from the North wreathed in smiles, bringing with him a beautiful pair of pea-green leather gloves he'd bought for Ethel in Fenwick's. She gasped when she saw them, because they must have cost a small fortune.

'I'd been saving up for them because I wanted to give you something special, pet,' he said, as he drew her into an embrace. 'I know I've not been much good as a husband lately. Kitty gave me a bit of a talking-to. I promise I'll try to do better.'

Ethel tried not to show it, but it rankled with her that his sister held such sway over his moods, whereas she was powerless to stop them, even though she was his wife. As she kissed him, the guilt about what she had done with Len on Christmas Eve sat leaden in the pit of her stomach. She'd sneaked back into the house in the early hours of

Christmas morning, when Da was still sound asleep, and he hadn't said a word about her staying out late beyond asking if she'd enjoyed herself. She had replied, truthfully, that she'd had a wonderful night.

William tugged at her sleeve. He had a toy aeroplane and a set of tin soldiers that his Aunt Kitty and his grandmother had given him for Christmas. Da swept him up into an embrace. 'There's my bonny lad! You come and tell me all about the big ships you saw on the Tyne and give your mam and dad a moment's peace.'

As Harry sat down in the scullery, it became clear what had really lifted his black mood.

'I've got a job offer, Ethel, back up in Newcastle,' he said excitedly. 'It's engineering for the ships, like I used to do, and it's good money, too. We can all go home.'

'But our home is here, in London!' she cried, before she could stop herself.

His face fell. 'I thought you missed the North, Ethel, and you'd want to get away from the smog and be back where we grew up, where we belong.'

She turned her back and bustled over to the sink to compose herself for a moment. All she could think of, every waking moment, was Len, the fella from around the corner. Being in his arms had ignited something in her and she knew it was wrong, but she wanted more. The thought of being miles away in Newcastle was more than she could bear.

'I like it down here, Harry,' she said, as if she were reasoning with a small child. 'We're settled now and I'm making friends. William loves it and he'll be starting school soon and Da's got a job. What about him? He'll be on the dole if we go back up to Newcastle. There's more work down here in London . . .'

Harry stared at his hands, as if the answer to their problems might magically appear at his fingertips at any moment. He pursed his lips. 'I've accepted the job, pet. It would be madness to turn it down.'

'Well, you should have asked me first!' she shouted, hurling a tea towel to the floor and running from the room. 'Nobody cares what I want! I won't leave London and you shan't force me to either!'

Ethel's tears had dried by the time Harry came up to bed. He stroked her hair and she turned to face him.

'I'm so sorry,' he said, putting his arms around her. 'I only wanted to make you happy. You needn't come with me back up North just yet if you don't want to. I'll go to Newcastle, just to get us some money saved up, and you can have time to think about things and come when you are ready. If things pick up in London and I can get an engineering job back here, I'll be back like a shot. I'll send you my wages, Ethel. I want to be able to buy you nice things, to treat you right and look after you properly. I know I haven't done a great job of it until now.'

He went on: 'There are so many men out of work now, pet, I don't know how long my job at the cardboard-box factory would have lasted in any case. With a job offer like I've got back in Newcastle, you can't look a gift horse in the mouth, not these days.'

'Oh, Harry,' she said, gazing up at him. She was secretly

delighted that she wouldn't have to leave London and her tone softened. 'I wasn't trying to be difficult. It's just with losing Mam, we've been through so much upheaval. You'll only be away a little while, won't you?'

He kissed her, and she felt herself responding to his embrace, but when they made love, she closed her eyes and it was Len's face she saw, not Harry's.

As January gave way to a freezing cold February, Harry moved back up North to start his new job.

He wrote to her often, sending her most of his wages just as he had promised. She did her best to write back, with snippets of news of what William had been up to as he had not long since started school, but she wasn't much of a letter writer and, in any case, she had other things to think about.

Ethel had started to feel rather queasy. It was a familiar feeling, a sickness and a hunger all at the same time, and it was at its worst first thing in the morning. She'd taken to putting a biscuit on her bedside table at night to try to stave off the urge to retch when she woke up by nibbling it.

When the waistband of her skirt began to get tight a month later, she went to see Dr Perkins and sat in his damp, crowded waiting room, fidgeting with her fingers, avoiding catching anyone's eye in case someone asked why she was there.

Once she was in his consulting room, she lay on the examination table, staring at the ceiling as the doctor prodded and poked around in places she didn't want to think about.

Then he glanced up, took off his glasses, and said, 'Congratulations! It looks like you're going to be hearing the patter of tiny feet soon.'

'How far gone am I?' she said, her throat parched.

'Well, from what you've told me about your last monthly bleed being early in December, I would say about twelve weeks or so. You're the third I've seen in here this morning. It must have been all that fine food at Christmas dinner. There'll be quite a baby boom in Clapham come September!'

He laughed at his own joke as she got down from the table and dressed herself behind the screen. The ticking of the clock on the wall seemed to grow louder and the world appeared to be spinning. She had to steady herself for a moment. 'I think I might need a glass of water.'

After a quiet sit-down with one of his nurses, she hurried home but there was only one person she wanted to share this news with.

And that was Len.

Ethel waited until William was asleep in bed and Da had gone out to his church meeting before pulling on her coat and sneaking out of the house.

She hadn't seen Len since that fateful evening, although she'd spent ages peering out of the front window in the hope of spotting him walking up the street. He seemed to have changed his route, perhaps to avoid any awkwardness between them or, more likely, any gossip from the neighbours.

The cold air nipped at her as she hurried up the road

and around the corner, her footsteps echoing as she went. It was gone eight o'clock and dim gaslight glowed through curtains all along the street as families gathered together to keep out the winter chill.

In her dreams, she'd imagined herself back at Len's house on Christmas Eve so many times. Everything that had happened just seemed so right; how he'd taken her in his arms and how natural it had felt when they were in bed together. Afterwards, he'd held her for ages and told her tenderly, 'You are such a beautiful woman, Ethel.'

Now her heart was in her mouth as she rapped on Len's blue front door.

He answered with a look of surprise, but the warmth in his eyes was unmistakable. 'Ethel! What are you doing here?'

She glanced down at her stomach and back up at him.

'You'd better come in,' he said.

She followed him through to the scullery, where his shoes were sitting, neatly polished, on some newspaper on the kitchen table. A pan of potatoes was boiling on the stove and the smell of cooking meat made her stomach rumble; she'd been too nervous and sick to eat anything for her tea earlier.

He moved the shoes off the table and pulled out a chair for her to sit on.

She glanced around the room, taking in the traces of the life he'd led before he was widowed. There were some ornaments on the mantelpiece – a flowered jug and a china dancing girl – and an apron hung from a peg by the back door. A crocheted mat had pride of place over the radiogram on the sideboard. Everything was spick and span.

'Len, there's no easy way to say this,' she began. 'I'm expecting. And I think it's yours.'

He sat down opposite her and clasped her hands in his. 'Oh, Ethel, I shouldn't have gone as far as I did on Christmas Eve, forgive me. It's just you're such a treasure, I couldn't help myself. I wasn't trying to break up a happy home.'

Before she knew what was happening, all the longing of the last two months without seeing him spilled out.

'I'm not happy, Len,' she said. 'I'm not happy at all. Harry's not the man I thought he was when I married him. He's away working up North now and the worst thing is, I don't miss him; I miss you. I know that sounds silly because we barely know each other, but he doesn't talk to me like you did that night. Sometimes I think he can't stand the sight of me. And he's got troubles of his own that, well, they get in the way of us being together.'

Len's face lit up. 'I only stayed out of your way because I didn't want to cause trouble, but I can't stop thinking about you, Ethel. I would give you all the tea in China if I had it. If you ever need a listening ear, I'm here. What do you want to do about us?'

The way he said 'us' made her stomach flip. He really did see them being together; it wasn't just a drunken fling.

'We can't be seen to be having an affair,' she said. 'Not round here. And we can't tell anyone about the baby.'

The woman in the next street over had just about been tarred and feathered for cheating with the tallyman.

'Are you certain it's mine?' said Len. 'I mean . . .'

'From what the doctor said about the dates, yes, it's yours, Len.'

'But what about your husband?'

'Well, that's the problem, isn't it?' she said conspiratorially. There was a little well of excitement building inside her at the thought of this shared secret with Len. Only they would know the truth. This baby would bind them forever, no matter what. It wasn't a betrayal of Harry, no. He had betrayed her by not being the person she thought he was, with all his selfishness and strange ways. He'd let her down and she'd ended up in Len's arms. That was the truth of the matter.

'It wouldn't be too hard to make him think it was his, but it would just be a case of convincing him that the baby had come a bit early, that's all,' she said, staring at the floor. For some reason she felt guilty admitting to Len that she'd been with Harry, as his wife; it was as if the betrayal was the other way around.

'Ethel, please don't misunderstand me,' he said. 'I know I have no rights over you and if you were mine, I wouldn't expect a thing anyway. I'd just be glad you were in my life. A man can't own a woman or expect things of her. That's not what marriage is about, is it?'

Ethel looked at him. He was older than Harry, maybe five years or so, greying, and his eyes crinkled when he smiled, but she thought he was the most handsome man she'd ever seen. For the first time in her life, a man was treating her with respect. Da had controlled her, Harry had neglected her, and now Len wanted to care for her, to treat her as his equal. She felt almost giddy with desire.

She leaned in closer. 'We can get through this, can't we, Len?'

He gazed at her adoringly. 'Yes, together we can face anything, Ethel. If you'll let me, I'll be here for you, as much as I can. It's nobody's business but ours, that's the way I see it; it's our secret.'

Ethel stood up and walked over to the back door. She slipped the apron on. It fitted her perfectly, even with her growing bump.

'Yes, it's our secret. We'll find a way, won't we?' she said, beaming at him. 'But first, I'd better get your dinner out of the oven before it burns to a cinder.'

Harry was over the moon to find out that Ethel was expecting but when the baby came a full three weeks early at the end of September, instead of mid-October, he was so worried, he jumped on the first train down from Newcastle.

Ethel lay in bed glowing with happiness, with the baby nestled in her arms, wrapped in a beautiful shawl knitted by her friend Doreen. William was so curious about the new arrival, he kept poking his fingers through the bars of the cot when the baby was sleeping and Ethel had to tell him to keep off. He had a mind of his own, just like his father, and that drove Ethel up the wall. There were questions from him morning, noon and night about how things worked and he wouldn't take no for an answer. It was exhausting having to deal with that on top of the baby. Da was good with him, he kept him busy, tinkering about in the back yard. In fact, they were managing so well without Harry, she barely noticed he was gone these days.

She tensed as she heard the front door slam followed by his footfall on the staircase and as he came into the bedroom, she gave him a tight little smile.

Harry rushed to her side and gazed down at the bundle in her arms. He leaned in and kissed Ethel. She tried not to tense at his touch. She felt nothing for him now.

'My daughter,' he said, stroking the baby's cheek. 'My little girl. Daddy's here.'

20

Ethel

Clapham, August 1932

It was one of those long, hot London summers, when the tarmac on the roads melted and the stifling heat made sleep impossible.

By the middle of the month, half the families in Edgeley Road had taken advantage of factory holidays to get out of town altogether and go hop picking in Kent to earn a few shillings more, where the air was fresh, and the grass was still green.

Ethel stayed put. She had no intention of picking hops until her fingers bled or living in a ramshackle wooden hut while William picked up bad habits – and nits – from the local urchins who would run wild while their parents worked in the fields. He was the image of his father, with his grey eyes, and Ethel knew it was wrong, but she couldn't help being hard on him because of it.

He was always pawing at his baby sister too, asking to hold her. Ethel wanted to keep the baby's clothes looking beautiful, just as Mam had done for her when she was a little girl living in Benwell. Da had saved up and bought the baby a pretty dress, in crisp white cotton, with smocking on the front in pink thread. She looked like a little angel in it.

She'd gone along with Harry's idea to call her Zena, after his French grandmother, Zelina. It was a beautiful name – glamorous and a bit exotic. It certainly set her apart from all the other girls in the street – the Maggies, Beryls and Adas. Ethel loved that; her baby was her little jewel.

Zena was crawling now and getting into everything. Ethel couldn't help being anxious about her; she was so precious, with her sweet little face and mop of black hair. She was forever telling William off for playing too roughly. It wasn't that he was a bad lad, he was just a bit clumsy and Zena was so dainty; she reminded Ethel of the little china dancing girl on the mantelpiece round at Len's house.

Len was as pleased as Punch with his daughter and they'd worked out a plan for him to spend time with Ethel and Zena, away from the prying eyes of the Clapham folk. Once a fortnight, she'd get Da to take William to Battersea Park for the day, and she'd wheel Zena out in her pram and walk for miles, across the river, where she'd meet Len on the Embankment, and they'd stroll along, arm in arm, just like any other couple.

Twice a week she'd sneak off to his house in the evenings, usually with a pie she'd made, telling Da she was visiting one of the old dears who lived in Clapham Manor Street. No one suspected a thing. Harry wrote to her still and sometimes she'd reply but more often than not she'd forget because she was just too busy these days. He had suggested she should come and spend the summer up there, but she made an excuse that she was so worn out with running around after Zena and William, she couldn't possibly face the journey. She dreaded his visits because they disrupted her carefully planned routine that gave her time to be with Len. Thankfully, Harry only managed to get down to see them twice a year because of the cost and he just couldn't get time off work that easily.

Ethel ruled the roost and that was the way she liked it. Da treated her with more respect now than when Mam was alive. He was much gentler these days, making sure to thank her for all the work she did around the house. The grandchildren were the apple of his eye and he'd tell William, 'Listen to your mam, she knows best and don't grumble, that is the way things are,' while giving Ethel a little wink. It was unspoken between them, but Ethel knew that having Harry out of the picture made Da feel a lot happier. He was the man of the house but there was no need for him to be bullish about it.

With so many houses in Edgeley Road deserted over the summer, it was as if she was the queen of the whole street. And the best thing was, with no one around to gossip, Len had taken to popping in some afternoons when Da was out at work. He'd get off his shift early at the Pall Mall East Furniture Company, where he worked as a cabinet maker, and come in for a cup of tea, if no neighbours were loitering.

And today was one such afternoon, when the coast was clear and they were free to be together. William was away playing down at the common with some of the other boys on the street, so they took the chance to snatch a moment upstairs while Zena was sleeping soundly in her cot. Ethel put on the peach satin chemise Len had bought her as a gift; he was so thoughtful, and he spared no expense where she was concerned. She liked that.

Afterwards, as they lay in each other's arms, Len told her some big news. 'I'm thinking of setting up a business with my brother, Fred. I've always wanted to be my own boss and there's a dairy on the corner of Clapham Manor Street that's coming up for sale. The couple running it are just getting too old to manage now.'

'It sounds wonderful, Len,' she said. 'If anyone can make it work, you can.'

'I'd love to make a go of it, Ethel,' he replied, hugging her. 'It would be hard work, but I want to be able to provide for you and the baby. I know it's difficult for you, but we should be thinking about the future, *our* future.'

She was turning to kiss him again when she suddenly heard footsteps coming up the stairs. She sat bolt upright, pulling the bedclothes up to cover herself, and shouted, 'Not now, William, I'm having a lie-down. Just leave me in peace for a while and play in the yard like a good boy.'

Len jumped out of bed and was just pulling his trousers on when the bedroom door swung open. It wasn't William standing there, but Harry. Time stood still for a moment and a look of utter shock crossed his face.

'What in the name of God is going on?' shouted Harry, running at Len with his fists raised.

Ethel screamed and lunged forward to stop him. 'Harry! No! Let me explain . . .'

He slapped her, hard, across the face and she fell backwards onto the bed with a scream. Before she knew what was happening, his hands were around her throat and she was gasping for air.

'Leave her be!' shouted Len, trying to push Harry away from her. 'For God's sake, you'll kill her!' But Harry seemed to have the strength of ten men and he swatted Len away like a fly and continued to throttle Ethel, his eyes bulging with rage.

The sound of Zena crying carried through the bedroom wall, just as the room around her was turning black and her lungs felt as if they were about to explode.

Suddenly, Harry relaxed his grip and staggered backwards, wild-eyed, with tears spilling down his face. 'Oh my God, Ethel. What have I done?'

She sat up, gasping for air. 'Get out!' she screamed. 'Leave us be. You tried to murder me!'

He sank to his knees. 'I'd never do that. I love you, Ethel, please, don't say that. Think of our children.'

All the years of being bossed around by men, of being such a good girl and a dutiful wife, seemed to swell inside her like a giant wave.

'Zena isn't yours! She's Len's,' she spat. 'I love him, not you. I've never loved you. You don't understand what I need, Harry, and what's more, I think you've got a screw loose.' She tapped the side of her head.

Each word seemed to strike him, and he looked up at her with hurt and confusion, just as William did when she walloped him for breaking Zena's toys or hurting his baby sister with his rough games.

'Get out! I don't want you near me or the children ever again,' she said, putting her hands to her throat, which was horribly red and blotchy from his vice-like grip.

Len picked himself off the floor and put himself between the two of them. 'I think you should leave now, Harry,' he said. 'Ethel's telling you the truth. The baby is mine.'

The two men glared at each other for an instant.

Then Harry stood up and turned to go, his hands hanging limply by his side. Ethel stared at his departing back, shaking with shock.

As the front door banged shut, she heard William, outside in the street, shouting, 'Dad! Dad! Where are you going? Dad, come back!'

But Harry never did.

21

Harry

King's Cross, February 1933

The bitter cold cut through the newspaper he'd stuffed inside his jacket, chilling Harry to the bone as he walked the streets of London.

Travellers bustling in and out of the station gave him a wide berth. Glancing at his reflection in the window, he realized why; to them, he was just another tramp. He couldn't blame them. His collar was frayed, his trousers and jacket were filthy and after spending yet another night in a dosshouse near King's Cross station where the beds were ninepence and the fleas came free, he stank to high heaven.

That was preferable to having to wash in the blocked sink with its pool of murky water and thick head of scum on the top. The only towel in the communal bathroom was black with grease, so anyone brave – or daft – enough to try some ablutions only came off looking worse.

Most fellas lay in bed until it was chucking out time, literally sometimes, when the dosshouse owner would come along and tip the stragglers out of their beds and onto the bare boards. They kipped six to a room, sometimes more. A good night's sleep, like a decent meal, was the stuff of dreams and the subject of much discussion among the hostel dwellers, who gathered on street corners or loafed occasionally on park benches during the day.

You couldn't stay put for long, because the law would be on you, and have you for loitering or begging and then you'd be up before the beak. Harry was always on the move, looking for any work he could find to get himself enough money for a bed for the night.

Sometimes he'd get up to Covent Garden early on the off chance that some of the costermongers might spare him a few pennies for helping them to move their barrows. Other days he'd queue for hours to earn sixpence for handing out some flyers to shoppers along Oxford Street. But as the weeks turned into months and he looked more down-at-heel, he was always passed over for someone who reeked less of poverty.

When he was hungry enough to stomach religion, he'd throw himself on the mercy of the Salvation Army, or the Sally Bash, as all the men like him called it. The strict rules there rankled and served only to bind the rag-tag bunch of down-and-outs closer together in their misery: no booze, no ciggies, no gambling of any sort, no talking after lights out and enforced attendance at an evening service, where they were urged to repent their sins and turn to Jesus.

As the homeless crammed in together in long rows of narrow pews in the desolate, whitewashed hall which served as a free 'sit-up' night shelter for the poorest, the Sally Bash soldiers handed out dog-eared hymn books to their unwilling congregation. Elbows were shoved into ribs to wake the destitute, preparing them to hear the word of God – or else they'd be out on their ear.

The superintendent, resplendent in a peaked cap and a matching navy uniform adorned with a row of shining buttons, raised his hand to speak and a hush fell over the room. 'We are all sinners here and the punishment of the wicked shall be endless. Let us pray.'

The tramp next to Harry snorted himself back to consciousness as they started to mumble the Lord's Prayer in unison: 'Forgive us our trespasses, as we forgive those who have trespassed against us . . .' A young lad on the other side of him clasped his hands together tightly in prayer and was mumbling a few Hail Marys.

Harry closed his eyes and pretended to pray for a minute, but the room slipped away from him, just as it did every time that he tried to get some rest. His head was pounding as the Sally Bash brass band struck up the nightly hymn and row upon row of London's downtrodden and dispossessed started to stamp their feet in time to the music.

Harry willed himself not to, but in his mind, he was back in the bedroom in Clapham again, finding Ethel in bed with another man.

His hands were closing around Ethel's throat and as he squeezed more tightly, he caught the look of panic on her face but the voice in his head was telling him to keep going and he wanted to, he wanted to snuff her out, to stop all the lies and make it all go away.

Then it wasn't Ethel he saw beneath him but the German soldier he'd struck with his rifle butt in an assault on one of their trenches. He throttled him, until his face went purple and his blue eyes bulged. He held him there, down in the mud, until his enemy went limp and it was over.

Harry heard a baby crying and he relaxed his grip, but it was too late. The soldier had gone and Ethel lay there in bed underneath him, lifeless. 'Oh, Ethel, forgive me,' he sobbed.

Men around him were singing 'Onward Christian soldiers, marching as to war' but the soldiers were in the hall, and they were in front of him, clad in khaki, clambering forward over the pews, bayonets fixed.

Somewhere, a cymbal crashed, and the big guns went off, firing their shells into no man's land.

'Fire two rounds for twenty seconds, two rounds for twenty seconds!' said Harry, putting his fingers in his ears.

Men around him went over the top. 'It's a long way to Tipperary, it's a long way to go . . .' and they marched onwards to war, into a hail of bullets, into the mist and cordite, screaming as they fell.

Domino whinnied, and Harry reached out his hand and felt down the animal's flank, which was sweating from the effort of hauling the eighteen-pounder to the front. 'It's all right boy, we'll be back at camp before you know it.'

The stamping grew louder, boots on boards, but they were inside his head too. There was another crash of a cymbal and a flash of white light. He was lying in a shell hole, blood gushing out over his tunic, he was cold, and his legs were shaking.

'Cease fire!' he whispered, digging his fingernails into his palms. 'Cease fire!'

*

The Sally Bash dormitories were cleaner than the ninepenny-a-night lodgings, but they were vast and cheerless, with about fifty men packed in there. At least in the dosshouse there was the camaraderie of the kitchen, with its roaring fire and shared bread and dripping. Once you got used to the stench of your neighbours and the occasional fist fight – usually over a card game or stolen food – it wasn't such a bad place. In some ways, it reminded Harry of his time in the trenches. There was death in the dosshouse too, but it was a lingering affair, signalled by the hacking cough of consumption, hastened by near starvation and finished off by the old man's friend, pneumonia.

The passing of another unfortunate was usually marked by a moment's silence and a brief reflection on 'good old so-and-so' before someone piped up about how much he'd owed for tea and two slices, or in gaming debts.

Harry settled himself onto his narrow bed at the Sally Bash, which had a mattress so lumpy he'd have been better off sleeping on the floor, and a lad next to him introduced himself. He recognized him as the boy who had sat next to him during the Sally Bash service.

'Tom,' he said, stretching out a hand across the six-inch gap between them. He was slim and blond, almost girlishly pretty, with green eyes and long lashes. 'I'm new here, just down from Liverpool, looking for work.' He can't have been more than fifteen.

'Does your mother know you're here?' said Harry, offering him a crust of bread he'd shoved in his jacket pocket earlier.

'Well, I'm one of nine, so I doubt she'd know if I was missing!' he joked. 'I was hoping to try my hand down at the docks tomorrow. What do you think?'

'I think you'll get beaten to a pulp down there, lad,' said Harry, pulling off his boots. 'London's no place for a boy like you. You should go home, while you've still got the train fare.'

'I don't get on with my stepdad,' said Tom, looking downcast. 'I've got a character reference from my priest back home. Look, it says I'm trustworthy. I'm hoping I might get a job as an errand boy in one of the shops instead.' He thrust a piece of paper into Harry's hands. 'Do you think I should write a letter, introducing myself to my future employer? I'm educated, I've got good copperplate handwriting, my teachers always said so.'

Harry shook his head in disbelief. 'Just do yourself a favour and go home.'

A whistle sounded and one of the Sally Bash officers yelled, 'Lights out!'

As darkness descended, Tom started to snivel.

Harry reached out across the divide and patted him on the shoulder.

'Harry?' Tom whispered. 'Where are you from?'

'Newcastle upon Tyne,' said Harry.

'So, you are a Geordie, then,' said Tom.

'And you're a cheeky Scouser,' said Harry, with a laugh.

A body on the other side of Harry turned over and grunted, 'Shurrup, will you?'

Tom ignored him and carried on whispering; he was quite the chatterbox. 'Don't take this the wrong way,

Harry, but when we were in the church service, were you remembering your time in the war?'

Harry hesitated for a moment. There was something so honest about this young lad's concern that he found himself answering truthfully. 'Yes,' said Harry. 'I was. At least, I think so. I don't like all the noise. It sets my nerves off.'

'So, who is Ethel and why don't you go home to her?'

His question hung in the air, amid the nightly cacophony of grunting, snoring and the coughs of those living below the breadline trying to catch forty winks. Harry lay awake, staring into space until dawn broke and the whistle sounded again, this time for them to get up and be on their way.

When Tom arrived back at the Sally Bash shelter that evening, he was sporting a proper shiner.

He sat on his own, in the furthest recess of the hall, nursing a bowl of watery soup he'd bought for a penny.

Harry sat down beside him and offered him some bread and cheese. 'You ignored my advice and went to the docks, didn't you?'

Tom nodded, blushing. 'I think I'll stick to trying to get a job as an errand boy instead. They let me off lightly because they realized that I was from out of town, so I didn't get a proper hiding, just enough to see me on my way.' He gave a weak smile.

'It's still not too late to get on the next train home back to Scouseland,' said Harry gently.

'It's not too late for you either, Geordie,' said Tom, with a laugh.

'Careful or I'll black your good eye,' said Harry, pretending to take a swipe at him, which finished with him ruffling Tom's hair.

'You're more of a dad to me than my stepdad has ever been,' said Tom. 'Have you got kids of your own?'

Harry gazed into the distance for a moment.

'I have a son,' said Harry. 'But I had to leave him with his mother in Clapham.'

'You left your son?'

'I did,' said Harry. 'I couldn't go back, not after what she did – and what I did to her.'

'What do you mean?'

'I could have killed her.'

The colour drained from Tom's face so that his skin looked almost translucent. 'But you didn't, did you?'

'I wanted to,' said Harry, chewing thoughtfully. 'I caught her in bed with another fella and then she told me our little girl was his, not my own. It was a wicked thing, enough to destroy a man.'

'That's awful,' said Tom. 'But what about your boy? He's still your son.'

'Tom, when you're young it all seems so simple, but life isn't like that. I'm frightened of what I will become if I go back there. More than that, I'm frightened of who I might be in any case. He's better off without me in his life. It's like those Sally Bash God-botherers say, we are all sinners and our punishment will be endless. Well, my punishment is endless. I see it every time I close my eyes.'

'Don't you have family up North still?'

'Yes, I have my mother, but she isn't in the best of

health, so I don't want to worry her. And then there's my sister. But what's happened to me here is too shameful to share with them. I couldn't look them in the eye . . .'

Tom pulled a piece of paper and a pencil from his jacket pocket.

'You write to your sister and I give you my word I will be on the first train back to Liverpool tomorrow,' he said. 'You can take me to the station yourself – unless you've got something better to do.'

Harry laughed but he picked up the pencil and then hesitated.

'What have you got to lose?' said Tom. 'Look at the fellas in here, wasting away, fighting over ha'pennies. That'll be you in a few years' time if you don't get back in touch with your folks. You can have a fresh start, sort yourself out.'

'Well, there's a wise head on young shoulders,' said Harry. 'Maybe those dockers knocked some sense into you, lad.'

'Go on then,' said Tom. 'Get on with it.'

Harry licked the end of the pencil and then began to write.

My dearest Kitty . . .

One week later, Harry waited at King's Cross station, just as he had promised Kitty in his letter. He skulked by the entrance, as he'd already been moved on once by the stationmaster, who thought he was just malingering to keep out of the rain, which was coming down like stair rods.

Passengers emerged through great clouds of steam, bustling down the platform as porters rushed forward with their trolleys to assist those who looked like they'd give a good tip.

Harry had almost given up hope when he caught sight of her.

She looked older, with the first streaks of grey in her auburn hair, but when she smiled, she was his sister, just as she'd always been for as long as he could remember.

He ran forward to greet her with arms outstretched, as people turned to stare at this tramp who was rushing down the platform towards a well-dressed woman.

A porter came to Kitty's aid, stepping in front of Harry. 'Clear off! I don't think the lady needs your help.'

'No, please!' said Kitty, sweeping the porter aside and ignoring the astonished glances of the other passengers. 'He's my brother!'

They fell into each other's arms.

'Oh, Harry,' she cried. 'Where on earth have you been? We've been so worried about you!'

The pot of tea that Kitty bought for them at the station cafe was possibly the finest brew that Harry had ever tasted.

He wolfed down an iced bun in a flash and almost licked his fingers too, until he remembered his manners.

Kitty sat watching him, with her handbag on her lap, and pushed a teacake towards him, which he accepted hungrily.

'You must come home with me today, Harry,' she said.

'Whatever has happened, we can put it right. But you need to find your feet again, back where you belong. Mum is desperate to see you; the worry has nearly broken her. She's got your room ready for you. Will you come with me?'

Harry nodded. There was nothing here for him in London, he could see that now.

Kitty went on: 'I wrote to Ethel countless times, but she didn't write back. Are the children all right?'

He looked away and in the station a train whistled its departure. There were tears in his eyes.

Eventually, he said, 'She's with another man. She told me that Zena isn't mine.'

Kitty gasped. 'That good for nothing! I knew she was trouble, Harry, from the moment you met her. And there was something fishy going on with her being down in London and refusing to come back up North with you.'

'It wasn't like that,' said Harry. 'I spoiled everything. It wasn't her fault.'

Kitty reached out across the table and held his hand. 'It isn't William's fault either. Whatever has happened, you have to be there for your son. Surely you can see that? You have got to find a way.'

'I can't,' said Harry. 'I can't go back. She won't have me there and look at the state of me. My boy is better off without me in his life.'

'Harry, we can put this right,' said Kitty. 'A boy needs his father. He's your flesh and blood and for all we know, Zena could be too. She could be lying about that. We have to be strong together, remember? Other people don't understand, they can never understand, what we have been through. What's done is done and it's hard, but we have to find a way to carry on. Dad made us promise.'

'I nearly hurt Ethel very badly,' said Harry, looking up at his sister as pain and fear filled his eyes. 'I could have done it. Who's to say, Kitty? Everything seems so mixed up in my head. Perhaps I'm not the full shilling, just like Ethel said when she told me to go.'

Kitty was crying now, tears running down her face. 'No, Harry, you mustn't say such things. You've been through some terrible times, that's all. You're a good man, you're my brother.'

Harry glanced around at the other people in the cafe and whispered, 'Well, perhaps I'm more like our father than either of us might like to think.'

22

Kitty

Newcastle, March 1910

The *Northern Echo* lay spread out on the dining table, the headline screaming about a murder on a local train: 'THE RAILWAY CRIME!'

All the talk in the accountant's office today was about the killing, and the robbery of the pitmen's wages. More than £300 in cash was stolen and the poor colliery clerk carrying the money was shot dead in one of the carriages. Kitty picked up the newspaper and began to read as Mum came in with her best steak and kidney pie. Harry was busy at the other end of the dining room with his homework. He was more studious than most twelve-year-old lads and enjoyed getting his nose into a good book, thanks to Mum being a teacher.

'Honestly, the pair of you would eat words rather than my cooking if you could,' she tutted. 'Kitty, put the paper down, will you?'

Kitty did as she was asked. Mum nodded in the general direction of the front-page story and added, 'And don't go talking about that in front of your little brother, please, it's a dreadful affair.'

It was indeed a shocking thing. The clerk had been shot five times in the face. His wife only lived down the road in Heaton and she had waved to him as the train went through the station on the way up to the colliery at Stannington, just as she did every week when he delivered the miners' wages. But when the train arrived at its destination, he was dead – murdered – and his body had been shoved under a seat in one of the carriages. It sent a shiver down Kitty's spine to think that anyone could do such a thing.

Harry looked up from his algebra homework. He was oblivious to everything once he got his head stuck into numbers.

'Harry, go and wash your hands before you eat,' said Mum, bustling off to the kitchen to bring the vegetables, as Kitty hurriedly got the silver knives and forks and some freshly ironed napkins from the drawer and laid the table.

Dad liked things to be done a certain way, and supper was part of their family tradition. Most Newcastle folk had tea at five o'clock but Dad liked to make the distinction that they were white-collar workers and so they had supper – a cooked meal – closer to six o'clock, with the table laid properly.

Kitty heard his footfall on the stairs and shooed Harry out to wash his hands, just as Mum had asked. Dad appeared in the doorway, the ends of his neat moustache freshly waxed and his dark hair swept back from his forehead. He'd been into the city on some business. He didn't ever go into much detail about what he was working on, mainly because Mum didn't like him talking about the part of his job that involved placing bets for his main client, who was a wealthy coal merchant. Being a book-keeper was illegal – Mum and Kitty knew that – but it wasn't something that Harry was really aware of and Mum preferred it that way. He patted Harry on the head as he strode past him into the kitchen.

Dad had eager little hazel eyes which had just a hint of mischief about them. 'Have you been putting the world to rights at work with the other lasses again, our Kitty?'

'No, Dad,' she laughed. 'Just listening to the men talking nonsense all day long, as usual.'

That made him roar with laughter. 'Oh, you would give that Mrs Pankhurst a run for her money. You're worse than your mother!'

Kitty went to help Mum with the plates and they were just sitting down to eat when there was a knock at the door.

Dad sighed and put down his knife and fork. 'I'll get it.'

He was wearing his favourite brown leather slippers, the ones Mum liked to warm for him in front of the fire every evening, and so his walk was more of a shuffle. Dad pulled the dining room door shut as he left the room, to keep the heat in; the first daffodils were coming up in the garden, but Newcastle could be cold in summer, never mind the springtime, and so the fires had been lit.

There were murmured voices in the hallway for a few moments and then Dad appeared, ashen-faced. He spoke directly to Mum, as if Kitty and Harry were no longer there.

'There's a policeman here,' he said, his jaw set firmly.

'There's been a terrible mistake. It's to do with this train business. I don't want you to worry. Keep my supper warm for me, I'll be back soon.'

Mum's mouth gaped in shock. She was suspended for a moment, half in, half out of her chair as his words registered and then she ran to him, throwing her arms around him. 'What on earth do they want with you, Jack?'

'Just some questions,' said Dad. 'It's a mix-up, that's all. A few questions and I will have everything answered and then I'll be back here in no time, you'll see.'

He took off his slippers and Harry ran to get him his boots.

'Good lad, that's right,' said Dad, beaming at him. 'You make me proud, son. Just carry on the way you are, and look after your sister and your mother while I'm out.'

He lowered his voice to a stage whisper: 'Because the women think they are in charge in this house, Harry, but we know it's us men, don't we?'

And with that, he ruffled Harry's hair and turned to go.

Kitty went out into the hallway, where a tall, thin gentleman, with cheekbones as sharp as razor blades, was waiting, idly blowing smoke rings from his cigar and gazing around him. When he saw Kitty, he smiled and tipped his bowler hat to her. She didn't smile back.

Dad gave her a peck on the cheek as he made his way towards the front door. 'I won't be long.'

They stood at the front gate, all three of them, as they watched Dad walking down Lily Avenue, away from their home, as the policeman fell into step beside him.

*

Mum spent ages getting Harry to go to sleep, reading to him until he finally dropped off, while Kitty waited patiently at the front gate for Dad to return.

Just as it was beginning to get dark and Kitty was getting cold, she saw half a dozen policemen in uniform, led by another man – short with his hair clipped high above his ears – marching down the street.

Kitty ran back into the house to tell Mum, as the whole lot of them made their way up the front path. Mum greeted them on the doorstep with her arms folded.

'What on earth do you think you are doing?' she said. 'It's night time and this is a family home! I have a child asleep upstairs.'

'I'm Superintendent John Weddell, and I have a search warrant,' said the short man, waving a piece of paper. 'And we need to come in. I must also inform you that your husband has been arrested in connection with the murder of John Nisbet and he will be brought before magistrates at Gosforth police station tomorrow. You are welcome to attend. Now, can I come in?'

Kitty grabbed Mum by the arm to steady her as the policemen entered. Mum retreated to the kitchen, where she sat, mute, watching as half a dozen pairs of hands tore her home apart.

It wasn't long before the noise of the police rootling through drawers and Dad's bureau, lifting carpets, opening and closing cupboards and stamping around woke Harry, who stood at the top of the stairs in his pyjamas, clutching his reading book, fighting back tears.

'Come on,' said Kitty, running upstairs to embrace

him. 'Let's all go into the kitchen and have some cocoa.'

She raised her voice loud enough for the superintendent to hear, anger swelling inside her. 'They won't find anything because there is nothing to find in our home. Our dad is innocent and these charges against him are an outrage.'

As she did so, the discordant clatter of musical notes emanated from the dining room as the piano was dismantled in the search for clues.

The following morning all the newspapers in the city carried full reports about Dad's arrest.

Kitty hurried back from the corner shop with a sheaf of papers tucked under her arm, avoiding stares from their neighbours. Word carried fast and before long, a little gaggle of people had gathered on the other side of the street. Kitty drew the front curtains to stop them peering in.

Mum kept Harry off school so that he could see his father, but he was tired after being woken last night and he didn't really understand what was going on. He played marbles up the hallway and when that got on their nerves, he went into the back garden and thwacked a stick aimlessly against a tree.

'It's as if they have convicted him already!' cried Mum, once Harry was out of earshot. Neither she nor Kitty had slept a wink after the policemen had finally left in the early hours. The house looked like it had been turned upside down but that was the least of their worries; they'd sat up in the parlour downstairs, talking over what Dad was doing on the train in the first place.

They knew he'd been up at one of the collieries – Stannington – on business yesterday, but that wasn't unusual. He often went up there to speak to coal merchants and businessmen who had an interest in sinking new pit shafts. Dad had an intricate knowledge of the mining industry because of his previous job as a secretary to the Morpeth Colliery Company. He also acted as an agent for speculators and placed bets for them on the side as well as at the races to make a bit of extra cash. Dad had talked about having a few run-ins with some of the gangs controlling the racecourses, as well as the Bigg Market lads, who'd try to take a slice of winnings sometimes, but there'd never been any serious trouble and never with the police.

'He'd never hurt anyone,' said Mum, over and over, wringing her hands. 'How could anyone even suggest such a thing?'

The morning newspapers didn't seem to share that view and they were certainly having a field day with the latest twist in the tale: 'MAN DETAINED AT NEWCASTLE IN CONNECTION WITH TRAIN MURDER'

Kitty's heart sank as she read, word for word, what her father told the police. It was all there in black and white.

He admits that he travelled on the same train. He denies, however, that he was in the same compartment as the murdered man, stating that he was travelling on business in connection with a small colliery between Stannington and Morpeth.

The worst bit was the description of the identity parade that happened. Two other men who'd travelled on the train with the murdered clerk had picked Dad out of a line of a dozen men, and one of them said, as he pointed the finger of blame, that although he wasn't 'absolutely sure if it is any one of these, it is he.' They were wages clerks, just like the victim, John Nisbet, and they knew him by sight, but they worked for the Netherton Coal Company and the murdered man worked for a different firm. The men, Percival Hall and Thomas Spink, said that they had seen Mr Nisbet get into a compartment with another man, while they had got into a carriage further down the train. That seemed a bit strange to Kitty because she'd pored over every detail in the papers and the train guard at Newcastle station, who knew the victim well, said that he'd watched him getting into a train carriage on his own.

'They are making him look guilty!' cried Mum. 'I won't have it!'

Later that afternoon, Mum picked out her best skirt and jacket, in a light fawn tweed, and carefully pinned her favourite black straw hat, adorned with green feathers, into place. Dad had bought it for her and he always said she looked beautiful in it.

They walked the mile or so to Gosforth police station, with Kitty holding Harry's hand the whole way. 'I want to see Dad,' he kept saying. 'Why have they taken him?'

Mum turned to him and smiled, with such love in her eyes that Kitty almost burst into tears. 'You shall see him today, pet, I will make sure of it. This will all be sorted out very soon and you are not to worry because your father has told you not to and we must do as he asks.'

But when they got to the police station on Hawthorn Road, a crowd of men and women had gathered outside the front door. They were rough-looking types, dockers and their wives. 'Come to see the murderer?' said one bloke. "Cos they won't let you in.'

'I'd like to give him a good hiding,' said another. 'They're burying poor Nisbet down at Jesmond later. No man deserves to die like he did.'

Mum glared at them as she ushered Kitty and Harry through the heavy wooden doors and into the building. 'You shouldn't presume a man is guilty of a crime. Shame on you.'

The next hour passed in a blur. The policeman at the front desk was more than civil – he offered them tea and biscuits – and Mum went off to speak to the superintendent while Kitty and Harry waited in a side office. Eventually she came back and explained, quietly, that she would be allowed to sit through the hearing in which Dad would be charged but they would have to stay put. Kitty covered her mouth with her hand to stifle a gasp so as not to alarm Harry but she couldn't contain her anguish. 'They can't charge him with anything,' she said. 'You have got to stop them, Mum!'

Harry looked at the floor and Kitty saw that he was crying.

Mum kneeled down before him and said, 'We have to be strong. Your father is innocent and we all know that. The truth will come out but there is nothing we can do now to stop them charging him. We have to be calm. That is what your father and I want.'

She glanced over at Kitty. 'Do you both understand? It

is very important that we behave properly. We are a decent family. Dad has done nothing wrong. He was on that train going to the colliery on business and a court hearing will clear everything up. There is no other way. Can you see that now?'

They both nodded and Mum smiled at them, before she stood up, smoothed her skirts and left the room.

Kitty peered through the office window as official-looking men in sombre suits swept into the building with briefcases in hand and were directed to another room, down a long corridor with cream tiles on the walls. Mum waited by the front desk for a moment.

Then, a horde of scruffier-looking men swarmed in, waving notebooks and chattering incessantly. The press had arrived. Kitty heard her mother's voice ring out, clear as a bell, across the foyer. 'You do not have my permission to take any pictures of either me or my husband. Do I make myself clear? And I won't have any sketches made either.' Then she swept off down the corridor with about a dozen journalists trailing in her wake.

When she returned, thirty minutes later, she had shrunk visibly, and her eyes were red-rimmed from crying. 'Righto,' she said with enforced jollity. 'Dad is waiting to see you both, so come along with me.'

All the pressmen had gathered in the foyer and as Kitty and Harry walked past, she heard one murmur, 'That's his kids! Look at the boy, he's the image of him!'

Kitty put her arm around her little brother protectively and hurried him along.

They were shown into a side room. Dad was there, still

wearing the same suit he had left Lily Avenue in the previous evening, but he was pale as a ghost. The room was bare apart from a wooden table and chair and the worst part was, it had bars on the windows. He got up as they entered, and they fell into his arms and hugged for what seemed like forever. Harry started to sob, before a policeman coughed loudly and said, 'That's enough now, leave the prisoner be.'

Kitty could barely believe her father was being called a prisoner. She wanted to scream, but instead, she shot the policeman a pitying glance, as if he was just a fool who had no idea what he was saying.

'Come on, son,' said Dad, placing his hands briefly on Harry's shoulders. 'No tears. I will be home very soon, but now I need you to be brave.' He sat back down and Mum kissed him goodbye.

He smiled at Kitty. 'We will get through this. Be there for each other.'

The policeman stepped forward and opened the door, and motioned for them to go through it. They walked down the corridor and back to the entrance hallway in silence.

As they stepped into the street outside, a few of the men who were still loitering about came up to them, their caps pulled down low, and one of them spat on the ground, right in front of Kitty.

'Murderer's child!' he said.

'No,' she said, looking him straight in the eye. 'I am my father's daughter.'

As she spoke, she knew that whatever the future held, life would never be the same again.

23

Kitty

Newcastle upon Tyne, July 1910

The family existed in a twilight world of shame and fear.

Life went on around them, but they were no longer part of the community.

Ever since the day Dad was charged with the murder, they'd endured taunts from complete strangers whenever they were recognized; eggs had been thrown at their windows and kids took delight in chalking abuse on their front path.

Even the sounds of children playing hoopla or the milkman clip-clopping past with his cart set Kitty's nerves on edge. The clatter of the letter box brought fresh terror because of the hate mail they'd been getting – postcards and letters filled with such vitriol, Kitty scarcely would have thought it possible. Mum had tossed them on the fire to spare Kitty from dwelling on the spite.

Kitty had practically stopped going out, other than to work. She wanted to block it all out, to get away from everyone. Thankfully, she had one good friend, Emily, from the office, who stood by her through it all. Emily would walk to the tram stop with her and accompany her to the shops because in some places, Kitty could no longer get served. She'd got used to shopkeepers pretending she wasn't there because if they were seen to help her, they risked getting a brick through their own window.

Poor Harry was bullied mercilessly by the other boys at school and in the end, he begged to be allowed to stay home but Mum wouldn't hear of it. 'We have to face the world, Harry, we have done nothing wrong.' Kitty wanted to protect him from it all, but she was powerless. Whenever he came home with a black eye or his legs covered in bruises, he'd scamper upstairs to his room and shut himself away. He was sullen and moody with her and she knew that although the bruises would heal, the scars ran deep.

Mum seemed to have found the strength to carry all of them over the past months and Kitty was in awe of her. Mum wrote to Dad nearly every day, getting him to recount all the things that he could remember about that fateful train journey, to see if there was any clue, anything at all, that could help prove his innocence in the forthcoming murder trial.

So far, they'd suffered only setbacks. The worst was the coroner's inquest where a jury had concluded a verdict of 'wilful murder' against Mr Nisbet by her father and the reports of that were plastered all over the papers, which only swayed public opinion even further against him. Dad's solicitors had instructed him not to speak, to save his evidence for the trial, which Kitty thought was a mistake, because he could have protested his innocence.

Mum could barely bring herself to speak about the inquest. She referred to it as 'that witch-hunt'. At the hearing, another witness, an artist called Wilson Hepple, had come forward to say he had seen Dad walking along the platform at Newcastle station beside the victim on the morning of the murder. What's more, he had known Dad since he was a lad. Hepple couldn't swear that he saw Mr Nisbet and Dad getting on the train together but as every morsel of information about the case was devoured by a public ravenous for justice, it had only strengthened the case against him.

Dad told Mum that he hadn't got into a compartment with Mr Nisbet, but he had been with him in the ticket office because Mr Nisbet was ahead of him in the queue. He had known him by sight because of working in the collieries for years but they weren't friends. Dad was sure there were other travellers in the carriage with him at various points during the journey, but he was so engrossed in the sporting pages because of the Grand National on the Saturday that he'd barely taken any notice of them. In fact, he'd missed his stop and got off at Morpeth, paying an excess fare. As the weeks passed, Kitty hoped that someone would come forward to help support her father's version of events, but nobody did.

And then there was the question of the guns that Dad had ordered. Kitty had never seen him with a weapon, but a local gunsmith told the coroner's inquest that he had sold Dad a pistol in 1907 and a lady at a local newsagent's said that Dad had received packages at her shop under the name 'Fred Black'. Once she had a revolver turn up for him but that was sent in error and he returned it swiftly. It wasn't against the law to have a gun, but Kitty had to admit, it did cast a shadow of suspicion over Dad. When she lay in bed at night, she wondered if he'd got mixed up with rough types at the racecourses or if wealthy clients asked him to collect packages on their behalf, no questions asked. Perhaps he'd got out of his depth in the murky world of gambling, speculating and betting but she didn't believe for one second that he would have killed someone. Mum wouldn't talk to her about the guns other than to say she hadn't known about them either but her faith in Dad was unshakeable.

When Dad wrote back to Mum, he poured out as much love as he could fit onto two sides of prison notepaper. But no matter how hard Mum tried to jog his memory, to find something to help his case, there was nothing.

A date had been set for the hearing at the Moot Hall in the city, which lay just a stone's throw from the River Tyne and the whole of Newcastle was buzzing with anticipation, excitement even, about the train murder case coming to court.

Dad was held in Newcastle Gaol, which squatted like a huge, grim fortress at Carliol Square, just to the east of the city centre. It was surrounded by blackening walls of thick stone which stood twenty-five feet high. As it lay less than a mile from St Nicholas's Cathedral, where Dad had walked Mum up the aisle on one of the happiest days of their lives, he could hear the peal of the bells from his cell, bringing him a stark reminder of everyday life going on in the world outside.

Once a week, Kitty, Mum and Harry took the tram into the city and walked up to the prison gates to visit Dad. Those visits brought little comfort because although they were allowed to see him, they could not touch him. They were separated by an iron grille and it was torture to watch him becoming more gaunt with every visit, as the bleakness of his situation sank in. The missing money bag had been found down a disused pit shaft while he was in custody with all but a few last farthings taken and there was nothing to link him to it, but still his name was cursed in the city as the killer.

They always left the gaol in tears, often running the gauntlet of a gaggle of hostile men and women, who would hiss or spit at them, but Kitty reminded herself that what-ever she suffered, it was nothing compared to what her father was enduring in that dank prison cell, day after day.

It was unthinkable that he could have done anything to hurt anyone. Dad was a gentle and kind man. Yes, he was strict with Harry when he got too rough with his games but that was all. It was like stepping through the looking glass, into a world in which innocent people were blamed for terrible crimes and no matter how often they told the truth, the powers that be wouldn't believe them.

Kitty couldn't help but wonder how he could possibly get a fair hearing, and now she knew that her father would be on trial for his life.

The bugles glinted in the morning sun as heralds on horse-back trumpeted the arrival of a gleaming black landau filled with judges, resplendent in wigs and flowing scarlet robes. The horse-drawn Black Maria carrying her father, with bars at the windows, followed on behind as the whole party arrived at the grand, colonnaded entrance to the Moot Hall.

It was a spectacle like no other and as Kitty and her mother stood resolutely on the steps of the courthouse, an old woman next to them remarked that the King himself wouldn't have been disappointed with the ceremony or the turnout. Kitty silently thanked God that Harry wasn't here to see the circus that this whole sorry affair had turned into. Sending him to school was a hard decision but she'd supported Mum in cajoling him to go.

Hundreds of people swarmed about in front of Moot Hall, elbowing each other out of the way and craning their necks to see. Half the kids in the city had played hooky to catch a glimpse of the notorious prisoner and Kitty thought factories must have been standing idle too, if the number of working men in flat caps was anything to go by.

The sight which upset Kitty most was the women, in headscarves and shawls, who'd queued up early to get tickets for the proceedings, guaranteeing themselves a seat in the court. Many had brought their knitting with them and the sound of their needles clicking away was a constant, sickening accompaniment to the spectacle, like the hands of a clock, counting down to the start of the case.

The crowd fell silent as Dad got out of the prison carriage, his hands cuffed in front of him, flanked by two prison warders. He made his way up the steps into the hall and Mum smiled at him. He seemed to grow taller in that moment and he caught Kitty's eye. She had to fight the urge to run to him, as she turned to go inside, to take up her place in the gallery of the oak-panelled courtroom.

The courtroom was full to bursting and in the heat of a summer's day, so stifling hot, it was almost unbearable. Barristers sweltered under wigs and gowns, flicking through sheaves of paper. Women fanned themselves as the morning dragged on, with the prosecution outlining the case against her father – witnesses who swore they'd seen him walking up the platform at Newcastle station beside the man who was later murdered and robbed. Sightings of a mysterious passenger in the same coach as the murdered man and suggestions – but no proof – that it was Dad.

There was a lot of discussion about his business affairs: gambling, speculating, working for businessmen who had an interest in the mines and placing bets for them on the side. The prosecution tried to suggest he had money problems because he had pawned some jewellery but both he and Mum had money in their bank accounts. Kitty knew the pawn tickets were just a ruse in case the Bigg Market lads asked for credit when they placed bets. Everything was being twisted to make him seem guilty but one ray of hope came when a weapons expert revealed that the bullets were of two distinct calibres, meaning that two guns had most likely been used. Why would a lone assailant have done this? And the gun which had been linked to her father was not capable of firing any of the bullets which killed John Nisbet. Another was that the victim's missing money bag had been found down a disused pit shaft when Dad was already being held in Newcastle Gaol and there was no sign of the money anywhere in their house or bank accounts.

When it was time for Dad to give evidence, he entered the witness box and glanced over to the jury for a moment. A ripple of shock swept over the room as he revealed that one of the men who had picked him out of the identity parade at the police station had been intimidated into doing so by a policeman, who'd pushed him back into the room and forced him to pick someone.

The prosecution summed up the case, saying that although the evidence against her father was circumstantial, the jury would have to make up their own minds as to whether he was telling the truth or not. The barrister argued that if all the pieces of evidence created a chain which proved, beyond reasonable doubt, that he was the killer, then they should find him guilty.

The defence barrister then argued that many of the circumstantial facts of the case had been provided to the police willingly by Dad, which would be a strange thing for him to have done if he were guilty. The identification evidence against him was at best circumstantial and in the case of Hall and Spink, very shaky. And it was agreed that the likely scenario was that two weapons had been used to kill the victim. Looking around the courtroom with a growing sense of trepidation, Kitty didn't think that argument had persuaded anyone that her father was innocent.

On the third day of the trial, the judge spent several

hours summing up, before sending the jury away. They were gone for more than two hours and most folks left the courthouse to stroll about outside in the sunshine and get some fresh air. A court clerk took pity on Kitty and Mum, who couldn't face the stares and catcalls of those awful women from the Quayside, and he ushered them into a side room and gave them a cup of tea, which they sipped at. Kitty felt the hot liquid gnawing away at her insides; they hadn't eaten since breakfast, but she had no appetite. Mum seemed to be fortified by the drink and, balancing the empty cup and saucer on her lap, turned to Kitty, and said, 'We'll have to get the house tidy for him when he comes home, won't we? I've barely been around with the duster in months.'

It was such an unexpected comment, with all the odds stacked so heavily against them, that Kitty didn't know whether to laugh or cry.

Mum went on, with a faraway look in her eye: 'I'll try to get down to the butcher's so I can make him a steak pie. I think he will like that, won't he? He's missed my cooking so much . . .'

Kitty felt her words sticking in her throat and looked at her mother, whose hair was greying. All the softness of her features had been worn away by sleepless nights of worry.

'Well, what do you think, Kitty? Will you help me get the house ready for your father when he comes home?' Mum was more agitated now and the court clerk looked up from the pile of papers he was quietly reading at his desk.

'Yes, of course,' said Kitty, fighting back tears. 'We'll

make it a day to remember when Dad comes back home to us all.'

When they returned to the stifling courtroom, they watched as Dad was brought up from the cells to stand in the dock, and the usher said, 'All rise!' as the judge, Lord Coleridge, swept in wearing his scarlet robes and wig. He was a haughty-looking man, with a fine, long nose and a high forehead, and Kitty had long since decided she didn't like him at all.

You could have heard a pin drop as the judge, speaking in clipped tones, asked the jury foreman, 'Do you find the prisoner guilty or not guilty?'

The foreman stood up, with almost indecent haste, and addressed the court: 'Guilty!'

Dad was asked if he had anything to say and he clasped the edge of the dock, his knuckles white, as he spoke: 'I can only repeat that I am entirely innocent of this cruel deed. I have no complicity in this crime. I have spoken the truth in my evidence and in everything I have said.'

Kitty watched aghast as the judge put on his black cap. 'Prisoner at the bar. The irrevocable decision has now been given and the jury have found you guilty of the crime of murder. In your hungry lust for gold you had no pity upon the victim whom you slew. It is only just that the nemesis of the law should overtake the author of the crime. The scales of justice are now balanced by the verdict which your fellows have pronounced. The punishment is death.'

There were gasps from the gallery and Mum covered her face with her hands.

But Dad hadn't finished yet. He looked around the courtroom and shouted out, 'I declare to all men that I am innocent!'

As he was taken down to the cells, the incessant chatter of the women of the Quayside started up again. It felt as if the eyes of the entire city were on Kitty and Mum as they stumbled out of the courthouse clinging to each other, with the catcalls of 'Murder!' and 'Hang him!' ringing in their ears. A kindly solicitor hailed a horse-drawn taxi and they clambered aboard, shutting the door behind them as people peered through the window.

They knew Harry would be waiting for them at home at Lily Avenue, hoping against hope that Dad might be set free.

'Don't worry, Kitty,' said Mum, drying her eyes as the taxi set off for Heaton. 'This isn't over yet. We will fight on.'

Over the coming days, Mum wrote letters to the newspapers, protesting Dad's innocence and pointing out that all the evidence against him was circumstantial. She was tireless in her arguments, insisting that despite being on trial for his life, he had been kept in solitary confinement and had not even been allowed a book or a newspaper to read. He was starved, left without food or water during lunch when he was locked away, so that when he gave evidence, he was hungry and thirsty.

Dad's solicitors had launched an appeal and a fortnight after that dreadful day, the case was up before three justices of appeal.

They had some startling new evidence, from the two

men who had travelled on the same train as Dad and later picked him out of an identity parade. An investigation by the Chief Constable of Northumberland had revealed that officers had pointed Dad out to Hall and Spink, the colliery clerks who were witnesses, as he sat in a room at the police station, on the night he came in for questioning but before the identity parade.

Neither of them could remember which officer was responsible, but the door was deliberately pushed ajar, and they saw Dad. One of them remarked that from the back, he didn't look like the suspicious man who had been in the carriage with the murder victim, but he noticed that Dad was wearing his light overcoat and that was the same coat he was wearing when he was picked out of the identity parade later on – so the whole procedure was a sham.

Mum felt certain this crucial flaw in the handling of the case – pointing Dad out before an identity parade – would be enough to spare his life.

'I knew that there was something amiss with the whole thing, the way he was picked out of that line-up,' she confided over her nightly cup of cocoa, which was one of the small pleasures she still afforded herself. 'Surely they will see sense and set him free?'

But when the case came to court again, this new evidence was ruled inadmissible and Mum sank back into despair as the justices ruled there were no grounds for an appeal.

One afternoon, when Kitty had just got back from work, a visitor knocked at the front door and she nervously opened it, half expecting to find herself facing a barrage of hatred from a total stranger. But as she peered through the crack in the door, she saw a cleric standing there, holding a small bundle of papers.

'I've been collecting signatures around the city, from people who believe your father is innocent and should be reprieved,' he said. 'They've read your mother's words in the newspapers and we want to send the petition to the Home Secretary himself.'

Little by little, the petition grew until there were several hundred names on it, and then – almost unbelievably – this number increased until it included more than a thousand people. They may not have been willing to offer the family friendship in their darkest hour, but there were enough kind souls in the city to plead for a reprieve and that offered a tiny glimmer of hope. The document was sent off to Winston Churchill, the Home Secretary, who reviewed the case and went through all the evidence. He had the power to commute the sentence, to spare Dad's life.

As they waited for his decision, Mum renewed her letter-writing campaign, revealing to the newspapers how they were forbidden to have any physical contact with Dad because the police thought that they might use 'daring and cunning' to slip him poison, so that he could take his own life. The thought was a ridiculous one but that is how the police saw it.

In one letter to the papers, pointing out the flimsy nature of the evidence against Dad, she wrote:

Only a few days ago, I got off the car at the foot of Northumberland Street at the same time as a gentleman, whom I had never seen before and

*probably never will see again. We walked together,
side by side so far as a casual observer could tell,
until we reached Worswick Street, because neither
of us could get out of the road of the other. If
shortly afterwards I had been found murdered,
would the fact of us having apparently walked
down Pilgrim Street together have been proof that
the man was my assailant?*

Dad also wrote a personal appeal to the Home Secretary, telling Mum in a letter from prison:

*I am still hoping and trusting that something or other
will be disclosed, which will prove my innocence.*
    *For your own great and untiring efforts under all
these heart-rending and benumbing blows, I cannot
say all I wish, but to your own self and to Kitty
and Harry, my feelings are more and more deeply
sunk in my heart, forever and ever.*

But when a letter arrived in a thick, white envelope
bearing a London postmark, Kitty brought it to Mum and
she opened it, with trembling hands. She knew that Dad's
life depended on what was inside.

*I am directed by the Home Secretary to inform
you that he has given careful consideration to the
petition submitted by you and I have to express
to you his regret that after considering all the
circumstances of the case, he has failed to*

*discover any grounds which will justify him in
advising his Majesty to interfere with the due
course of the law.*

With all avenues for appeal exhausted, the date for the execution was set for just two days' time. The hangman was due to arrive at Newcastle Gaol and nothing could save him now.

That evening, Harry came home from school and rushed into the kitchen before Kitty could even greet him. She found him at the sink, scrubbing at his face with soap and water.

When he turned to her, she saw that his face had been daubed with black paint.

'Who did this to you?' said Kitty, rushing to get a cloth to help clean him up before Mum saw him.

'Just some lads,' said Harry. 'They pinned me to the floor while they did it.'

'What on earth for?'

'They said it was like the hood the hangman will put over Dad's head,' he said, his shoulders drooping in defeat.

24

Kitty

Newcastle upon Tyne, Monday, 8th August 1910

It was the cruellest goodbye.

Standing in the airless prison visiting room, with Harry sobbing at her side, Kitty ached to feel her father's embrace one last time.

But he was separated from them by iron bars, with warders at his side. There would be no farewell hugs or kisses, the authorities insisted on that, no matter how hard Mum begged for a final farewell together.

'Don't be afraid for me because I love you so much,' he said, smiling weakly at them all through the grille. 'I will face what comes with dignity, I won't let you down.'

At that, Mum let out a sob.

He went on: 'I feel certain that one day, someone will clear my name. Live your lives with your heads held high in the knowledge that I am innocent, but what's done is done and we cannot change it.

'You are a brave young woman, Kitty. Now it's time to

be strong and always speak your truth. If you ever doubt yourself in this life, I will be walking beside you.'

Dad told Harry to strive to be honest and to lead a good life, and Kitty watched as her brother nodded, understanding that these would be the last words he would hear from the man who had raised him. He crumpled in her arms, like a broken doll.

To Mum, he said, 'I will burn your letters and make an end of it all, just as I promised. I love you, always.'

After just half an hour, they were told their time was up and they had to leave. Dad waved at them and blew kisses, with tears running down his face, as they were ushered out of the room and that was the last Kitty saw of her father.

The clock on the mantelpiece hadn't been wound for over a week, so it couldn't strike the hour of the execution at eight o'clock the following morning.

It seemed almost unfathomable that five months ago they were just a family from Newcastle. Now they were notorious, and Dad would meet his fate at the end of the hangman's noose.

Time passed.

THE NORTHERN ECHO
Wednesday, 10th August 1910

Alternate light and shadow prevailed yesterday when morning dawned on the day of John Alexander Dickman's execution and for some it seemed uncertain whether the day would be fine or wet.

The air was cold and raw, but this did not deter people from

assembling at a very early hour in Carliol Square to gaze at the
gaunt walls of the prison. Policemen were on duty and the
front of the prison was kept clear, although at other points
people were allowed to assemble and, fully, a thousand were
present at the appointed hour.

Extraordinary precautions had been taken to ensure privacy
and in front of the scaffold a huge canvas screen had been
stretched to shut out the view from an adjacent school roof
once used by an enterprising reporter. Even the doors of the
trap had been padded so that in falling they would not make a
noise loud enough to be heard outside the walls, although in
this the authorities were not absolutely successful.

There had been nothing to see for a long time so the arrival
on foot of the prison governor and prison doctor was itself
quite an event.

The clock in St Anne's steeple, with its harsh bells, began
first to chime the hour and before it had concluded the prison
clock struck eight with a haste that was almost unseemly. St
Nicholas was the last to take up the chorus, the Canterbury
chime preluding Big Ben's solemn striking of the hour.
Hardly had the last gong sounded before a slight thud was
distinctly heard by several assembled outside. There was
some doubt as to whether this was actually the noise of the
falling trap, but corroboration was afterwards forthcoming in
the fact that the execution was really about half a minute
late.

People began to parade in front of the prison and took
increasing interest in a placard posted there, headed 'Capital
Punishment Amendment Act, 1868' and declaring that the
sentence of the law passed on John Alexander Dickman, found

guilty of wilful murder, would be carried into execution at eight o'clock.

At 8.30, a warder removed the notice and substituted ten minutes later two others. One issued by the governor, who certified that 'judgement of death was this day executed on John Alexander Dickman at His Majesty's Prison in Newcastle and the other by the surgeon, stated that he had examined the body and certified that the man was dead.

It is understood that the prisoner slept well and arose from his bed before seven o'clock. He had bread and butter for breakfast. The prison chaplain waited on him and urged him to confess the truth but to this request, the prisoner made no reply. He did not, as expected, declare his innocence on the scaffold and from the moment his cell was opened for the executioner, Ellis, and his assistant, Dickman never spoke a word. He braced himself up to meet the executioners and arose to his feet on their entrance. He was apparently calmly awaiting the end and submitted passively to the process of having his arms pinned behind his back.

The chaplain, reading the burial service, headed the procession to the scaffold, where Dickman met his death unflinchingly and calmly.

It is stated that in his last letter to his wife, Dickman repeated his statement to her that he felt certain that some day all would be made clear.

'I can only repeat that I am innocent,' he concluded.

25

Annie

Acton, June 1944

The silence when the doodlebugs' engines cut out over-head was the most terrifying thing in Annie's world.

You'd hear them before you saw them, the horrid metal beasts with wings, as they soared into the skies above Acton making a noise like a lorry zooming along. The whole world stood still when they fell silent and people craned their necks to follow each bomb's dreadful down-ward path.

Annie stood in the back yard, with baby Patricia in her arms and little Anita playing with her doll at her feet, as the doodlebug appeared in a clear summer's sky, its engine sputtering. John, thank God, was under the table in the kitchen with his toy cars. Time stood still.

'Dear God, no!' she screamed, watching frozen in terror as it sailed silently above them. 'Please, not us!'

'Mummy!' her little girl cried, clutching at her legs.

Just a few precious seconds saved their lives, as the bomb fell not on them but on some poor souls a few streets away, and as the boom of the explosion reverberated, Annie dropped to her knees in shock, making a grab for Anita and holding the baby close.

This time they had been lucky, but she knew that for some of the other residents of Acton, that fine summer's day may well have been their last.

At least half a dozen V1 bombs had fallen on the town in recent weeks and in one of the most terrible tragedies, a bus full of people was hit. Harry had tried to spare her the worst of the details but, ever since Vera had died a year ago and it had seemed they were drifting apart, he'd agreed to tell her the truth about what he was dealing with as an air-raid warden. Just being able to talk, even if he told her very little about the awful things he saw in the aftermath of the bombings, had brought Harry back to her.

She'd made him promise not to bottle things up any more. It was never going to be easy. He wasn't a big talker, but in the dark of the blackout, he seemed to find the courage to share his feelings and, little by little, his thoughts wandered from the devastation of the air raids to the battlefields of France and Flanders.

At first, he was full of apologies, as he clammed up and his hands started to shake.

'Please, Annie,' he said, turning to face the wall, 'I don't want you to see me like this. I can't bear to be weak. That's not right for a man.'

'It's not weak to tell me about the things that are troubling you,' she soothed. 'We are married for better and for worse and I'm here for you, Harry.'

Some memories were just a blur, but she understood now how he had been little more than a boy when he had gone away to war and had returned, like so many others, haunted by nightmares of what he'd seen, suffering shell shock.

'I lost my father when I was just turning thirteen, so it was harder for everyone when I went away to the war,' he said, his voice little more than a whisper. 'They needed my wage and when I came back, I wasn't fit to work for a long time. Kitty helped me get better. She just had a way of calming me down, of talking sense into me.'

Annie made a little murmur of understanding. She didn't like to push him to talk about Kitty, because she still hadn't met his sister, and it seemed to upset him so much to suggest it. She often watched him reading his sister's letters, wondering what news was being shared, but he always kept them closely guarded, locked away in the little tea chest, and the key was kept in his jacket pocket. There had been times when he was having a nap that she'd been tempted to take that key and have a little look but then she'd thought better of it. A husband had to trust his wife and she wasn't about to let him down.

'What happened to your dad?' said Annie.

There was a long pause and then Harry said, 'He died, and it was sudden, very sudden, and a big shock to all of us. I don't think any of us have ever got over it.'

'I understand,' said Annie, who'd never known her father because he'd died when she was just a baby. Some wounds were just too raw and time would never heal them. She was sure Harry would talk about the memories of his father when he was ready to but for now, she was just grateful that he was sharing some feelings with her because it brought them closer.

He went on: 'I wanted to go away to war, to fight, to make my family proud of me but, God knows, I was terrified most days and once you were there, there was no going back. Some days, it seemed you were going to get a bullet either way because the deserters got shot at dawn and the rest of us then got blown to bits on the battlefield. I envied the dead because at least they had some peace.

'My horse, Domino, kept me going. That dumb animal was so faithful, he'd have followed me through the gates of hell if I'd asked him to. And in some ways, Annie, I did.'

He turned on his side to face the wall and she knew he was crying. She put her hand on his back to offer some comfort.

'When the bombs started dropping on us here, I wanted to help, there was no question of it,' he said, his voice muffled. 'But it brought it all back and I started to see things and hear things, every time I shut my eyes. I've been afraid, Annie, afraid I would lose my mind.'

'You won't ever do that,' she said.

He turned to her and she traced the line of his cheek with her fingers.

'You don't know that. A man can lose his mind and not get it back. The nightmares start creeping into everything. I'm scared, Annie. There's so much more I want to tell you but I can't, I can't.'

'Shh, don't upset yourself,' she said, hugging him so tightly, and they kissed.

'Let me be here for you, Harry,' she said. 'We have so much to look forward to in this life. You just have to trust me. The past is gone and we will get through this war, we cannot give up on that, and we can't give up on each other either.'

Not long after the New Year of 1944 she'd given birth to their third child, a little girl who had a mop of black curls. She hadn't enjoyed the pregnancy as much as the others because of the guilt she felt when she jumped the queue for rations with her special green book, which was given to mothers when they were expecting. People had been going without for so long now, it was just an accepted part of life, to get your coupons for butter, bacon, eggs and so on. Pregnant women had the first choice of fruit at the grocer's, as well as double rations of eggs and a full pint of milk a day. But Annie hated to feel like she was getting special treatment because they were all in this together as a community.

After baby Patricia had come along in January, they'd moved into a new flat in Horn Lane, just a few streets away from her mum's in Grove Road. With the three little ones it was getting crowded in their old place and this was more spacious than anything Annie could ever have dreamed of. She'd put by as much as she could from her stint of war work and Harry had been saving hard so they could afford it. These days, they tended to stay there during raids, even with the threat of the flying bombs, because people had got tired of all the discomfort of the air-raid shelters night after night.

Annie had got used to gathering the kids and huddling under the kitchen table and saying her prayers. Harry would have preferred her to go to one of the shelters – even the public ones – but she just felt, after Vera had died, that if a bomb was going to drop, there wasn't much you could do about it. It was strange how many people felt that way after nearly five long years of war.

Their flat was the upstairs rooms above the United Dairies shop and once you came in through the front door, there was a black and white tiled passageway down to the kitchen, which overlooked a yard where a haulage firm parked its lorries. It was home, so Annie didn't mind. She just put some curtains up at the window to make it prettier.

They had to share the indoor lavvy with the fella who ran the shop, who was nice enough, but he could come in and out of the hallway through a door which was locked from his side when he needed to. Apart from that, the rest of the place was theirs and it had three bedrooms, which was like living in a palace as far as Annie was concerned. There was an inside bathroom, gas laid on to cook with and a boiler for the hot water.

They had a sitting room too, with a radiogram in it. Harry loved nothing more than to relax in there after work, in an easy chair he'd picked up down the second-hand shop in South Acton for next to nothing, and listen to the BBC World Service.

Most days she'd spend the morning doing the house-work and then she'd take a daily trip out to the shops before heading down to her mum's in Grove Road. Today she stopped to buy Anita a carrot on a stick for a penny – the poor little mite had never even seen a lollipop because sweets were on the ration. She was pushing the pram with the two youngest in it and Anita walking alongside down Churchfield Road when she caught sight of Dennis, her old boss from the Acton Works. She hadn't seen him since she left before she had Patricia and he had barely spoken to her once he saw she was in the family way, in any case.

Now he blushed and pretended not to see her, turning his head to gaze into a shop window as she passed. There was something faintly odd about the way he did that; he couldn't even look her in the eye, which made him seem rather shifty. It wasn't as if anything had happened between them, other than that silly dance, but being around him when she and Harry were having problems had been a real comfort to her – she accepted that, with a pang of guilt. Perhaps he had felt it too and had expected more and she'd led him on? She had never crossed the line with him but it could have happened, she knew that, and she might well have enjoyed it; the war had seen plenty of people having affairs. There was a live-for-today attitude, and with women spending more time in the pub, and with husbands away overseas, it gave them more opportunity to stray if they wanted to.

But that had never been Annie's intention. She'd just wanted to feel close to someone and when it came to it, the person she wanted more than anyone in the whole world was Harry, she realized that now.

'Good morning, Dennis,' she said loudly, as she pushed

the pram along with her children. She didn't bother looking back to see if he acknowledged her. Those days had gone.

While Mum played with the children down at Grove Road, Annie mixed up some 'mock crab' which was an unholy-sounding mix of margarine, dried eggs, salad dressing, a bit of cheese and some vinegar, before serving it in sandwiches.

Annie loved to listen to the BBC Home Service to get tips on how to make food go further. Marguerite Patten made it all sound so easy, but she'd had a few culinary disasters. Harry still laughed his head off about her 'goose' made of lentils that they'd managed to force down last Christmas.

When Bill came in from the back garden, where he'd been bailing water from the Anderson shelter, he poked at her mock crab mixture suspiciously before tucking in.

'Dear God, Annie,' he said, struggling to swallow it. 'You should send this to Hitler, it'll bleeding finish him off!'

'Don't be so ungrateful,' said Mum, taking a dainty bite. 'It ain't so bad.'

She showed Annie the letter she'd just received from George, who was fighting in Italy, and Annie swapped it for a postcard she'd received from him. He'd now been gone from home for more than two years. All his letters were chirpy, but Annie couldn't help wondering, after speaking to Harry so honestly, what dreadful things her brother might have seen.

She didn't mention that to Mum, of course, because of her heart trouble, and there was no point making her worry over things that couldn't be changed. Mum was too busy chortling about George's latest joke in any case.

Can't wait for this war to be over so I can come home and make good use of that Anderson shelter, he wrote. *I'm planning to keep chickens in it. It will make a lovely hen house. Please tell Bill not to dismantle it!*

'Well, I read in the paper that the aircraft factory got fined for serving their workers too much tea,' said Mum conspiratorially over a cuppa that was as weak as dishwater. 'Blooming cheek if you ask me and serves them right.'

Annie had heard the same about the De Havilland factory up on Western Avenue. Even the number of cups of tea served to workers was tightly controlled these days and while everyone else was scraping by or going without, it did cause ill feeling if others were getting more.

The one place Annie and the family looked forward to going to once a month, as a special treat, was the British Restaurant down at the King's Rooms on Acton High Street. Churchill had set up the restaurants where people could eat a decent meal, off the rations, for about a shilling a head. It was wholesome stuff, stews, usually with plenty of seasonal vegetables on the side and always a pudding of some sort. Elsie was cock-a-hoop about their forthcoming trip because she was planning to introduce her boyfriend, Josh, from Ohio, to the entire family.

He'd taken her up to Rainbow Corner, the GIs' club in Shaftesbury Avenue, last Saturday night and she'd come home fizzing like one of the Coca-Colas he'd bought her, having danced the night away to tunes on a jukebox.

'Joan's coming along too,' she told Annie, as she pulled out a heap of faded cotton dresses from the wardrobe, holding them up to the light, one after the other, to select the prettiest. 'I've got to look my best and you know I can't hold a candle to her.' There was no way that Elsie could get a new dress; clothing had been strictly rationed for years and the coupon allowance cut from sixty-six per year to just forty-eight. Besides, she'd had to get a new winter coat in January, because the moths had been at hers and that had set her back sixteen coupons. She'd shelled out five for a new pair of shoes for the dance later that evening, but Mum had warned her to make do with whatever else was in her wardrobe.

'Oh, Elsie,' said Annie, hugging her sister, whose hair fell in curls almost to her shoulders. 'You are just beautiful. Josh wouldn't mind if you turned up wearing an old sack, I'm sure, but why don't I go through my sewing box and see if I can find some nice bits and pieces to smarten up one of your frocks?'

It didn't matter that she was worn out from running around after the three children, Annie wanted to make Elsie feel the best she could for her special night, even if she'd be burning the midnight oil to do so.

Elsie's eyes sparkled. 'Would you do that for me? Annie, you are the best sister in the whole wide world!'

Annie's stomach was rumbling as she caught a whiff of the rabbit stew that was on the menu tonight down at the British Restaurant.

It was lovely not having to cook and her sister Ivy had agreed to mind the little ones so she could go out with Harry. Ivy tended to stay in, even though Charlie was away with the army. There was nothing anyone could do to persuade her otherwise. Annie got the feeling that his mother ruled the roost in his absence with her 'Charlie wouldn't like its' and Ivy didn't want any trouble indoors, so she stayed put. Harry had promised to join them as soon as he clocked off from work and Annie was looking forward to having a dance with him, just like they used to before the war broke out.

'Ooh, it's dead man's leg,' Elsie joked when she saw that jam roly-poly was for pudding. She was in such good spirits and Annie put it down, in part, to the fact that she looked so pretty. Annie had taken her sister's old gingham summer dress and added new buttons down the front and some lace around the collar. Annie had found some red ribbon and Elsie had tied that around her waist, as a little belt. A lick of lipstick and the excitement of introducing Josh to Mum and Dad seemed to do the rest.

Even Bill had cheered up, but that could have just been at the prospect of sneaking off for a pint later when Annie and the others went dancing at the town hall.

They waited patiently in the queue for their food, handing over their money to one of the WRVS ladies, before sitting down at one of the tables. There were other families there too, although some of them were certainly less fortunate than Annie's because they looked dishevelled. The restaurant was used by the poor souls who'd been bombed out and were staying over at the rest centres at Acton Congregational Church Centre. Her friend Esther and the other women from the WRVS who served up the meals always made sure that the needy got the biggest helpings, which was only fair.

They were just tucking in when the double doors to the dining room swung open and a tall, blonde young man in a sand-coloured uniform stood there. He was so striking, with his chiselled jaw and commanding air, that the whole room fell silent. He caught sight of Elsie, who gave a little squeal of delight as she waved, and he strode over, reaching out to shake Bill by the hand.

'Charming fella,' said Bill, who was as bowled over as everyone else and put down his knife and fork to gaze at the young GI, who had ambled over to the servery.

It was a stark contrast to his grumblings in the scullery about the Yanks being 'overpaid, oversexed and over here'. Mum beamed at Josh as he returned and leaned over to plant a kiss on her cheek. 'Elsie's told me so much about you all.'

Bill was just asking Josh about the farm back in Ohio when the dining room doors opened again and Joan sashayed in, wearing a dress that shimmered as she moved.

'That's silk!' gasped Elsie as her friend drew up a chair and gave Josh a shy little smile. 'Where on earth did you get that?'

'Ask no questions, I'll tell you no lies,' said Joan with a giggle.

'Looks rather flashy for a dance at the town hall,' said Mum curtly, just loud enough for Annie to hear.

If Joan heard the comment, she didn't let on, because

she was too busy drowning in Josh's baby blue eyes, which were fixed on her. 'My mum cut up her wedding dress to make it for me, if you must know,' she said, giving Elsie a little poke in the ribs. Elsie forced a faint smile. 'She said there's no time like the present, what with the war on. Ain't that right, Josh?'

'Well, you certainly look like you're ready to make the most of the evening, Joan,' he murmured, blushing a bit. He turned swiftly to Elsie and added hurriedly, 'But you look stunning in your dress too. I think you must be the prettiest girl in London tonight, Elsie.'

He had done his best to be convincing but everyone knew that Joan was the belle of the ball.

The band struck up a tune and the dance floor filled with people, as Annie glanced around to see if Harry was here yet. Elsie twirled in Josh's arms as couples formed up behind them, to go forward and back across the dance floor in time to the music. People started singing along: 'Don't sit under the apple tree, with anyone else but me, till I come marching home!'

The steps all looked a bit complicated to Annie, who didn't mind a nice foxtrot but wasn't sure she could cope with all the moves that Elsie was gliding through with such ease. Her sister had warned her that the Americans had a completely different way of dancing; it was much livelier than anything she was used to. As the band struck up an even jauntier tempo, Joan leaned over to Annie and explained, 'It's the jitterbug. We do it all the time up in the West End!'

Joan sat on the sidelines, tapping her feet and refusing all the smart young GIs who asked her to partner them, until Elsie was tired enough to sit out. Then she sprang forward and was away onto the dance floor in Josh's arms.

Josh gazed down at her as they moved in time to the music. As Joan's honey-blonde tresses cascaded down her back and her lithe body moved like water in her silk gown, they seemed to be the most perfect couple from a Hollywood film. He was Fred Astaire to her Ginger Rogers.

Elsie sat glumly on the sidelines, her hands in her lap, looking for all the world as if the Germans had just won the war. She only perked up when she caught sight of Harry ambling in to join them, fresh from his work shift.

'Cheer up, Elsie, it might never happen!' he quipped.

'Oh, it already has,' she said, nodding in the direction of Joan and Josh as they glided around the dance floor.

'Might I have the pleasure of this dance then?' he said, giving a little bow, as Annie looked on, suppressing a fit of the giggles.

Elsie shook her head. 'Thanks all the same, but I'll sit this one out. I've got a lovely friend here who you might like.' She gave Annie a nudge in the ribs and she burst out laughing.

'Oh, yes,' said Harry, pulling Annie to her feet and stealing a kiss. 'Do you come here often? I'm sure we must have met . . .'

In a split second they were swaying to the music. As he smiled down at her, she knew that she was where she belonged, in his arms.

*

Only a few days after the dance, all the US servicemen disappeared from Acton overnight and the town was buzzing with expectation that something big was going to happen. Annie tuned in to the BBC news on the wireless at lunchtime down at Grove Road only to hear a special broadcast.

'*D Day has come. Early this morning, the Allies began the assault on the north-western face of Hitler's European fortress,*' the announcer said in a sombre tone. The children played at their game of hide-and-seek under the kitchen table, oblivious to the news unfolding around them or the battles being waged for their future.

Annie shushed them for a moment, hanging on to every word as Mum swivelled round, looking at the wireless in disbelief.

'*Under the command of General Eisenhower, supported by strong air forces, Allied Armies began landing on the northern coast of France.*

'*It was announced a little later that General Montgomery is in charge of the army group carrying out the assault. This army group includes British, Canadian and United States Forces.*'

Mum dropped her tea towel in shock. 'That means George is there! What if it's Dunkirk all over again?'

Annie ran to her mother and hugged her tightly. 'It won't be. We have to believe that our boys can do it.' After so long, they had the Germans on the run now, didn't they? The tide had turned in their favour, that's what everyone was saying these days.

But by the time Harry came back to Grove Road

clutching a copy of the *Evening Standard*, Mum was a nervous wreck and Annie had been forced to open the last bottle of sherry stashed under the stairs to calm her.

Harry almost had to fan Mum with the front page to get her to listen to him. 'Look! It says here that Churchill says it's all going to plan. The landings are a success. We have broken through Hitler's defences. This is it!' He pulled Annie into an embrace. 'I think we are going to win, Annie, I can feel it. We've done it before, we can do it again.'

He poured them all a little glass of sherry.

Moments later, Elsie came home from work, her eyes red-rimmed from crying. She ran upstairs without so much as a cup of tea.

'She's probably worried sick about Josh,' said Annie. 'I'll take her up a cuppa.'

But when Annie gently opened the bedroom door, Elsie was lying face down sobbing on her bedspread, refusing to budge.

'Be brave, Else, he's going to make it home,' said Annie, kneeling at her side. 'Things are going to go our way from now on. You'll meet again, just like the song says.'

'But I won't,' said Elsie, crying into her pillow. 'I won't. He's gone and slipped a ring on Joan's finger. No matter what happens in this war, nothing will ever be the same for me again, because Joan's won his heart!'

26

Annie

Acton, May 1945

The whole town was festooned in a sea of red, white and blue.

Every sewing box had been raided to find ribbons for the children's hair and even the dogs sported patriotic rosettes on their collars. Bunting, which had last seen action during King George's coronation in 1937, was pressed into service and strung across the street from lamp post to lamp post.

The air almost crackled with expectation of the big announcement, due later that day, from Prime Minister Winston Churchill, who had guided the nation through its darkest hour. Ever since Hitler took the coward's way out a week ago in his Berlin bunker by shooting himself, the writing had been on the wall for the Nazis.

Some people had taken that as their cue to start celebrating a few days early. Annie had heard about a raucous victory party down in Shepherd's Bush, but the air-raid wardens had put paid to that with stern warnings. 'Don't you know there's a war on?' was still the constant rebuke.

Yesterday, the woman from opposite and all the neighbours who didn't have a wireless set had crowded into the little scullery at Grove Road to hear the momentous news from the BBC: Germany had finally signed an unconditional surrender and the war really was coming to an end. Churchill himself was to make a speech about it, drawing the whole thing to a triumphant close.

They listened, mouths agape, before Bill broke the silence.

'About bleeding time too! They were never going to beat us!' he said, raising a mug of chicory coffee in a toast to the radiogram. 'Now, I'd better start getting those bunk beds out of the Anderson. No time like the present, is there?'

Mum rolled her eyes. 'Honestly, I swear he'll miss that shelter.' And everyone collapsed in fits of laughter. It was true, the Anderson seemed to have developed more leaks than the *Titanic* given the amount of time Bill spent out there. If George got his way and used it as a hen house, what on earth would Bill find to do?

The housewives put their heads together to make Victory in Europe Day an occasion to remember. Even though sugar and eggs and just about everything else needed to make a cake were on the ration, ovens were soon heated as hot as furnaces and sweet treats were baked as if by magic. Kids had grown up with carrots being grated into cakes to sweeten them and apple pies were always a treat, especially with a bit of evaporated milk poured over instead of cream.

Annie peered out of the net curtains to spot a boy on a bicycle riding up and down the street whistling to himself. It seemed incredible to think that just a day ago, they were living in fear but now, everything was going to change for the better, after nearly six long years of struggle. One by one, people came out of their houses, bringing tables, chairs, china and anything they could muster to give to the little ones as a treat for the party until the whole street was transformed. Neighbours who only days ago had been worn down by years of struggle started smiling and laughing together and it was like the sun coming out in their street.

Bottles of beer and sherry were pulled from under floorboards and dusted off from the backs of cupboards and poured into teacups while the kiddies had their fun, dressed as pirates, nurses and anything else that their mums could find around the house to make a costume with. John was determined to be a cowboy, so Annie had made him a pair of chaps from an old towel and she'd altered an old black felt hat by attaching some string under the chin. He roamed the street with two sticks for guns, terrorizing anyone who crossed his path, to whoops of delight from the other little boys. Anita wanted to be a princess, like the girls in her favourite book of fairy tales, so when Mum's back was turned she took down one of the net curtains in the front room and tied it around her daughter's waist with a bit of spare ribbon.

Mum burst out laughing when she saw what Annie was up to and hastily took the other one down so that Anita could wear that as a headdress.

As Mum fixed it in place with a spare yard of lace from her sewing box, she cooed, 'Don't you look lovely! Now, run along and play with the other children.'

As Anita skipped off, Mum smiled in a way that Annie

hadn't seen since before the war. One little mite came dressed in a pillowslip with a ribbon tied around her middle and no one minded. There were bobbing apples and games of hopscotch and running races and the street was alive with the shouts of excited children as Harry helped judge the winners.

At three o'clock precisely a hush fell over the proceedings as the wireless set took pride of place at the head of a long row of tables and the unmistakable voice of Winston Churchill resonated over the airwaves, bringing the news that they had all been longing to hear.

'*My dear friends*,' he began. '*This is your hour. This is not a victory of a party, or of any class. It's a victory of the great British nation as a whole. We were the first in this ancient island to draw the sword against tyranny.*

'*After a while we were left all alone against the most tremendous military power that has been seen. We were all alone for a whole year.*'

Annie thought of all the terrifying nights spent during the air raids and silently thanked God that they had been spared.

'*There we stood alone,*' said Churchill. '*Did anyone want to give in?*'

The whole street erupted with shouts of 'No!'

Churchill continued: '*Were we downhearted?*'

Again, the cry went up and fists punched the air: 'No!'

'*Every man, woman and child in the country had no thought of quitting the struggle,*' he said. '*London can take it!*'

Within moments of the speech ending, church bells all over the borough started peeling and aeroplanes zoomed overhead, flying into the city of London in celebration. Buses and cars honked their horns in a jubilant cacophony down on the High Street. Neighbours hugged each other and children danced. Only one person stood on the sidelines, smiling but not really joining in. It was Elsie. She'd lost so much weight due to her heartbreak over Josh that Annie had been forced to put darts in all her waistbands; she was almost as skinny as Ivy. The end of the war would mean the one thing she was dreading – Josh and Joan would be getting married.

'Come on!' said Annie, running to her sister and pulling her over to where the children were playing ring-a-roses and a bottle of sherry was doing the rounds. 'Come and join in the fun! We've got to celebrate.'

Elsie shrugged. 'I feel a bit tired, Annie. Maybe I could look after the kids so that you and Harry can go down the pub with the others? You deserve some time together.'

Annie couldn't accept that her little sister's dancing days were over. 'Tonight of all nights it will be a huge party and there are plenty more fish in the sea. You owe it to yourself to get out there and have some fun.'

But Elsie wouldn't be persuaded. She just shook her head, helping Mum to clear some of the plates and teacups. It was as if she'd lost the magical thing, the sheen which made fellas look twice. The Blitz hadn't broken her but that damn GI had stolen her spark.

The next day was declared a public holiday, so the bloke Annie watched being pushed home in a wheelbarrow because he was three sheets to the wind wouldn't mind too much about the hangover he'd have in the morning.

By early evening, the people of Acton had drunk the pubs dry, but no one was downhearted; they had the spirit of victory to sustain them.

As night drew in, bonfires were lit for the first time in six years and word spread around the pub about a huge one down on the green at South Acton. Annie and Harry joined the good-natured gaggle of folk heading over there, linking arms, singing at the top of their voices.

Kids had made an effigy of Hitler, stuffing an old boiler suit with straw and using a sack for a head, inking on his unmistakable moustache for good measure. They chucked it on the top and whooped with glee as the fire was lit. Hitler crackled and popped as a rowdy conga line snaked its way down the road towards the gathering in a jumble of arms and legs.

Someone darted out of the pub with a chair and chucked it on the bonfire, sparking other people to follow suit. They pulled chairs from their own homes, just to make the flames leap higher. Who cared if they'd have to sit on the floor in the scullery tomorrow? They'd just won the blinking war!

Annie caught sight of Bessie standing there, staring into the flames, and went to join her.

'Vera would have loved this, wouldn't she?' said Bessie, wiping a tear from her eye as the conga line skipped and kicked its way past to hoots of laughter.

'Yes,' said Annie, knowing that nothing she could say would ease Bessie's torment over their lost friend. 'She would.'

As the night wore on, fireworks exploded, lighting up the sky, and it seemed as if the town would celebrate forever. It made such a difference from the tracer fire and the resounding ack-ack of the anti-aircraft guns.

They were a joyous mass of humanity, endlessly singing, dancing, kissing. All the agonies of the war were swept away as pianos were hauled out of smoky bar rooms and into the streets, so that everyone could join in the knees-up. They belted out 'Roll Out the Barrel' and when they did the 'Lambeth Walk', lumbago was forgotten for the night. People smiled and laughed more than Annie could ever remember.

Harry, her Harry, was there with Annie through it all until they'd sung themselves hoarse and their feet were blistered from dancing.

As dawn was breaking, they made their way home through the streets they knew so well, past the places that had been reduced to rubble by the terror from above which had made the nights of London a living hell for so long.

Dunkirk and the Blitz and everything they had suffered had united the community more than Hitler could ever have foreseen. Their homes lay in ruins, but their faith had not been shaken.

Stopping for a moment outside their front door, Harry pulled her into his arms and they kissed. She knew then that whatever the future held, they could face it together.

They had gone out during war time but they came home at first light, to peace at last.

27

Ethel

Clapham, May 1945

'Go on, Zena! Give us a twirl!'

Ethel beamed with pride as her beautiful, raven-haired daughter led the dancing in the street, to the cheers of their neighbours at their VE Day party.

She was the brightest, the prettiest of all the girls and what's more, she was kind too; she'd sung her way through many an air raid in the tube stations during the blackout, to keep everyone's spirits up. Even when she was almost dead on her feet from dancing, she still found time to entertain the folks who'd been bombed out down at the rest centres.

No one knew where she'd got it from, but Zena seemed to have the most extraordinary talent for making people smile. When she walked into the room, it was like the sun coming out. Ethel and Len doted on their daughter, and now this dreadful war was over, they were even thinking of setting up a dance school for her, so she could achieve her dream of being a teacher. She was fifteen now and lovelier with every passing day.

Len's dairy business and shop in Clapham Manor Street was doing well and he treated Ethel like a queen. Zena was his princess and William, well, he was growing up to be a young man, who was nearly twenty now. He looked the spitting image of his father and he was prone to his moods, too, which Ethel despised. Len knew how to handle him, though. He'd get him working away in the shop or, better still, pushing the handcart full of milk around the streets on his daily rounds. Len always had a spring in his step when he went off every morning and Ethel loved him dearly.

Ethel felt a little tug at her sleeve and gazed down to see one of the snotty-nosed local tearaways looking up at her.

'Can I have some of that jelly, Mrs Ebdon?' he said, pointing to the bowl on the table.

'Of course you can,' she said, serving him a big helping. She'd put by a whole stash of tinned fruit and jelly when the war broke out and it was wonderful to be able to share that with the children, to make the day one to remember.

Everyone called her Mrs Ebdon as a mark of respect because she helped run the shop; she was a pillar of the community. It almost made the long hours standing on the freezing floor of the dairy worth it, although she hated having to turn the greying sausages over to the pink side to make them look a bit more appealing so they'd sell.

Her life now in London was everything she could have wished for. Well, except for one fly in the ointment. Sometimes she'd lie awake in bed at night and worry about what would happen if Harry ever came back. That dreadful afternoon when Zena was a baby and he'd caught her with Len still haunted her. In fact, she carefully locked the front door and checked all the windows every night, just in case. She didn't want him barging his way back into their lives. He could be dead for all she knew – not that she cared. There was always that sister of his in Newcastle who she could ask, but Ethel wasn't going to chase her; they'd never got on in any case. It was best to let sleeping dogs lie, that's what Len said.

As far as the local community was concerned, nobody spoke about where Harry had gone or why she was living with Len. She'd just put the word out to Doreen that he'd walked out on the family and it was good riddance to bad rubbish, and neighbourhood gossip did the rest. Da took her side about Harry and he seemed to approve when she took up with Len, who worshipped the ground that Ethel walked on. It had been tough for a while when she and Len had first moved in together, because Da knew that she was still married to Harry, but he was so captivated by his beautiful granddaughter, Zena, that he was prepared to overlook that. And Len was charming to Da, who now lived in a flat around the corner, and was always welcome in their home.

With every passing year, it got easier to think less about Harry – except for the fact that William was so like him, not just in looks, but in his bookish ways and his interest in politics. That rankled with Ethel, but she allowed him to go off to the library on his bicycle or spend hours alone in his room, just to keep him out of her way, which she preferred.

Sometimes, when she was down the pub, she found herself spinning yarns about how she'd run away from Newcastle when she was just eighteen to start a new life in London. Perhaps it was wrong to do that but she couldn't help it; it was just easier to gloss over the truth, that's all. Meeting Harry had been her stepping stone to being here, with Len, where she was meant to be and it was better if he didn't feature in her life story, which sounded more glamorous and entertaining when she told it the way she did.

Len had bought her a beautiful wedding band which she wore with pride, but they weren't married, not that she'd ever let on, not even to the children. Len wanted to marry her, of course, but they couldn't walk up the aisle together because she was still married to Harry.

They couldn't afford a divorce and if they'd tried to trace Harry and he refused, it would have spoiled everything they'd worked for. She did not want that lunatic back in their lives. Len was well respected and she was the queen of the street – the woman everyone looked up to – and that was before she got onto all the attention she got because of being Zena's mother. The child had star quality, like an actress from the films she still adored watching at the cinema most weekends. Yes, Ethel was living the life she'd hoped for and now this blasted war was over, they could all start to enjoy themselves a bit more, even if there was no end to rationing in sight.

Living on rations didn't bother her – she was thin as a pin anyway because her clothes fitted her better that way and Len liked it. But she wanted to take some days off from the shop, to go to the seaside or up West, to the theatres, to wear the lovely mink stole Len had bought her before the war and really let her hair down a bit.

She spotted William at the end of the trestle tables, pouring himself another drink from a bottle of sherry. He was already glassy-eyed.

'I think you've had enough,' she said, going over to his side.

'It's a party, Mum!' he said, rocking back on his heels and laughing. 'Don't be such a spoilsport!'

He was a big lad now, taller than Len, and handsome with it but he had a determined streak and a liking for the drink, which worried her. And when his grey eyes settled on her, it was like going back twenty years, to the Hoppings fair in Newcastle, where she first met Harry.

William had cried for his dad so much that first year after he left but when Ethel put her foot down and said that was that, the tears had stopped and the moods had started. She'd slapped him once, when he was unforgivably rude to her. But Len had handled it all in the end, explaining that his dad had problems and didn't want to be with the family in London for his own reasons. That seemed to do the trick and William accepted Len as his stepdad because he was such a kind, caring man. Zena didn't know anything about Harry, of course, other than what she might have overheard in whispered conversations – that he had deserted the family before she was born. William knew better than to raise his name within earshot of Ethel or she'd give him what for. Just a glance from her was enough to let him know he was sailing close to the wind.

The truth about what had happened with Zena was a secret she kept, uneasily, but out of necessity, for all their sakes. As she watched William pouring himself another drink, she had a fleeting sense of unease about whether she'd been too hard on him when he was growing up.

But then Zena skipped over and hugged her and the fella from the pub brought out his accordion, to the delight of the kiddies, who started waving their Union Jacks in time to his version of 'Rule Britannia', amid shouts of 'We won the war!' In that moment, the past was forgotten.

Ethel only wanted to look to the future now, a future that was as bright and sunny and vivacious as her beautiful daughter. She wasn't anything like her father, Len, in looks, but then, daughters didn't always take after their dads, did they?

28

Annie

Acton, January 1946

Some tatty bunting left over from the VJ Day celebrations was still tied to the top of a lamp post on Grove Road. It had hung resolutely through the winds and the rain of a London winter as a little reminder of the happiest day when the war finally ended.

There had been another big street party after atomic bombs were dropped by the United States and Japan surrendered soon after, but when pictures of skeletal-looking soldiers who'd been held prisoners of war in Japanese prison camps began to emerge, alongside stories of their horrendous suffering, the appetite for celebration had been muted.

The bunting fluttered in the wind, as Annie and the children made their way up to the grocer's shop to see if the bananas had finally arrived. A big ship had docked a week or so ago down at Avonmouth and children were going to be allowed to have the first ones. They were chattering amongst themselves about what this strange new yellow fruit would taste like as they rounded the corner and saw a big queue forming outside the shop.

'I'm going to share it out between us,' said Anita, puffing her chest out a bit. She was the eldest and there was no way she was going to let her little brother and sister snaffle it.

'But I want it!' cried Patricia, toddling along. 'It's my banana!'

'You won't get anything if you carry on like that,' Annie chided. 'We all have to queue and wait our turn and share things fairly, you'll see.'

In some ways, life after the war hadn't changed that much. People accepted long queues for food as just one of those things. Annie didn't mind because it was a nice way to catch up with neighbours and pass the time of day.

There was still rationing for milk, tea, sugar, meat, butter, lard, cheese and sweets and some said that flour shortages meant that bread was likely to be put on the ration soon – which seemed daft to Annie, now the war was done, but folk like her were not to question these things. It was up to the powers that be.

Her friend Esther was standing at the end of the queue, with her shopping basket, looking a bit forlorn. She seemed rather rudderless now the war had ended and with her kids in school, the days were long. There was still a lot of voluntary work to be done, with so many people having lost their homes or their loved ones, but the sense of urgency that had provided the focus for her work had departed. What's more, things were a bit difficult for her indoors because the children had got so used to living without a father that they found it hard to adjust to having their dad, Paul, back at home from the Royal Air Force.

'How's everything?' said Annie, giving her a little hug.

Esther had dark circles under her eyes, as if she hadn't been sleeping.

'It's not easy,' she said. 'Paul's gone back to his mother's for a while. I think it's for the best.'

Annie lowered her voice, so that the woman in front of them in the queue wouldn't hear.

'But what happened?'

'He's just so moody and regimented, he's treating the house like his barracks and he wants to impose so many silly rules on me and the kids,' she said. 'I can't live like that, Annie. I'd rather be alone.'

'You don't mean that, do you?'

'He just seems to snap over the silliest of things,' she went on, staring into space as the queue inched slowly forwards. 'He'd shaved his moustache off when he was demobbed and because I didn't notice, he treated that as a betrayal. It was as if I had slept with another man. He didn't speak to me or the children for a week and then when he did, he started barking orders at us.'

Annie thought for a moment of all the things Harry had told her about how men suffered mental scars from being in the war.

'He's probably seen some terrible things, lost friends in those fighter planes in all those battles,' she said. 'It can take time for men to readjust to life at home, that's all. Give it a chance, Esther.'

But Esther shook her head sadly. 'I've seen things too, in the rest centres. Mothers who have lost children, wives who have lost husbands. People suffered and made sacrifices on the home front too for so long. I can't go back to having him rule the roost. Nothing can ever go back to the way it used to be before the war. I don't want him telling me what to do any more.'

Annie bit her lip to stop her saying anything to upset her friend further. Esther had the right to make her own choices.

Just then, she spotted Bessie hobbling along Churchfield Road with her book of coupons in her hand to join them at the grocer's. 'Why don't you let me get your shopping for you and you can go down to my mum's and take the weight off your feet?' said Annie to the old woman.

Poor Bessie, she'd spent her entire life standing on freezing-cold stone laundry floors and now she struggled with the daily pain of having worked in such harsh conditions. On bad days, her walk was a hobble and her legs looked like a pair of tree trunks under her wrinkled stockings.

She nodded gratefully and was just shuffling off when a wild-eyed young bloke, who couldn't have been more than twenty or so, almost knocked her flying.

He was wearing an army greatcoat which he clutched to his thin frame and he jabbered away to himself before grabbing a great handful of apples and trying to make off with them. He was so scrawny, his eyes seemed to be eating up his face.

'Oi!' cried one of the other women in the queue. 'Put those back, you bleeding tea leaf!'

The grocer ran out to see what the fuss was about, and he collared the thief. As luck would have it, a copper came strolling past but when the man caught sight of his uniform, he did the strangest thing. He fell to the floor, weeping, and curled himself into a ball with his hands over his head and started whimpering, 'No! Please, no!'

'He was in the camps in Burma,' someone whispered. 'It ain't his fault.'

The copper took off his helmet and kneeled down beside him before offering him his hand. 'It's all right son, there's no enemies here. Come on, we'll get you home.'

The grocer prised the apples from the fella's grasp and stuffed them into a brown paper bag, before quickly handing them back to him. 'These are on the house. Just come and ask me if you want anything and you'll have it, no charge, see? We're your friends here.'

'Why is that funny man lying on the ground?' said Anita.

'Don't stare, it's not his fault,' said Annie. 'He's scared because a nasty person did something terrible to him during the war, that's all. But we are not like that here. This whole town is his home and we must all look after him.'

George returned from the war to a hero's welcome.

He was tanned but so much thinner and his khaki uniform hung off him in a way that had Mum piling extra dumplings onto her boy's dinner plate, much to Bill's annoyance.

The children clambered all over him like excited puppies

and he was such a good uncle, he was barely back in his civvies before he was busy building a wooden fort for John and a doll's house and a cot for Anita and Patricia.

The next plan, true to his word, was to buy some chickens and keep them in the Anderson shelter, which he lined with hay. Tending those birds provided hours of entertainment for the little ones, as well as free eggs, which were still on the ration. Mum was pleased as Punch with that turn of events.

'I knew you'd make it home safely,' said Annie, as they stood in the back garden watching Bill showing John how to feed the new family pets.

George turned to say something but was caught out by yet another coughing fit.

'Have you seen a doctor about that cough, George?' she said.

'There's no need, really,' he replied with a wave of his hand. But Annie wouldn't be dissuaded. Her brother had been seriously ill as a little boy, with TB, which was rife in the laundries of Soapsud Island, where the family had worked for so long. He'd suffered damage to one lung because of it.

'George, please,' she began. 'You know you need to look after your chest . . .'

His voice fell to a whisper. 'I don't want to worry Mum but yes, it's TB. I saw a lot of doctors in the army when I was over in Italy and France and the fresh air there seemed to help but there's nothing to be done about it. I just have to keep myself well, that's all.'

Annie nodded. She'd seen so many women with the

condition in the laundries; thin, white as the sheets they were scrubbing at the washboards. People lived with it because there was no treatment, only long stays in sanatoriums and operations too gruesome to talk about, which some said left you worse off than if you'd just let the disease take its course.

'We're all going to die sometime, Annie,' he said, smiling down at her. 'I'm home now here, with you all, and I want to live each day to the full.'

He was true to his word and within a few weeks of coming home, George had got himself a job as a carpenter and was walking out with a girl from Ealing, who he'd met at the varieties in Chiswick.

Mavis was introduced to the family over a cream slice at the Lyon's tea room in Ealing Broadway, although Ivy stayed at home with Charlie, who was back from the army. A visit to the Lyon's tea room was definitely a cut above as far as Acton folk were concerned. Annie had never set foot in the place before; she'd only admired the white and gold lettering on the frontage, not to mention the gleaming liveried van which was always parked outside. George had put on his best bib and tucker and was nervously adjusting his tie when Mavis hove into view, puffing away on a cigarette.

She was generously proportioned and as she grabbed George in a kind of a bear hug to plant a wet kiss on his cheek, Annie thought she might break him in two. When she ate, she sank her teeth right into her food, consuming it with gusto, flicking fag ash everywhere.

'Ooh, fag ash Lil!' said Elsie under her breath.

Mum looked a bit concerned when George started coughing. 'Maybe you could put that out while we eat?'

'Oh, no!' cried Mavis. 'He don't mind a bit, do you, George? In fact, I keep telling him to take it up because smoking opens up your airways in the morning.' George wheezed a little as he laughed. 'Cough up,' said Mavis.

But despite everyone's worries, Mavis was a good sort and George was very fond of her. So fond, in fact, that before long, Mavis was stomping up the aisle, so he could slip a ring on her nicotine-stained finger.

After they were married, they moved to Ruislip, which might as well have been the moon as far as Mum was concerned.

'Ruislip!' she muttered to herself, running some sheets through the mangle in the back yard, as George's hens pecked aimlessly and wandered in and out of the Anderson shelter. 'What on earth did he want to go and move to Ruislip for?'

In some ways, Annie thought her mother might have preferred it if he were still abroad fighting. At least then he would have sent a postcard.

Annie had only sent her eldest daughter up to the shops two minutes ago to get Harry's evening paper, so she couldn't be back already, surely?

The knocking at the front door got louder and she turned the gas down on the stove, so that the bacon she was frying for tea didn't get burned to a cinder.

'All right, I'm coming!' she shouted, bustling up the

hallway. 'I don't know why you didn't take the key with you!'

She opened the door to find that Anita wasn't standing behind it after all. In her place was a well-dressed woman with a brolly hanging over her arm and a suitcase in her hand.

'I've come to see Harry,' she said, with a determined look in her eye. 'I'm his sister, Kitty.' She stepped over the threshold without waiting to be asked and handed her hat to Annie. She glanced around the hallway with its peeling paint and sniffed at the air. 'You must be his landlady?'

'No,' said Annie, who was unable to hide the look of surprise on her face at the very suggestion. 'I'm his wife!'

Harry ambled down the hallway to see who the visitor was and stopped in his tracks when he caught sight of Kitty. Her face was set like stone.

'Well, Harry, you've been busy in London, haven't you?' she said. 'Too busy to come up and visit me and Mum in Newcastle and now I see why.'

Right on cue John and Pat bundled out of the kitchen brandishing Anita's favourite dolly, which they liked to pinch to tease her. Anita then came in the front door with the *Evening News*, handed it over to her mum and scampered up the stairs in hot pursuit of her little brother and sister.

'Are these your children?' said Kitty. She addressed the question to Harry, but Annie answered.

'Yes,' she said. 'All three of them – Anita, John and Patricia. Come down here and say hello to your Aunt Kitty, children.'

Three little heads bobbed over the bannisters before there was a stampede down the stairs.

Kitty's expression softened a little as they gathered in front of her. 'Why, they remind me of us when we were young, Harry!'

Harry didn't smile. He looked at the floor, as if he was waiting for it to swallow him up.

There were so many questions in Annie's mind about why Harry had been so secretive, but it wasn't her way to make a fuss, so instead, she took off her apron, smiled at her sister-in-law and said, 'Shall I put the kettle on?'

Harry and Kitty settled in the sitting room upstairs and Harry shut the door firmly behind them. Annie knew, without him having to say anything to her, that he needed to have some time alone with his sister. Kitty certainly was every bit as forceful as Harry had warned her, so it was no surprise when she heard raised voices from both of them.

Annie brought them some tea and sandwiches on a tray and when she went in, Kitty was sitting, crossly, with her arms folded and Harry was gazing out of the window. You could have cut the atmosphere with a knife.

Annie left the room but hovered in the hallway outside. She shouldn't have done so, really, because it was eavesdropping, but she just couldn't help it. Harry's sister had turned up without so much as a by-your-leave and had mistaken her for the landlady! Why on earth hadn't Harry told her the truth? Anger knotted itself into a furious little ball inside her stomach but she didn't want to spoil the visit and so she willed herself to be calm, for Harry's sake and the children's.

She pressed her ear to the door.

'What else was I supposed to do?' Harry said crossly. 'There was a war coming and I fell in love, of course I married her. We wanted to start a family together! I don't need your permission to live my life.'

Annie couldn't catch Kitty's reply, but she heard Harry say, 'There was no way I could go back there, Kit, you know that, so please let's not go over that again. You've got to let it lie. Promise me that.'

Perhaps Kitty had been insisting that he should have moved the family to Newcastle during the war, after all? Their voices grew quieter so that she really had to strain to hear and Harry murmured something which she couldn't make out.

Then Kitty erupted: 'But I must have the children come to stay with me. It's only right. You cannot cut them off from their Newcastle family like this. It's not what Dad would have wanted. You've made your choices and you've done what you've needed to do but we are family and I won't let you keep me apart from the children, not any more.

'We both want the same thing. We both know what's done is done, so there's nothing to worry about. It would be good for your eldest to get out of London and see something of the city where you grew up, wouldn't it?'

Annie heard the chinking of china being loaded onto the tray and hurried away downstairs to the kitchen to check on the children, before she was caught out being a nosy parker.

When Kitty came into the kitchen she was wreathed in smiles and gave each child a hug, before asking Anita, 'Perhaps you'd like to come and stay with me in Newcastle very soon?' She added hastily, almost as an afterthought, 'If your mother will allow it?'

Their eyes met and Annie nodded. She'd waited so long to meet this woman who knew Harry better than anyone. She wanted to be friends with her, even if they came from very different worlds. And Kitty had a point – it would be good to show the children where their father came from. Besides, it was clear to Annie that Kitty was clever and that might lead to better opportunities for the children.

The world was a different place since the war: things were being rebuilt, there had been a general election and the working man had had his say, to the extent that a Labour government had swept to power. Working-class people like them had a bigger voice because of the sacrifices they'd been prepared to make fighting for their freedom and Annie wanted to make sure her kids had more chances than she'd ever had, toiling in the laundries from the tender age of twelve, just to help her family make ends meet.

'It's a long journey, though, King's Cross,' Annie said, turning to Harry. 'Perhaps we should wait a year or so until she's a bit older?'

'Of course, you wait as long as you like,' said Kitty. 'But she will come one day soon and that will be enough to keep me happy. And if she takes a book along with her on the journey, the time will fly by.'

Anita clasped at her dolly for a moment before replying: 'Would you meet me at the station in Newcastle?'

'Yes,' said Kitty. 'We can arrange everything and I will meet you at Newcastle Central Station.'

She caught Harry's eye. 'It's where some journeys end and new adventures begin.'

Kitty was animated with the excitement of it all. 'And when you come, you can stay in your dad's old room. He was always my younger brother, you see, and he still is, really, and you are very much like him. You are your father's daughter, such a clever little girl, I can see that.'

Then she turned to Annie and said, 'Thank you.'

29

Annie

Acton, February 1952

Long after the war had ended, Annie still woke up in the middle of the night, listening out for the dreadful wail of the air-raid siren.

She'd have to pinch herself to remember that it had all happened in the past, and there was nothing to fear now. Harry slept soundly at her side, just as he had done before the war, when they were first married. She couldn't remember the last time he'd had a funny turn with his nightmares and if he was troubled by them, she took that as a sign that he needed to talk to her more about things. He'd never be someone who found that easy, but she accepted him as he was because she loved him so much.

The way his grey eyes twinkled whenever he saw her was enough to let her know she was adored.

People didn't talk about the Blitz much these days, but the reminders of those terrible war years were all too visible in the craters and the rubble of the bomb sites which had become playgrounds for the next generation. It didn't matter how many tellings-off worried mothers gave their kids, they'd be scrambling over fallen masonry and playing soldiers in the ruins every chance they got. Annie didn't like it – not only because of the tragedies that had unfolded there but also because they were blooming dangerous places – but boys would be boys, wouldn't they?

Everyone knew someone who'd suffered in the war, whether it was losing their house to a German bomb, or a loved one in the conflict. Emotional scars were quietly acknowledged with a listening ear, tea and sympathy, but the Dunkirk spirit still prevailed. People wanted to look forwards, not back, and the politicians had promised new houses, built by the council, which were springing up all over town. They were boxy-looking, modern and clean and people were pleased as Punch to get one, although Annie still loved their flat above the dairy on Horn Lane.

And that wasn't the best of it. Once word got around that the government was offering free healthcare for everyone, the queues to see the GP were longer than anything that Annie had ever seen outside the grocer's or the butcher's during the war.

The new National Health Service was the most wonderful thing for people like them, who'd had to count every last farthing to make sure they had enough money to pay their health insurance.

A trip to the doctor had always been a last resort, and for the children only. Everyone else just struggled on regardless, relying on old family cures or whatever they could get for a few pennies from the chemist's.

But now things were different, although older folk like

Bessie couldn't quite believe it and Annie practically had to drag her to the GP for a tonic when she got a nasty bout of the flu, which laid her low for weeks.

The saddest thing was that although doctors' bills were a thing of the past, and politicians talked endlessly on the wireless about building a healthier Britain, the NHS wasn't able to save George.

Annie wiped away a tear as she looked over at the only photograph she had of her brother. It had been taken in the back garden at Grove Road, just before he headed off to North Africa, when Anita was still a babe in arms. He was smiling, just as he did on the last day she saw him in the hospital. That had never left him, even when the tuberculosis made it almost impossible for him to speak and his body was little more than skin and bone.

George had only lived two years more after he and Mavis got married and although they visited every couple of weeks, Mum always grumbled that she barely saw him. After he died, Mavis came round to Grove Road with his war medals, which he had left to John, still smoking like a chimney. Poor George. He'd dodged German bullets at Dunkirk, D-Day, El Alamein and the Italian campaign only to succumb, at the age of just thirty-six, to a disease he'd picked up on the streets of Acton as a child. But there was no sense to this life, war had taught Annie that much.

The children still played with the beautiful toys he had so lovingly crafted for them because he never had kids of his own, and they helped Mum to look after his chickens which ruled the roost in the old Anderson shelter.

Mum put a brave face on it all, but she was broken by

the loss of her son and on the anniversary of his death every year, she made a sad pilgrimage to lay flowers at his graveside and each time she returned from the cemetery, she seemed to grow a little bit weaker.

Annie was worried sick about her, because not only had she been right off her food, she'd lost a huge amount of weight too. Most things were still rationed, but not bread, and so Annie made copious amounts of Mum's favourite bread and dripping, toasting it by the fire down in Grove Road.

That was all well and good until the children came home from school and tried to snaffle it. Bill would swipe at them playfully and tell them to 'Sling yer 'ook', while secretly feeding them titbits; he really was a doting grandfather on the quiet.

He and Mum adored the children. Anita was a proper little bookworm and true to her promise to Kitty, Annie sent her up to Newcastle once a year. She always came back with a smart set of new clothes and a caseload of books from her aunt. Kitty visited them in London too, bringing with her copies of the *Shipbuilder* for John. She'd sit with him at the kitchen table and make him add up all the ships' specifications, to help him improve his maths.

It was a good thing for him, that quiet time studying, and Harry encouraged it because, like all the local boys, John loved nothing more than to hare about on his bicycle or use the bomb sites around Acton as a playground.

Kitty had none of that whenever she came to stay. As Kitty sat with John going through all the numbers on the page, Annie cooked their tea, quietly marvelling at this clever and determined woman. Kitty had carved her own path in a world which, even after everything that women had done in the war, still thought the best place for them to be was at the kitchen sink.

It wasn't that Annie had grand plans to go out to work like Kitty. In fact, Annie didn't mind being at home; she loved keeping house and watching her little ones grow up. It was what she was good at. Harry was still working at C.A.V. where he was one of the union leaders and they were saving up to go to the Isle of Wight on holiday this year. Annie had never been so far afield; she'd heard the beaches were beautiful.

Harry was happier now too, settled in himself. He liked to read the reports in the newspaper about football and he loved to follow the horse racing, but he was dead set against gambling of any sort, which was unusual for blokes. Annie could never quite work that one out. The only time he allowed himself a flutter was on the Grand National.

Harry had yet to break the news of their planned holiday to Kitty, because she'd been hoping to get them all up to Newcastle for a break. Annie would leave that to Harry. Those two still had their letters to each other and their whispered conversations behind closed doors in the sitting room. It had just become part of the routine whenever Kitty came to stay for Annie to bring in a tray of tea and sandwiches and for the door to be shut firmly behind her as she left them to it. She didn't listen at the keyhole as she had done that first time – why would she? It was just a brother–sister bond, their relationship, and the way they liked to be with each other to talk privately some-times. She had an inkling it was rooted in the loss of their father when they were both young, but she didn't pry because, well, it wasn't her place to do that.

Now clothing was off the ration, she had started taking on some sewing jobs for other people, to make a little pin money, which was nice because she was a dab hand with a needle and thread. She made all the children's clothes and things for her sister Elsie too, not least the new petti-coats which were all the rage.

They required yards of material and Mum laughed her head off at them the first time she saw Elsie swishing about in hers, which she'd starched so that it stuck out a street mile from her legs.

'You won't fit that bloody thing in the wardrobe, my girl,' said Bill, raising his eyes to heaven when he caught sight of her before she went out dancing.

'Oh, leave off, Bill!' Mum chided. 'She's entitled to enjoy herself and I think she looks smashing.'

Elsie was still living at home in Grove Road and she'd got herself a job as a secretary in one of the factories, which was a big step up. She was more sociable these days but as she gave Mum a quick peck on the cheek, she said, 'I'll be back before eleven, so don't worry or wait up, promise me?'

Annie secretly hoped that one night her sister might stay out late, returning flushed with excitement at having met someone she could go courting with, but Elsie made it plain she wanted nothing more to do with men.

Gone were the days when she'd gallivant all over the

West End or Shepherd's Bush with her mate Joan. In any case, Joan had disappeared off to Ohio to marry that dratted GI Josh at the end of the war and Elsie didn't complain when she failed to keep her promise to keep in touch.

Elsie confided in her sister Ivy quite a lot, probably more than she did Annie these days. Those two were close in age and they looked up to Annie as a mother figure because she was already working in the laundries when they were little. They'd always been as thick as thieves.

Ivy's husband Charlie had come back from the war safely and she was very quickly back under his thumb in a way which kept Annie awake at night, wondering if her sister was happy. Annie, Elsie and Mum all suspected that he was knocking her about a bit when he lost his temper. There were no bruises to show for it but there was something about the way Ivy was quieter around him, and smoked nervously, that set alarm bells ringing. No one ever broached the subject because it probably would have made matters worse and nobody wanted that.

Poor Ivy. It was just one of those things that families knew about but didn't like to mention. It caused a few awkward silences at get-togethers but nothing that couldn't be smoothed over with a nice cup of tea and a chat about how much the kids had grown since last time.

It was the same in streets all over town. You never really pried too much into what went on behind closed doors.

It was a grim and freezing morning, the sort of day when Annie was glad to be doing the housework in their flat on

Horn Lane with the wireless tuned to the BBC, rather than going out to the shops.

She was just running over the tops of the cupboards with her feather duster when the music stopped and a voice came over the airwaves speaking in a tone which sent a chill down Annie's spine. It was just like the darkest days of the war.

'This is London. It is with the greatest sorrow that it was announced today from Sandringham that the King, who retired to rest last night in his usual health, passed peacefully away in his sleep earlier this morning.

'The BBC is now closing down for the rest of the day except for the advertised news summaries, shipping forecasts and gale warnings.'

Newspaper headlines proclaimed, 'THE KING IS DEAD!' and within a day the heir to the throne, Princess Elizabeth, had been named as his successor. She seemed to embody everything that the new decade was about, with her fashionable haircut and beautiful clothes, her dashing husband Philip and their two sweet little children, Charles and Anne.

The state funeral would take place a week later and it was to be shown on the television, which caused a lot of excitement. Mrs Banks, who lived opposite her mum on Grove Road, had a set in her living room and so the whole street crowded in there to watch the funeral. The kids were herded in there by the dozen to see such an important event and clips around the ear were meted out to any child who dared to speak as the funeral procession made its way into St George's Chapel at Windsor Castle.

Winston Churchill was among the mourners, in his heavy overcoat and black top hat, looking so much older. It was as if the weight of the responsibility of leading Britain through the war had finally taken its toll on him.

There were three queens in attendance, all clad in black and wearing veils to hide their grief. Elizabeth, the young princess who would be crowned next year, old Queen Mary, looking as if she'd stepped straight from the Victorian era in her headdress and skirts to the floor, and the late King's grieving widow, Queen Elizabeth, the heroine of so many London families to whom she'd been a great comfort during the Blitz.

They were the past, present and future of the nation, frozen for a moment in their grief for their son, husband and father. Everyone shared in the sadness of their loss. The King had been a tower of strength for the nation during the battle with Nazi Germany, but there was something about the televised images which made it feel to Annie as if they were intruding, peering in on their world.

Mum didn't manage to watch the funeral; she was feeling poorly again and so she went for a lie-down. Within a few weeks, she was in hospital. Doctors did some tests and found she was riddled with cancer. There was nothing anyone could do to save her.

Mum didn't want a fuss, that wasn't her way, but Annie and her sisters tended to her every need, taking turns to spend as long as they could by her bedside. The nurses did what they could to make her comfortable but her face twisted with pain every time they tried to move her and in the end, she slipped in and out of consciousness, aided by morphia to relieve her torment.

She looked so small and shrunken, lying in hospital bedsheets stiff with starch. Annie thought back to her days at the laundry, when Mum would make light work of ironing those sheets. She'd seemed invincible, not just to Annie, but to all the laundry girls, and especially to Bill, who always joked she was too good for him. Annie had secretly agreed with that, until she was older and realized that for all his faults, Bill treasured her mother.

It was a mercy that he wasn't there when she finally went.

Mum had been asleep for a while but she suddenly coughed, her chest heaving with the effort of it, and opened her eyes to look straight at Annie.

'The children send their love,' said Annie. 'They're making you a get-well card and I'll bring it tomorrow . . .'

Mum smiled and Annie held her hand and, in that moment, Annie noticed her mother's fingers were as cold as ice. Mum closed her eyes and Annie watched as all the colour drained from her face.

'Please don't go,' Annie whispered. 'Don't leave me, Mum.' But it was too late.

A nurse came to the bedside and felt for a pulse. When there was none, she pulled the sheets over her mother's head and opened the window.

Somewhere outside, a bird was singing.

The first blossom of spring was on the trees when Mum died. Annie picked some and laid it upon her mother's grave. She was buried next to George, which was her dying wish.

Bill was lost without his Emma, the woman he'd wooed in the laundries of Soapsud Island during the First World War, who'd put up with all his grumbling and borne him beautiful daughters. The light went out in his world when she went.

A year to the day after her death, he was rushed into hospital with chest pains, taking with him his favourite picture of Emma, as she was when they first got engaged. The nurses found him clutching it when he passed away that afternoon.

Everyone said he'd died of a broken heart. Annie believed them.

Epilogue

Kitty

Newcastle upon Tyne,
April 1979

Kitty shuffled when she walked now, just as Mum had done when her legs gave out and the arthritis got the better of her in her final years.

Her auburn hair had long since turned grey, but it was every bit as thick and wavy as it had been when Harry cut a great chunk out of it in a game that got out of hand in the back garden when they were bairns. She wore it piled high on the top of her head in a bun but when she glanced in the mirror, the old lady in her eighties who looked back at her still had fire behind her eyes.

Newcastle had changed so much you could scarcely recognize it and with all the new building work that was going on down at Eldon Square, you could have spent four score years and ten in the city and still not recognize the place. Gone were the elegant Edwardian houses, to be replaced by tons of concrete and glass and a modern shopping centre.

She preferred it here, in her sheltered accommodation, where she at least had people her age to talk to, people who had manners like hers and who might enjoy a political discussion over a game of cards or a cup of tea and a biscuit. It was nothing like the wonderful afternoons she'd spent with Mr Philpott of the *Shipbuilder*, of course, but he'd died so long ago she struggled to recall his eyes as green as the emerald ring she wore.

'Charles.' She said his name out loud, twisting the ring he'd insisted on giving back to her. It sat on her finger, which was so swollen at the knuckle that she couldn't take it off. He would have liked the irony of that. She thought she heard him whisper, 'My dear Kitty,' and she glanced around the room, but he wasn't there. How could he be, when he'd been gone for so long?

Yes, her ears were definitely playing tricks on her. Sometimes, in the quiet of the evening, she could hear singing, almost like a choir, and she'd get lost in that music; the more she listened, the louder it got and the sweeter the sound. It reminded her of a Christmas Eve in St Nicholas's Cathedral a long, long time ago.

'Are you all right, pet? Who are you talking to today?' said the carer, sticking her head around the kitchen door, with a dishcloth in her hand. She had bleached blonde locks which stuck up on end; goodness only knows what the latest fashions were these days.

'I was just wondering if you'd left the wireless on,' said Kitty. 'I can hear that music again.'

'No, pet,' said the carer, giving Kitty one of her looks. Before she could stop herself, Kitty muttered something unkind about the carer probably coming from Benwell, so what would she know anyway? And then she felt ashamed of herself because she was sure the poor girl must have heard that, and she didn't mean to be spiteful. She just found herself saying silly things without meaning to, that's all.

The past crept more and more into the present and sometimes she'd doze by the fire and half expect to find herself back in Lily Avenue, with Dad smiling down at her and Harry charging about with a catapult or making other mischief, as Mum busied herself or went out to one of her suffragette meetings.

But Harry had been gone ten years now since the stroke that killed him. That had broken Kitty's heart, not to mention poor Annie's too, because the truth finally came out. When her son John went to sort out his dad's pension, he was told it was going to his wife. The woman at the social services gave him a name he'd never heard of – Ethel. Harry had never divorced Ethel, of course; Kitty knew that. How could anyone afford it back in those days? Divorces were so expensive and difficult to obtain, it was only the upper classes who did that. And then the war came along, and no one knew what tomorrow was going to bring.

Annie had come into his life, she had brightened his world after he'd thought he could never love again, and they had had their children together. Kitty had tried in vain to persuade him to get in touch with his first-born, William, but to no avail, and the guilt of what might have happened to that child without his real father in his life gnawed away at her.

Harry had never told Annie the truth about Ethel, even though Kitty felt it was wrong to keep it from her. 'Whatever has happened stops with us, Kit,' he said. Kitty said that out loud too. At least, she may have done because the carer gave her another funny look.

She still talked to him, and why shouldn't she? He was her brother. The burden of carrying so many secrets weighed heavily on her now she was alone. It was at its worst when Harry died. She stopped eating for a while and she had a funny turn and ended up in hospital, so she couldn't go to his funeral. She'd never really said goodbye, which made it easier for him still to be here with her, in Newcastle, didn't it?

Of course, Annie came to visit when she found out about Ethel, and Kitty could still see her, sitting at the bedside, clutching her handbag on her lap, with a look of such hurt and confusion on her face. Kitty finally told her the truth about Harry's first marriage and why he'd left Ethel and William and never went back. Kitty didn't hold back, making plain her disdain for the woman who had pushed her brother to the brink of his sanity with her affair.

'But how could he lie to me?' Annie sobbed. 'Why didn't he tell me the truth?'

Kitty reached out and held Annie's hand, doing her best to comfort her sister-in-law. 'He loved you, he was faithful to you, so you mustn't think ill of him. He was trying to do what was right and he was afraid if he told you the truth about Ethel, you'd leave him and take the children with you.'

'You were in on it!' said Annie, pulling her hand away. 'How could you deceive me like this, Kitty, for all these years?'

Kitty sighed. How could she ever explain it all to Annie without hurting her feelings or telling her the real reason Harry was so troubled? If Harry lost Annie, he might well have lost his mind for good after all he had been through. Kitty wouldn't have risked that for anything; she'd vowed to always protect him. She'd promised Dad. Besides, to tell the whole story would mean revealing the one secret she would never share with Annie or anyone else in the family, for that matter.

She gazed out of the window for a moment, gathering her thoughts before she replied.

'He just felt the past was best left in the past, Annie,' she said eventually. 'You were the present and his future. You were everything to him, can't you see?'

But Annie didn't see. She was weeping uncontrollably when she left the room.

Kitty couldn't expect her sister-in-law to understand it because she hadn't lived it. Both she and Harry were bound by the same promise, one which crossed the boundaries between this life and the next, out of a sense of duty to their father. They both wanted to protect the following generations from the shame of it all, from being tarred as the offspring of a murderer.

Times had moved on. Seventy long years had passed; Lord knows, Kitty had lived through it all, with two world wars. Harry had done his duty for his country and suffered enough in the first of them. He'd been prepared to sacrifice himself and when he was pulled from that shell hole, barely breathing, life had given him a second chance. It had taken her father from her but spared her brother.

Now Harry's children had children of their own. Why should they be troubled by the past, even if it meant that secrets had to be kept?

'Pet?' Kitty called out and her carer came through from the kitchen to join her at the dining table, which was as glossy as when Mum used to polish it, back in Lily Avenue.

She pointed to the boxes of photo albums, letters and papers which she had carefully sorted from Dad's old bureau and the tallboy, during those long afternoons, as the clock ticked endlessly on the mantelpiece.

'I want to have a bonfire. Can you help me?'

'Are you sure about this, Kitty?' said the carer, heaving yet another box into the garden and tipping the contents onto a scrubby patch of earth where this year's daffodils had refused to grow.

'Yes, I don't want my family to have to sort through all my old rubbish when I'm gone,' said Kitty, leaning on her walking stick and pulling her cardigan closed against the chill in the air. 'They're far too busy to be bothered with all of this.'

'All right, then,' said the carer, pulling out a cigarette lighter. She knew better than to argue with Kitty when she was in one of her funny moods. She picked up a piece of paper, flicked the lighter open and held it to the flame. 'Would you like to do the honours?'

Kitty nodded and threw the burning letter into the middle of the pile. The flames spread, little by little, until the wind caught them, and their progress was unstoppable.

'Seems a bit of a shame, though,' said the carer, chewing on her ragged fingernails.

'What's done is done,' said Kitty, with a little shrug of her shoulders.

The fire licked over old photographs, which crackled and twisted, almost as if they were resisting for a moment, before they were engulfed.

Kitty watched it all burn and the singing in her head started up again. There were so many memories on the bonfire, of a respectable family in happier times: Kitty in a bonnet and a white frilled dress with her hair in ribbons and Harry in his sailor suit, scowling a bit because Dad had told him to stand up straight. Mum in her favourite black straw hat with the green birdwings and Dad in his best suit of light tweed, his moustache perfectly waxed, carrying a walking cane with a silver top.

Bundles of letters turned to ash; the fine copperplate handwriting of Mr Philpott declaring his affection for Kitty, burning alongside the last desperate outpourings of love from a condemned man to the family who believed in his innocence to the last. They never forgot him.

All this, all of it; the shame and the sadness and the struggle, all were consumed by the fire, just as Dad would have wanted.

Kitty smiled to herself.

'Let's make an end of it,' she said.

Author's Note

This book is about family and friendships and the will to endure, in the face of adversity. These themes resonate with me as much today as they did for my forebears and I'm sure I'm not alone in that.

All families have secrets. Many people live lies and some believe passionately in the version of reality they have created, because facing the truth would be too catastrophic for their nearest and dearest. They must carry the burden of the choices they have made and in the dead of night, before sleep creeps over them, it must weigh heavily, just as it did for my grandfather, Harry.

From our twenty-first-century standpoint, it's easy to judge the decisions of previous generations, but while writing this story, I was struck by how different the world was then. That doesn't excuse people lying or cheating but drawing together all the threads sometimes gives you another perspective; it can help you see the other side of the story. We are all failed human beings doing our best but back then, against the dramatically changing landscape of two world wars, life must have seemed very fragile. It was possible to move from one side of London to the other and start afresh in the hope that the past would never catch up. You couldn't get away with it today – at least, not easily.

The terrible event of 1910 unveiled in this book had an earth-shattering effect on the victim's family, which cannot and must not ever be forgotten. The widow of the murder victim had to fight to get compensation after her husband's death. The family eventually emigrated. I have not detailed their struggle in this book because I did not feel it was my place to do so. I cannot imagine the pain and suffering they went through and I would not presume to speak for them.

From the age of fifteen, when my mother, Anita, told me about what had happened to her grandfather John Alexander Dickman, I grew up in the shadow of the shame and secrecy about this murder. How she came to find out about the murder and her father Harry's secrets is another story entirely and there isn't space to go into that here. It was a long and convoluted path, spanning forty years, with hurt for all involved, but ultimately, the will to resolve and to find strength in family bonds prevailed.

In writing this book, I felt it was time, more than a hundred years after the event which so drastically altered the course of my family's history, to finally lay the ghosts of the past to rest.

The quest for the truth is something that led me to become a journalist and it has shaped my character too. I have an unswerving drive to speak out when I sense injustice, to stand my ground and to be heard. I can trace that all the way back to the courtroom of the Newcastle Assizes in 1910 and the hangman's noose which silenced my great-grandfather, John Alexander Dickman, one of the last men to be hanged in Newcastle Gaol. I see it in the letters that my great-grandmother, teacher Annie Sowerby Bainbridge Dickman, wrote to the newspapers and the Home Secretary to fight for her husband's life. I come from a long line of very strong women and that is a powerful thought for me when facing up to any difficulties.

My Great-Aunt Kitty was formidable, ahead of her time, and I owe her for a lot of my strength and determination, not to mention my love of writing, although I used to find her scary when I was little. She grew up in a world in which women didn't have the vote and were not equal to men in the workplace. She was fiercely protective of all women's rights: to vote, to have a say, to be heard, and she instilled that in my mother, who passed it on to me.

Kitty didn't live to see me become a journalist, to write the front page articles of national newspapers, or be a published author. I like to think she would have been proud of me, but quietly so, without too much fuss because that was not her way. I knew her as an old woman, living in a sheltered flat in Newcastle, making cups of tea, which she served at her highly polished dining table. I was a child of the seventies, tomboyish, a bit wild, and my lack of manners made her look askance. She'd smile to herself when she watched me arguing with my brother. Perhaps she saw in me a kindred spirit, an echo of the auburn-haired girl who played rough and tumble with her brother Harry at the turn of the century, before their lives were turned upside down by a murder.

She died when I was eleven. It's a shame I didn't get to know her better, but I feel, in some small way, through writing this book, I know her now.

I would like to thank my Uncle John, the oldest surviving member of the Dickman family, for his insights, advice and memories which have helped me to shape this story. I would also like to thank Rowan and Michele, my 'secret' cousins, for their memories and help. I wish I could have known their parents, William 'Roy' and Zena, but that was not to be and we are now one family.

I would like to thank my editor, Ingrid Connell of Pan Macmillan, for her incredible support, kindness and advice. Working in such a great environment is a joy because the process of writing can feel very solitary at times. Ingrid was with me every step of the way and I would also like to thank assistant editor Charlotte Wright for her eagle eye and valuable input, and copy-editor Lorraine Green for her help.

I am very lucky to have the total support of my husband Reuben and my boys, Idris and Bryn, as well as my dear friends Sally and Marcus; Jo, Mark and Clare; and Hannah and Tania.

There is no substitute for true friends and the love of your family.

Whatever has happened in the past, tomorrow brings with it the possibility that we can make different choices, because our actions in this life define who we really are.

What's your story?

Acknowledgements

I am grateful to the Acton History Group for their support and research, including the lovely book *Tin Hats, Doodlebugs and Food Rations* by Maureen Colledge, which relies on newspaper reports from the time, as well as oral history from local people. This helped me confirm stories about the war told to me by my grandmother Annie, my Great-Aunt Elsie and my mum. I am also very lucky to have had the backing of the We Love Acton W3 Facebook group, which provided many memories of my gran's time in Acton.

The case against my great-grandfather John Alexander Dickman is studied by law students today and remains controversial because of the nature of the evidence used to convict him and the possibility that there was police collusion. It resulted in a change in identification parade line-up procedures.

Several writers have researched this case incredibly thoroughly and I can recommend the work of authors John J. Eddleston, *May the Lord Have Mercy on Your Soul*, and Diane Janes, *Edwardian Murder*, for further reading. I was able to form my own opinions about the guilt or innocence of my great-grandfather by reading their works and studying the Home Office records of the trial held at the National Archives at Kew. John J. Eddleston offers the intriguing possibility of having unmasked the real killers. He also scotches another theory, namely that my great-grandfather was responsible for another killing in 1908, of a wealthy woman Caroline Luard, in Kent, having allegedly fiddled a cheque that she sent him after he had requested financial help in an advert in *The Times*. Eddleston points out that the trial evidence included all the details of my great-grandfather's two bank accounts from that time, and there was no reference to a cheque from Mrs Luard. It seems to me that this other murder case was most likely to have been pinned on John Alexander after his execution when disquiet about the case was growing.

I also relied on local newspaper reports from the *Northern Echo*, where I spent many happy years as a reporter back in the 1990s, and also the *Newcastle Evening Chronicle* and the *Newcastle Journal*. I can still recall looking through the old bound copies for the first time and reading the reports of my relative's trial and hanging, which sent a shiver down my spine. I reproduced the front-page news story about the execution exactly as it was reported in the *Northern Echo* the morning after it happened and I would like to thank Newsquest Media Group for the permission to do so.

Experts from the Great War Forum were very generous with their time and help in identifying my grandad's regiment in World War One as many of the records were destroyed by a German bomb during World War Two, which makes research difficult. The kindness and enthusiasm of these experts made a real difference to me.

George Orwell's account of living in London dosshouses in the 1930s, in *Down and Out in Paris and London*, helped to put my grandfather Harry's experiences in context. Life for the underclass without the safety net of any welfare state was a very grim one indeed.

The last word of thanks must go to you, my readers, who have been so supportive and enthusiastic about me writing a sequel to *All My Mother's Secrets*. Thank you for reading me. You make it all worthwhile.

The official Facebook account for all my book news is beezymarshauthor and you can follow me on Twitter or Instagram @beezymarsh. You can sign up for book updates and all my news on my blog on my website beezymarsh.com.

Research Sources

Colledge, Maureen, *Tin Hats, Doodlebugs and Food Rations*, Acton History Group, 2014

Laybourn, Keith, *The General Strike of 1926*, Manchester University Press, 1993

Rev J.O. Coop, *The Story of the 55th (West Lancashire) Division*, Naval and Military Press, Amazon, 2018

Janes, Diane, *Edwardian Murder*, Sutton Publishing, 2007

Eddleston, John J., *And May the Lord Have Mercy On Your Soul*, Bibliofile Publishers, 2012

Salmon, Thomas W., *The Care and Treatment of Mental Diseases and War Neuroses (Shell Shock) in the British Army*, Old South Books, Amazon, 2018.

I also viewed archive material, films and pictures from the
   following sources:

Pathé News

British Newspaper Archive

The National Archives at Kew

Forces War Records

Acton Gazette, *Northern Echo*, *Newcastle Evening Chronicle*,
   Newcastle Journal, the *Shipbuilder*

Great War Forum: www.greatwarforum.org

The Long Long Trail website for World War One regiments:
   www.longlongtrail.co.uk

BBC news and radio archives: www.bbc.co.uk

THE INTERNATIONAL BESTSELLER

The powerful prequel to *Her Father's Daughter* – a true story of love, loss and a family torn apart.

Annie Austin's childhood ends at the age of twelve, when she joins her mother in one of the slum laundries of Acton, working long hours for little pay. What spare time she has is spent looking after her younger brother George and her two stepsisters, under the glowering eye of her stepfather Bill. In London between the wars, a girl like Annie has few choices in life – but a powerful secret will change her destiny.

All Annie knows about her real father is that he died in the Great War, and as the years pass she is haunted by the pain of losing him. Her downtrodden mother won't tell her more and Annie's attempts to uncover the truth threaten to destroy her family. Distraught, she runs away to Covent Garden, but can she survive on her own and find the love which has eluded her so far?

From the grimy streets of Acton and Notting Hill to the bright lights of the West End, *All My Mother's Secrets* is a powerful, uplifting story of a young woman's struggle to come to terms with her family's tragic past.

Out now in paperback and eBook